University and Corporate Innovations in Lifelong Learning

A volume in
Research in Management Education and Development

Series Editors:
Charles Wankel, *St. John's University*
Robert DeFillippi, *Suffolk University*

Research in Management Education and Development

Charles Wankel and Robert DeFillippi, Series Editors

University and Corporate Innovations in Lifelong Learning

edited by

Charles Wankel
St. John's University

and

Robert DeFillippi
Suffolk University

Information Age Publishing, Inc.
Charlotte, North Carolina • www.infoagepub.com

Library of Congress Cataloging-in-Publication Data

University and corporate innovations in lifelong learning / edited by Charles Wankel and
Robert DeFillippi.
    p. cm. -- (Research in management education and development)
   Includes bibliographical references.
   ISBN 978-1-59311-809-9 (pbk.) -- ISBN 978-1-59311-810-5 (hardcover) 1. Management--
Study and teaching (Continuing education) 2. Leadership--Study and teaching (Continuing edu-
cation) 3. Executives--Education (Continuing education) 4. Academic-industrial collaboration.
5. Business and education. 6. Professional education. I. Wankel, Charles. II. DeFillippi, Bob.
  HD30.4.U55 2008
  658.0071'5--dc22

                        2008003132

ISBN 13: 978-1-59311-809-9 (pbk.)
        978-1-59311-810-5 (hardcover

Printed in the United States of America

CONTENTS

EDITORIAL REVIEW BOARD

A RANGE OF UNIVERSITY AND CORPORATE INNOVATIONS IN LIFELONG LEARNING

Robert DeFillippi and Charles Wankel

Ongoing important changes in twenty-first century organizations mean the people who manage and work in them need ongoing important learning. This volume in the Research in Management Education and Development series address this with articles on a wide range of approaches to lifelong learning in university and corporate contexts.

The first chapter by Lindsay Ryan explores lifelong learning for employees in organizations with corporate universities in partnerships with accredited universities, and discusses the findings from research into university-corporate education partnerships.

Ryan notes that corporate education and links with industry are likely to continue to be of growing importance to universities as more organizations recognize the significance of lifelong learning and become committed to the education and training of their employees as both a source of organizational development and strategic competitive advantage. Universities have the potential to provide quality education programs that assist in developing the skills and higher level capabilities of corporate employees. In particular, Ryan emphasizes that these higher level programs should provide credit, or at least a pathway, for participants to achieve university qualifications to further encourage lifelong learning and integrate their learning into a holistic learning framework. The programs should center on leadership and developing management knowledge and understanding to complement those programs offered in-house by corporations. Both universities and corporations will also need to recognize the importance of building relationships in their university-corporate education partnerships which will necessitate having continuity and consistency of people to manage and operate their corporate education units and not rely on people on short-term contracts or sharing the responsibility for developing and managing university-corporate links among other diverse activities.

Judith Stevens-Long and Charles McClintock's chapter focuses on the concept of co-presence as a central interpersonal and group process that supports online learning through an emphasis on faculty-student interaction and peer collaboration. Co-presence is about the social context of learning, empowerment of the learner, and critical reflection through dialogue. We discuss ways to create these experiences in the online context and present exploratory data to examine the effects of this kind of collaborative learning in graduate management education programs. Co-presence is especially important in the retention of life-long learners who show a strong preference for learning that connects knowledge to experience, provides alternative ways for them to demonstrate their knowledge, and challenges them to reach beyond what they already know.

Elena Antonacopoulou's chapter advances the idea of reflexive critique and explores its contribution to management learning. Drawing on diverse literatures propounding a critical perspective, this chapter integrates the various propositions of "what it is to be critical" in advancing the notion of reflexive critique and proposes two additional forms of critique. It is argued that reflexive critique is supported by the critique of simplification and the critique of identity. These forms of critique have not been previously articulated in the relevant literature and they are presented here as a contribution to extending our understanding of what it means to be critical. These forms of critique derive from the experience of introducing an innovative course titled "Critical Thinking" offered to MBA students over a 5-year period. The chapter discusses the importance of critique in the business curriculum and explains the rationale for introducing the course and its objectives, as well as the learning and teaching techniques employed. The analysis considers how different forms of critique can instill a more reflexive approach to the analysis of management in relation to participants' experiences of managing thus, supporting their lifelong learning. The chapter concludes with a review of the main lessons learned from teaching this course and considers the implications that these lessons raise about future management learning research and practice seeking to support lifelong learning.

A premise of Armstrong, Thursfield, Landri, and Ponzini's chapter is that the European Council's focus on maintaining Europe's place among the world's most competitive and dynamic economies. Lifelong learning is seen as a focal point for realizing that ambition. Their chapter reports on the efforts of a group of European partners to develop and deploy an innovative lifelong learning course for managers across the continent. The specific aim was to construct a course was to enable managers to develop the requisite knowledge and skills to launch lifelong learning in their organizations. The diverse partners through negotiation among themselves produced a final course that provided participants with a toolbox of ideas, concepts, models, and methods that have been found to foster lifelong learning. The chapter begins with a description of the process of de-differentiation of lifelong learning among the different national groups. In each country adult education is a means of improving workforce skills to deal with change. Moreover, each country is shifting its focus from formal education that ends at a specific age towards lifelong learning. The chapter investigates various perspectives on lifelong learning. One perspective referred to as "economic instrumentalism" sees the needs of the economy and organizations as paramount. Another sees lifelong learning as focally about the supporting the personal needs of individuals, the development of society and making organizations more humane. Such a premise might lead to the incorporation of more liberal education elements than economic instrumentalism might. A social justice perspective might see lifelong learning as a vehicle to "up-skill" people to enable them to receive more from the economy.

Beechler, Yorks, and Ciporen's chapter introduces an integrative learning framework that represents key aspects of highly functional learning communities. In doing so, it draws on the findings from a case study that examines the impact of a senior executive program at a top-tier U.S. university as well as literatures from adult learning theory and management education. The chapter begins with a description of The Executive Program (a pseudonym) and its evolution over a 10-year period. They then present an integrative learning community framework that captures connections between the unfolding program design and its links to learning theory. They describe a number of findings from their longitudinal case study, showing that creating diverse learning communities facilitates learning in ways that challenge participants' existing mindsets and supports leaders in developing broader and more complex perspectives, a powerful outcome that supports individuals' and organizations' abilities to thrive in today's complex environment. They conclude the chapter with lessons learned in designing learning communities in executive education programs.

Maria Avdjieva's chapter begins with the premise that the capacity for a lifetime of management learning has become a critical attribute of business graduates. Her chapter presents an innovative assessment designed to develop students' capacity for lifelong learning. It uses participatory action research and a case study approach to look at the curriculum redesign and delivery of a first year undergraduate business course. She documents students' enhanced self-awareness about careers and learning, increased ability to deal with the challenges of the higher education environment, as well as capacity for creative learning strategies. The design principles and steps for embedding assessments that create a life-changing management education experience establish a platform for self-directed lifelong learning.

Robert Fulmer and Jared Bleak's chapter probes what things work in leadership development. From a survey of the germane literature, it details guiding principles. A study of best-practice firms grounds a discussion of best practices in leadership development.

Nick Nissley's chapter "Framing Arts-Based Learning as an Intersectional Innovation in Continuing Management Education: The Intersection of Arts and Business and the Innovation of Arts-Based Learning" begins with the premise that there is sense of disillusionment being expressed by those in continuing management education. Concomitant is the increasing criticism of management education for underemphasizing the creative skills that leaders and managers require for coping with a rapidly changing and complex global business environment. There is a growing recognition by management educators that many required skills can be found in those creative arts that have typically existed outside the business school. However, coupled with the disillusionment is a growing sense of possibility emerging at the intersection of arts and business. Continuing management educators are beginning to work in the intersection of arts and business and finding arts-based learning an expressive means to generate innovative and stimulating continuing management education experiences. Nissley explores the learning fusion or intersectional innovation occurring within continuing management education, the intersection of arts and business, and the emergence of the innovation of arts-based learning in continuing management education.

Steven Maranville and Wil Uecker's chapter notes that university providers have but a miniscule part of the huge market for life long learning for corporate managers. The lure of such a large market, however, is seen as irresistible to business schools in their quest for revenue to enable them to compete for the best faculty and students.

They found that the executive education literature has focused on top tier international research universities' experience in deploying executive education. Their chapter instead looks the challenges facing smaller regional universities in addressing this niche through the through the experiences of the Jessie H. Jones Graduate School of Management at Rice University.

Augustinaitis, Malinauskiene, and Wankel's chapter considers the use of lifelong learning in the transitional economy of Lithuania. Lifelong management learning is seen as catalyst driving changes in society, work organizations, and technological innovation. The role of Lithuanian universities in developing needed abilities and knowledge processes is discussed.

CHAPTER 1

LIFELONG LEARNING THROUGH CORPORATE UNIVERSITIES IN PARTNERSHIPS WITH TRADITIONAL UNIVERSITIES

Lindsay Ryan

Globalization and rapid advances in technology are having a swift and substantial impact on the way organizations do business and the need to have a highly skilled and flexible workforce. Corporations are starting to acknowledge that education and training is not a cost but rather an investment in order to attract and retain the best workforce. Some organizations are centralizing their education and training functions and establishing in-house educational facilities, or corporate universities. As corporations expand their range of education programs, many are forming partnerships with traditional universities to provide accredited university awards to complement their in-house programs. This chapter explores lifelong learning for employees in organizations with corporate universities in partnerships with accredited universities, and discusses the findings from research into university-corporate education partnerships.

University and Corporate Innovations in Lifelong Learning, pp. 1–14
Copyright © 2008 by Information Age Publishing

1

INTRODUCTION

Globalization and rapid advances in technology have had a swift and substantial impact on the way organizations do business and the need to have a highly skilled and flexible workforce (Meister, 2000). In order to attract the right staff and to be regarded as an employer of choice to retain capable people, corporations are increasingly centralizing their education and training functions and establishing in-house educational facilities, with some labeling these centers as corporate universities. Corporate universities are in-house training units providing educational programs for staff from basic training to high level programs that equate to courses traditionally offered by higher education bodies and universities.

As corporations expand their commitment to providing education programs for staff, many are forming partnerships between their corporate universities and traditional universities in order to provide accredited university awards to complement their in-house study programs. This chapter investigates lifelong learning in organizations with corporate universities working in partnerships with traditional accredited universities and draws on current global quantitative research by the author on corporate-university partnerships for business education programs. This research, involving a total of 79 corporations, government agencies, and universities in the United States, United Kingdom, Europe, and Australia, explores the findings and emerging trends from university-corporate education partnerships and the implications for management learning and development. Approximately 65% of respondents indicate their corporate university unit has been established for 5 years or longer, which implies the concept of corporate universities is not just a fad that has a lifecycle of 3-5 years and therefore provides impetus for investigating university-corporate education partnerships.

THE GROWTH OF CORPORATE UNIVERSITIES

According to Nixon and Helms (2002), the first corporate university was established in the United States by General Motors as the GM Institute in 1927. Examples of corporate universities include Motorola University, McDonald's Hamburger University, Disney University, and GE's Leadership Center at Crotonville. Some of these corporate universities have operational size and scale equal to large traditional universities. The growth of corporate universities is not limited to the United States. Since the late 1990s corporate universities have also spread to the United

Kingdom, Europe and in more recent times to north and south Asia and to a small extent in Australia.

Although some large corporations have invested significantly in the physical aspects of their corporate universities there are many others that focus more on the concept of structured education and training as a means of strategic and coordinated development of their employees and their organizations. Bersin (2005) finds that some corporations have moved on from the corporate university as a place to go to learn to a more holistic and integrated approach of corporate learning services where "learning must be on-demand, it must be job-relevant, and it must be constantly changing. It manages courses and content which can be delivered anywhere" (p. 3).

While a number of corporations are seeking partnerships with universities for higher education programs and to award degrees to employees, increasingly universities are seeking to form partnerships with corporations. Blass (2001) claims that traditionally there has been a clash of philosophies between accredited and corporate universities as the accredited universities have an interest in developing students with liberated minds while corporate universities have an interest in assimilating individuals into a corporate culture. However, Hagen (2002) observes that traditional universities are changing due to economic pressures of global is at ion, competition and the challenge to find new sources of funding. Public universities are exploring opportunities to generate new sources of income as the primary source of funding from governments reduces or declines relative to escalating costs and demands on funds within universities. Nixon and Helms (2002) suggest that partnering between corporations and universities may offer the best of both worlds, with universities creating new income and opportunities for themselves by responding to corporate needs for fast changing skills and corporations benefiting from structured links to universities for management and organizational development programs and accrediting of their in-house programs.

From the research, 23% of all respondents state that the primary reason for establishing an in-house corporate university is to build the skills and competences of their employees in order to effect the strategies of the organization. As Meister (2001) finds, corporations now realize they have a role to play in preparing their employees to compete in a global economy "to meet and exceed service expectations, to adjust to changing roles and new technologies, and to respond to current and future global pressures" (p. 2). Corporations are starting to acknowledge that education and training is not a cost but, instead, an investment to attract and retain the best workforce.

The next major reason for establishing a corporate university indicted by 17% of respondents is to ensure consistency in the education and training programs offered to employees. The need for consistency in education programs is particularly relevant to organizations operating on a global or transnational basis that are striving to develop a consistent corporate culture and corporate values as well as have some consistency in product knowledge and customer service across the breadth of their operations. With increasing competition and the desire to achieve optimum returns on their training and education investment, organizations are also increasingly linking educational activities to their corporate objectives, which is the third main reason for establishing a corporate university by 16% of respondents. This helps to ensure that budgets are used effectively rather than each unit or division having their own interpretation of an organization's education and training priorities. The majority of programs delivered in university-corporate education partnerships are centered around: business/management, engineering/technical, computer science, and finance/accounting, consistent with Bedar's (1999) findings.

The fourth highest response by 14% of respondents indicates the purpose of their corporate university is to develop a learning organization, reflecting a growing awareness by some corporations to lifelong learning as a strategic approach to developing their organizations. The management of learning and knowledge creation within corporations in a more complex and competitive environment reflects the emerging importance for corporate universities in developing a competitive advantage (Holland & Pyman, 2006). Earlier research by Densford (1998) and the Association of Advanced Collegiate Schools of Business (1999) found that one of the primary purposes of a corporate university was to support or drive change within an organization. While facilitating change may still be a function, this current research finds only 13.5% of all respondents indicate change management as the purpose of the corporate university. Among the reasons for this could be that organizations are now constantly changing and evolving due to global trends, technology developments, and competitors' activities so change is no longer seen as an initiative but more as a necessity.

Given the looming skills shortage in many western countries, a commitment to lifelong learning could contribute to a corporation's reputation as an employer of choice to attract and keep good employees. Instead of training being used merely to address operational issues, some corporations are adopting a strategic commitment to education as a means of organizational development. Shah, Sterrett, Chesser, and Wilmore (2001) find that people are seeking more meaning in their work and the corporate university provides education programs to develop their skills, qualifications, and employability both within the organization and with other organizations should job security decrease.

Qualitative research undertaken by the author among human resource managers finds that mature workers, that is, those aged 45 and older, rarely receive investment in training and development. Corporations in most advanced western countries are facing the challenge of an ageing workforce and a looming skills shortage in some industries which could see the necessity of using their corporate universities to re-skill and up-skill mature workers as a means of keeping them in the workforce longer and to partially address anticipated workforce shortages. As many of these mature workers may not have received any formal or structured education and training for considerable time another role for corporate universities could be to assist employees to learn how to learn. This could involve providing a diverse range of teaching and learning approaches through their corporate universities to assist mature workers to understand the learning style that is most effective for them to acquire and apply new skills and knowledge.

One of the major imperatives for corporations to undertake corporate education programs is to develop internal leadership and management strength, with 55% of respondents indicating this as the most significant purpose for their corporate education programs. While such programs are usually targeted at senior managers, increasingly corporate education programs are being offered across organizations at all levels as leadership is no longer seen as purely a management function. Instead, leadership and initiative are now necessary at all operational areas throughout organizations and this necessitates developing people with the appropriate skills and knowledge and empowering them to be able to make decisions within certain parameters. Lifelong learning by employees in corporate education programs assists in developing the skills and capabilities of people to have the confidence to be leaders and make decisions to expedite smooth operational activities within organizations and reduce potential bottlenecks waiting for managers to make decisions.

GROWING CORPORATE-UNIVERSITY LINKS

While many corporate universities develop and deliver their own in-house programs or contract university academics and consultants to deliver programs specific to the organization's requirements, there is a growing trend for corporations to partner with accredited universities. A Corporate University Xchange Benchmarking Report highlights this growth in university-corporate partnerships with 51% of respondents placing medium or high importance on forming alliances with colleges and universities (Corporate University Xchange, 2004). The report also finds 46% of the responding organizations have partnerships with universities to offer courses on-site at the corporations' facilities and 45% partner with universities to offer customized courses or degree programs. This trend is influenced by a number of factors including the fact that as corporate universities align with corporation objectives, they adopt a more strategic approach to their programs and recognize the value in having universities contribute higher management education programs with sound management theory underpinning the content and for academics to integrate leading-edge research into the corporate education courses they deliver.

For those organizations seeking to be employers of choice, they realize that a qualification from a university holds more value and prestige due to its accreditation than an in-house certificate. From the research, over 22% of respondents indicate that being able to provide their employees with a university award as the main reason for establishing a partnership with an accredited university. Almost 19% indicate that they formed a partnership with a university in order to provide employees with a broader range of subjects to allow their staff to expand their thinking and knowledge. A further 17% indicate that the partnership with a university adds strength and credibility to their in-house programs. Only 9% of respondents indicate that the university brand name influenced their decision to establish the partnership. This finding is consistent with other research that the more innovative collaborations between corporations and universities are those involving new university business schools rather than the traditional university business schools. Prince (2000) finds new university business schools, formerly institutes of technology or colleges of advanced education, are more flexible and responsive to corporations in developing new programs.

A third of the respondents rate the value of their corporate-university partnership as very good, indicating it plays an important role in the organization, is linked to the corporate objectives and is providing a significant contribution in the skills development of employees. A further 53% respond that while the corporate-university partnership is good many people in their organization do not recognize the real value of the partnership. For universities, there is the opportunity to access new research projects, to have a learning laboratory in industry and to access real time information from markets to test or expand research hypotheses. For organizations, there is the opportunity to build the skills and capability of their employees in a nonthreatening environment using the neutrality of university academics to explore new and innovative ideas among employees while providing academic rigor to work-based projects that add value to the learning experience. Group projects involving employees from different discipline areas of a corporation, such as finance, marketing, production and human resources, can bring their diverse skills and knowledge together to work on specific projects. As Ellis (2005) finds, participants in corporate university programs develop an awareness of broader aspects of the business including an appreciation of the role of their colleagues in other parts of the corporation as well as a better understanding of how their role integrates with others.

Ideally, these work-based projects should be drawn from contemporary topics and issues that organizations need to investigate and work on as group projects that have relevance to the future of the organization as well as for academic assessment and credit towards a university qualification. The university academic can provide objectivity and ensure there is rigor and appropriate discipline and theory underpinning these work-based projects while a senior manager or executive from the organization should also be involved as a mentor to each group to provide access to relevant corporate information and materials to undertake the project, ensure the group maintains focus on the core issues and to demonstrate the commitment to learning by the senior management.

RELATIONSHIP FACTORS IN UNIVERSITY-CORPORATE PARTNERSHIPS

In order for lifelong learning to be effective in an organization there are a number of factors that need to exist in the relationship of the corporate-university partnership. Some of these factors are investigated in the research, such as trust and openness between the corporation and the university, which 40% of corporations indicate as being most important compared to 26% of university respondents. Arino, de la Torre, and Ring (2001) identify trust as an important factor that needs to exist in any ongoing corporate partnership and comprises four elements: (1) the reputations of the corporation and university that exist prior to the partnership being considered, (2) the opinions about each other's capabilities, technical competence, and ethical behavior during negotiations, (3) the experience with each other's behavior as the partnership starts to develop, particularly in regard to external challenges or internal difficulties and how these are managed, and (4) the partners' behavior outside the context of the partnership that affects their reputations and reveals their true commitment to certain values or business undertakings. Lang (2004) also emphasizes the importance of trust in partnerships especially in the knowledge sharing between the corporation and the university when initially establishing the strategic role of the corporate university and at a practical level as academics facilitate group discussions with participants where discreet corporate, competitor or market information is explored as part of the learning process within the corporate university.

Senior management commitment to the program and partnership is another factor in the success of partnerships identified by Elmuti and Kathawala (2001) who claim that for a partnership to have any significant impact on an organization's strategic plans they need to be developed, implemented, managed, and monitored with the full commitment of senior management. Senior management commitment is also important to demonstrate to others throughout the organization the importance of the corporate-university partnership. This factor is reaffirmed in the research with 95% of corporate and university respondents indicating that senior management commitment is significant or most significant in the success of the program.

The means by which senior managers demonstrate their commitment to the university-corporate partnership varies with each organization, however 73% of respondents indicate senior management involvement in signing or endorsing a formal corporate education agreement between their organization and the university partner. The respondents also indicate that in 54% of their organizations senior managers are involved in meetings with their university partner, 46% are involved in selecting or approving participants in the corporate education programs, 46% of senior managers attend as guest lecturers in corporate education programs and 19% actually participate as students in the programs. Visible senior management support is important at crucial times such as the approval of budgets to ensure corporate education programs receive adequate resources to be effective, attending sessions when participants present their findings and recommendations on work-based projects and attending graduation ceremonies.

Meister (2000) suggests another important factor for organizations exploring corporate-university partnerships is the careful selection of the university partner. The research finds 44% of corporate respondents regard selection criteria and the selection process as most important in contrast to 24% of universities that claim this is of little or no significance. This would suggest that many universities are still looking from the inside out with a view that corporations seeking certain business education programs have little choice than to purchase their programs from their university. This attitude could have implications for the financial future of some universities as industry now has increasing choices of higher education programs and growing accessibility to programs to meet their specific needs through globalization and new technologies. The pendulum for acquiring business higher education programs and qualifications is swinging away from universities having total control. This reinforces the importance for universities to understand more about industry and the potential opportunities, and implications, of considering university-corporate partnerships for business education programs.

While price or value-for-money will always be included in the criteria by corporations when selecting a university partner, the intangible nature of education programs means there are many other more important elements that need to be considered. Some of these elements will include: the level of understanding by the university of the purpose of the corporate education program, the willingness of the university to listen and understand the issues and future challenges facing a corporation and its industry, the flexibility on the part of the university to customize the content and assignments associated with the delivery of its corporate education programs, previous experience in working with corporate clients to deliver customized corporate education programs, the quality and experience of the university lecturers and the attitude and ability of the university to managing relationships with corporate clients.

As lifelong learning can involve a holistic program comprising many smaller and specialist courses, it is important for corporate universities to develop a customized program of educational development for all employees taking into account their career aspirations, capabilities, and the organization's plans for their career. These individual program plans will often be linked with an employee's performance review to identify areas for skills and educational development as well as monitor the benefits of the program on the employee's actual performance. Some training programs will continue to be delivered through an organization's in-house training unit and by contracting external providers and consultants. For those organizations providing more advanced education programs and pathways to higher education programs in partnerships with universities, it is important for the universities to understand the role and context of their program in relation to other programs delivered in the corporate university.

The research finds that a close working relationship between key people in the corporation with those in the university in the development and delivery of education programs is valuable. Almost 68% of all respondents indicate that a shared vision and understanding of the purpose of the education program is quite or most significant. Those organizations having partnerships with universities have evolved to a more strategic, longer-term view of employee development as an investment in education that often does not demonstrate real returns until 2-to-3 years after completing a program of study. This contrasts with training programs that usually have a short-term focus to address immediate or imminent operating issues. Therefore, both corporations and universities need to approach the relationship as partners and not as a customer-supplier arrangement. Education is not just a commodity with fixed specifications and parameters; often the most successful education programs evolve through collaboration between key people from both the corporation and the university with consultation from industry specialists and feedback from program participants themselves.

One of the major criticisms by corporations to emerge from the research is that universities need to take the time to meet with key people in the corporate environment to obtain an understanding of the purpose of the education program as it relates to their organization and the challenges their particular industry is facing into the future. While employers are increasingly prepared to support and pay for the educational development of their employees, including the achievement of a university degree, the prime purpose is about developing the organization by developing the skills of the employees. Paton, Peters, Storey, and Taylor (2005) find that corporate university managers need to work closely with their academic partners to jointly determine course content and methods of delivery and the tailoring of content and assignments to ensure they are relevant to the corporation while also drawing on research generated by the universities.

It is also important to have lecturers who are capable and confident to work in a corporate environment away from the relative security of the university lecture theater. Courses delivered in-house in a corporate environment can be intimidating for some lecturers as they are the outsiders on somebody else's territory and corporate students will often test lecturers in their first session to ascertain their knowledge, experience and their ability to apply theory to a real world situation.

Despite thorough planning and good intentions there will be times when scheduled education programs need to be revised or suspended at short notice according to changing circumstances. This implies there needs to be a good working relationship between the corporation and their university partner. The research finds that 58% of the respondents from both the corporations and universities claim a close working relationship is most or very important to the success of the partnership. On the topic of flexibility to make changes to the delivery dates of courses or other corporate requirements, 62% of universities claim they provide considerable flexibility. This contrasts with the response by 31% of corporations that their partner universities provide flexibility. A possible explanation for this difference is that as universities have the power to self-accredit their degree programs, the process involved in making changes can be tedious and limit the potential for greater flexibility. Universities could also argue that corporate education is not their core business and their first priority is to maintaining the integrity of their programs, which is one of the attractions for corporations to seek to partner with certain universities. Only 2% of corporations indicate there is no flexibility in the arrangements with their partner universities.

Corporate education programs are increasingly being adopted as a strategic initiative to assist in the corporate development of organizations and the research finds 65% of the corporate respondents link their education programs to specific corporate objectives compared to 53% of universities delivering corporate education programs to industry. While corporations often look for a return on their investment in corporate education, the research reveals that only 38% of corporations have specific goals for measuring the success or outcome of the corporate education programs. Perhaps corporations have traditionally relied on universities to measure the performance of participants in educational programs and that completion of a program and awarding of the appropriate degree qualification has been the main measure of success. Two-thirds of the university respondents indicate they have performance criteria for monitoring and evaluating the content and delivery of their corporate education programs.

This is likely to change as universities and corporations form partnerships to develop and deliver customized programs, both degree and nondegree, to industry as part of organizational development and lifelong learning strategies. While corporations may establish their own measures for the success of university-corporate education programs, often these will be quantitative in nature, such as: the amount spent on corporate education and training, the number of programs delivered, the number of people in each program, the number of people to successfully complete each program and staff retention.

However, corporations should not overlook the qualitative benefits of corporate education programs and seek to establish some measures to reflect the additional value to the organization. While qualitative measures will often be more subjective than quantitative measures, there should be some mechanism for identifying the value of the corporate education programs in such aspects as: staff morale, teamwork, and cooperation across the organization, the development of confidence among program participants, the contribution to the development and retention of corporate knowledge, and the innovative ideas generated in such learning environments.

As well as providing structured educational programs for employees through their corporate-university partnership, corporations should view the program as part of a broader context for learning and development. The educational programs should be supported with other activities that allow employees to apply what they learn to special workplace projects, to discuss what they learn with a mentor, to be part of special project teams to create new and innovative opportunities for the corporation and to develop their skills in leading and developing others by also becoming a mentor.

Another criticism to emerge from the research is the issue of succession planning in university-corporate partnerships. This criticism is mainly aimed at universities where corporations claim there are often academic or administrative staff appointed as their point of contact but have other job responsibilities as well that preclude them from spending any significant time on maintaining or building relationships with corporate partners. The research finds that over two-thirds of corporate universities are managed as separate entities with their own dedicated staff whereas just half of the universities responding indicate they are managed with dedicated staff. This level of commitment is also evident with almost 83% of corporations indicating that their educational partnership with a university is recognized as a valuable part of the organization's development plans. For universities seeking to expand their corporate links, a consistent point of contact within a university can play an integral role in developing and managing corporate relationships and assist in maintaining and building corporate education opportunities.

Succession planning also emerges as an issue for universities in their dealings with corporations, especially when senior managers who have been instrumental in the establishment of a corporate education program or a corporate university partnership are promoted or leave a corporation. Often their successors do not have the same vision or commitment to the corporate education program or corporate-university partnership, which can lead to a deterioration in the relationship and the continuity of the lifelong learning program leading to participants having to make a business case to complete their program or find alternative educational arrangements.

CONCLUSION

Corporate education and links with industry are likely to continue to be of growing importance to universities as more organizations recognize the significance of lifelong learning and become committed to the education and training of their employees as both a source of organizational development and strategic competitive advantage. Universities have the potential to provide quality education programs that assist in developing the skills and higher level capabilities of corporate employees. In particular, these higher level programs should provide credit, or at least a pathway, for participants to achieve university qualifications to further encourage lifelong learning and integrate their learning into a holistic learning framework. The programs should center on leadership and developing management knowledge and understanding to complement those programs offered in-house by corporations. Both universities and corporations will also need to recognize the importance of building relationships in their university-corporate education partnerships which will necessitate having continuity and consistency of people to manage and operate their corporate education units and not rely on people on short-term contracts or sharing the responsibility for developing and managing university-corporate links among other diverse activities.

REFERENCES

Association of Advanced Collegiate Schools of Business. (1999). Corporate universities emerge as pioneers in market-driven education. *Newsline*. Retrieved January 15, 2008, from http://www.aacsb.edu/publications/printnewsline/NL1999/spcorporat.asp

Arino, A., de la Torre, J., & Ring, P. (2001). Relational quality: Managing trust in corporate alliances, *California Management Review, 44*(1), 109-132.

Bedar, S. (1999, October). Corporate universities—for better or worse? *Engineers Australia*, p. 70.

Bersin, J. (2005). *Death of the corporate university; Birth of learning services.* Retrieved January 15, 2008, from http://www.bersin.com/tips_techniques/05_nov_death_cu.asp

Blass, E. (2001, June). What's in a name? A comparative study of the traditional public university and the corporate university, *Human Resource Development International, 4*(2), 153-172.

Corporate University Xchange. (2004). *Sixth Annual Benchmarking Report, Corporate University Xchange, New York.* Retrieved January 15, 2008, from http://www.corpu.com/news/press/2004_11.asp

Densford, L. (1998). Many CUs under development: Aim is to link training to business. *Corporate University Review.* Retrieved January 15, 2008, from http://www.traininguniversity.com/magazine/jan

Ellis, K. (2005). The mindset that matters. *Sales & Marketing Management, 157*(7), 34-37.

Elmuti, D., & Kathawala, Y. (2001). An overview of strategic alliances. *Management Decisions, 39*(2), 205-218.

Hagen, R. (2002). Globalisation, university transformation and economic regeneration. *International Journal of Public Sector Management, 15*(3), 204-218.

Holland, P., & Pyman, A. (2006). Corporate universities: A catalyst for Strategic Human Resource Development?, *Journal of European Industrial Training, 30*(1), 19-31.

Lang, J. (2004). Social context and social capital as enablers of knowledge integration, *Journal of Knowledge Management, 8*(3), 89-105.

Meister, J. (2000). Corporate universities: Market-driven education. *Journal of Business Disciplines, 1,* 1527-151X.

Meister, J. (2001). The brave new world of corporate education. *Chronicle of Higher Education, 47*(22), 10.

Nixon, J., & Helms, M. (2002). Corporate universities vs. higher education institutions. *Industrial and Commercial Training, 34*(4), 144-150.

Paton, R., Peters, G., Storey, J., & Taylor, S. (2005). *Corporate universities as strategic learning initiatives. The Handbook of Corporate University Development: Managing strategic learning initiatives in the public and private domains.* London: Gower.

Prince, C. (2000, May). Strategic change: The role of in-company management education. *Strategic Change, 9,* 167-175.

Shah, A., Sterrett, C., Chesser, J., & Wilmore, J. (2001, Spring). Meeting the need for employees development in the 21st century. *S.A.M. Advanced Management Journal, 66*(2), 22-27.

CHAPTER 2

CO-PRESENCE AND GROUP PROCESS IN ONLINE MANAGEMENT EDUCATION

Judith Stevens-Long and Charles McClintock

This chapter focuses on the concept of co-presence as a central interpersonal and group process that supports online learning through an emphasis on faculty-student interaction and peer collaboration. Co-presence is about the social context of learning, empowerment of the learner, and critical reflection through dialogue. We discuss ways to create these experiences in the online context and present exploratory data to examine the effects of this kind of collaborative learning in graduate management education programs. Co-presence is especially important in the retention of lifelong learners who show a strong preference for learning that connects knowledge to experience, provides alternative ways for them to demonstrate their knowledge, and challenges them to reach beyond what they already know.

INTRODUCTION

The popular image of distance or e-learning is a technological one that essentially transfers face-to-face pedagogy to a virtual medium through the

University and Corporate Innovations in Lifelong Learning, pp. 15–32
Copyright © 2008 by Information Age Publishing
All rights of reproduction in any form reserved.

use of "shrink-wrapped" (i.e., digitized) lectures and learning objects or streaming video and audio supported by downloaded text-based materials (Stevens-Long & Crowell, 2002). This emphasis on the technology of online learning belies the significance of interpersonal relationships and group dynamics in the learning process. Whether in the classroom or mediated by technology, we suggest that the idea of co-presence, or a mutual sense of interaction (Palloff & Pratt, 2007), deserves more attention as critical to learning. In addition, in the area of management education, interpersonal relations are a critical success factor in the practice of the profession (Raelin, 2000).

In this chapter we describe collaborative learning practices for graduate-level online management education that create a sense of what we call "co-presence" and enhance interpersonal skills that are key to managerial effectiveness. Co-presence is the experience that someone is engaged with you in the online learning environment, and it is particularly important in retaining adult lifelong learners who thrive on the opportunity to connect their personal and professional experience to the classroom experience. Co-presence is a subtle experience that is not easily defined, but we argue here that it can thrive in the asynchronous environment (perhaps more so than in synchronous interaction) and can be built through collaborative learning practices and an appreciation of the life of the group. In addition, we report on our experience with student-centered, collaborative pedagogy at Fielding Graduate University and present data analyzing several of our online learning options in management-related content areas with respect to collaborative learning and co-presence.

SOME BRIEF HISTORY

Beginning in the late nineteenth century with the work of Anna Ticknor, who founded a society dedicated to the education of women through printed materials that could be sent through the mail, distance education took root in the correspondence schools of the early twentieth century. Many distance education programs still include correspondence, though it may now be accomplished by e-mail.

As early as 1932, University of Iowa attempted to use television to transmit college courses. After World War II, several important studies suggested that there were either no differences or very small differences in the learning of students who attended classroom lectures and of those who saw those lectures on TV (Childs, 1949; Parsons, 1957). Despite these promising results, however, attempts at televised education all but died during the 1960s due to the poor quality of much televised instruction.

Current interest in the use of DVDs and streaming video in Web-based courses seems to have revived this dimension of distance education.

With the coming of the Internet, early educational experimenters attempted distance learning via e-mail and bulletins boards where messages could be posted. In these primitive trials, only 2 decades ago, messages were posted by date alone. Threaded discussion was not possible and one could read text online as quickly as the computer could display it. Since that time, learning platforms such as WebCT, Blackboard, and Sitescape have developed along with streaming video and audio, graphic capabilities, and the wide variety of content resources available on the Web.

Many prospective students and teachers who approach online learning emphasize technological features without giving much thought to pedagogy. Yet, it is creative pedagogy that can make online learning meaningful, especially for adult professionals, through interpersonal interaction and peer exchange. In our last attempt to summarize this research, we found a frustrating lack of distinction between "distance education" courses that were offered by closed-circuit television, video or CDs and those that were offered via an external, Web-based resource such as WebCT or Blackboard (Stevens-Long & Crowell, 2002). More importantly, we reported then that the emphasis in the study of distance education was on media, rather than pedagogy.

> The pedagogy has remained an independent study model that has consistently adopted new communication technology (instructional radio, instructional television, later videotape, and now the Internet) to shorten the communication time between instructor and student, but those technology-based efficiencies have been largely both singular and unidirectional (applied only to the linkage from the instructor to the student). New technology sped up information transfer to the student; it allowed, in some forms, for more facile, concurrent access to a larger learner population. (pp. 152-153)

At that writing, much of what was available online was "shrink-wrapped" (i.e., digitized) workbook or textbook material that was to be downloaded and read prior to taking a text or writing a paper that would then be uploaded to the professor who would assign a student a grade. In some cases, students were attending optional asynchronous discussion groups or, even more occasionally, chat rooms. It is refreshing to see that just 4 years later the literature describing the use of the medium has become more sophisticated about both the pedagogy as well as the technology of online learning (Wankel & DeFillippi, 2003). As a part of this evolution, several interesting typologies have been proposed.

TYPOLOGIES OF ONLINE LEARNING

There are several classification systems that describe a continuum of online learning ranging from the technical to the interpersonal. Roberts and Jones (2000) proposed four models of online teaching as follows:

- The naïve model: lecture and reading material is posted to the Web, but no interaction is expected or required.
- The standard model: Materials are posted on the Web and interaction about those materials is encouraged, generally through Q&A.
- The evolutionary model: The method of course delivery remains fluid with some posting of materials and some class discussion that might influence selection of course materials.
- The radical model: This model dispenses with lecture altogether and proceeds through faculty-student interaction and peer collaboration.

More recently, Rungtusandtham, Ellram, Siferd, and Salik (2004) offered a similar typology of business online education. They identify four basic modes of delivery that include:

- Overview: Course materials are delivered through a one-way Webcast. The content is faculty designed and driven. There is little interaction.
- Overview with feedback: Course materials are delivered by Webcast in this mode as well, but limited opportunities exist for interaction such as question and answer periods.
- Technical skills model: the emphasis in this mode is on technical learning aids (like games and quizzes, puzzles and simulations). The learning aids themselves provide feedback to the learner.
- Managerial learning model: This model is designed to teach decision making and complex problem solving. Interaction is deemed essential. Students are expected to learn and apply course content, to receive feedback, make changes, and reapply.

In the first three modes, students may proceed at their own pace through the course content. In the managerial learning model, individual flexibility is sacrificed to some extent by the desire to have the group stay intact and benefit from interpersonal exchange and peer learning.

In many ways, these typologies can be applied to classroom instruction as well, and as is true of the traditional classroom, there is fairly widespread agreement on the importance of faculty-student interaction in creating effective learning on the Web. Arbaugh and Stelzer (2003) note, "There is more to delivering Web-based courses than building a series of Web pages and handing them off to students" (p. 23). Instructors make the difference in the classroom online in the way they design the syllabus, the success they have in creating a learning environment, and the interactions they have with students (Anderson, Rourke, Garrison, & Archer, 2001; Marks, Sibley, & Arbaugh, 2005; Swan, 2002).

There is also support for the proposition that a sense of interpersonal community built on student-to-student interactions can contribute to the success of the learning experience (Shea, Swan, & Pickett, 2003). However, the importance of student-to-student interactions has been more difficult to assess since the demand for and structuring of these interactions vary across subject matter, program or institution. In addition, research on Web-based instruction reflects a complex portrayal of the construct of "online learning" and the factors that affect the quality of student experience and learning, including class size, subject matter, use of multimedia, as well as student and instructor characteristics (Arbaugh & Stelzer, 2003).

In our view, the type and frequency of student-to-student interaction is one of the key instructional issues in the online classroom, particularly for lifelong learners who bring a wealth of experience to the learning environment. Research on the effectiveness of collaborative pedagogy that emphasizes interpersonal interaction is mixed, although it is not clear if this is due to poor implementation of this pedagogical approach or the approach itself (Arbaugh & Seltzer, 2003). Given that most higher education faculty members are not trained in pedagogy, it seems most likely that inconsistent research findings are due to variable instructional skills.

We argue here that the use of collaborative learning and an understanding of group process and critical pedagogy can improve the experience of mature students and faculty by cocreating a sense of presence and community by facilitating opportunities for adult learners to bring their experience to bear on the issues raised in the syllabus.

COLLABORATIVE LEARNING, CRITICAL PEDAGOGY, AND PRESENCE

Porush (2005) summarizes the Sloan-C Quality Framework for a successful Internet learning environment as active, constructivist, andragogic, and agentive. These are the student-centered graduate education principles that have supported the learning model at Fielding

Graduate University for the last 30 years. Futhermore, we see these principles as critical to the personal and professional development of adult students in general but most especially for those in management-related professions.

Fielding offers WASC-accredited masters and doctoral degrees as well as various continuing education and certificate programs for midcareer professionals. The management-related programs in Fielding's School of Human and Organization Development (HOD) enroll students who are human resource professionals, organizational consultants and trainers, internal OD practitioners, and managers at every level who want to expand their professional and personal horizons.

Mature adult students prefer learning that addresses their real life challenges. They expect to be involved in the design of their education and have the need for flexibility of time, place and pacing. They demand mutual respect between instructor and student and substantial constructive feedback (Maehl, 2000). Adult students "seek to be collaborative partners in the learning process" (Rudestam & Schoenholtz-Read, 2002, p. 7). Fielding was designed to meet the lifelong learning needs of mature students through its student-centered pedagogical practices. This philosophy has also guided the design of its online learning environment.

Critical Pedagogy

Using the Roberts and Jones (2000) typology described above, Fielding exemplifies the radical model of online teaching. We have dispensed with lectures almost entirely and have cast the teacher in the role of facilitator rather than instructor. Beginning with the work of Malcolm Knowles (1984), a founding faculty member in the school of HOD, Fielding built its learning model around the principles of andragogy. As articulated by Knowles, andragogy emphasizes self-directed learning and the integration of life, work, and education.

In recent years, we have augmented these assumptions with those of critical pedagogy (Cervero, Wilson, & Associates, 2001; Freire, 1970, 1973) as well as work on transformative collaborative and emancipatory learning (Mezirow, 1991; Mezirow & Associates, 2000; Schapiro, 2003). This work had led us to emphasize the social context of learning, issues of power and social justice, and the need for critical reflection and dialogue. Fielding's model has also been described as neo-humanist (Shapiro & Hughes, 2002) based on the work of Habermas (1970, 1990, 1994) who emphasized the goal of improved human understanding and affirmed egalitarian and democratic values. In the neo-humanist paradigm, it is necessary to discover the student's perspective, take it seriously, and attempt to make the environment fit his or her learning needs.

Richardson and Newby (2006) define cognitive engagement as the "integration of a student's own motives and strategies in the course of their learning" (p. 25). In their study, graduate students who continued to pursue online education showed higher levels of cognitive engagement and self-regulation. While Richardson and Newby believe that online education encourages students to take more responsibility for their own learning, it is also apt that students with a preference for self-regulation and cognitive engagement are likely to choose online learning. This has been our experience as an institution.

Schapiro (2003) provides a summary of the learning principles and practices in the School of Human and Organization Development. The weight of the model falls on the learners' needs, purposes, and goals rather than on the agenda and ideas of the instructor. The learning process is built around problems rather than subjects, inquiry rather than answers, collaboration rather than competition, and includes the emotional, kinesthetic, and spiritual dimensions of learning as well as the cognitive. It is constructivist and encourages students to learn from their own and each other's experience as well as books and instructor commentary. We are reluctant to say "lecture" here as we do almost nothing online that might be considered lecture in another setting. Faculty members engage students as colleagues and colearners in the educational enterprise. Students are expected to bring their own observations, their own questions and their own wisdom to the process using faculty as colearners and collaborators in building knowledge.

In research on our doctoral program (McClintock & Stevens-Long, 2002), we have found that alumni attribute important changes in their behavioral, emotional and intellectual development to the collaborative relationships they experienced with faculty and other students. Since the average age of our doctoral students is 47, we consider them lifelong learners from the moment of their entrance in the program. As alumni, they constitute one of the most important markets for our continuing education and certificate programs.

Both the principles that we espouse and the outcomes we have found imply a critical role for student-to-student interaction in the online learning environment. We require our students to engage in interaction with one another online. A large part of their grade depends upon the level and frequency of their participation. Typically, students are divided into small study groups. They post their assignments to separate forums provided for each study group in the course and comment on the work of others in the group. Different instructors expect different levels of commentary; some require that each student comment on every other student's work; some require that each student comment on the work of two or three other people each week.

Marks, Sibley, and Arbaugh (2005) point out that students often get out of participating in the course by rotating the leadership from one student to another so that everyone does not have to participate equally in the discussion. In other work, students are described as "lurking" rather than participating in many courses (Nicol, Minty, & Sinclair, 2003).

While online instructors at Fielding often rotate leadership through the small study groups by asking one of the students to pose the questions for a week's assignment, all members of each group are required to comment on each other's work regardless of who is assigned to lead. One student is often assigned to summarize the week's discussion as well. There is no shirking or lurking permitted.

NOVELTY, DRAMA, AND CO-PRESENCE

In the context of this frequent student participation, the faculty member is expected to demonstrate his or her "presence" and work to create a sense of community. Short, Williams, and Christie (1976) first used the term "social presence" to refer to the degree to which the medium is experienced as sociable, warm, sensitive, or personal, creating the impression that the person communicating is *real*. Lombard and Ditton (1997) talk about presence as an "illusion that a mediated experience is not mediated" (p. 1). Witmer and Singer (1998) refer to the subjective experience of being in an environment in which one is not actually present.

Presence is described in the online learning literature as a function of faculty behavior that includes the presentation of content and questions, attempts to focus or summarize student discussion, confirm understandings, diagnose misperceptions, inject knowledge, and respond to technical concerns (Anderson, Rourke, Garrison, & Archer, 2001; Shea, Swan, & Pickett, 2003; Swan, 2002). In other places (Arbaugh & Stelzer, 2003), presence is also discussed in terms of instructor "immediacy" behaviors. Based on work by Mehrabian (1971), immediacy behaviors include the use of personal examples and humor, providing and inviting feedback and addressing students by name. All of the behaviors that are outlined in the current literature on presence are quite consonant with the collaborative model. The role of the faculty member is to guide and expand the discussion, to model feedback and critical thinking rather than to lecture.

At Fielding, we have also drawn upon the literature that describes the experience of presence in novel or foreign environments (Fontaine, 2002). Fontaine shifts the emphasis slightly from the experience of the medium to the psychological experience of the participant and his or her awareness that others are "present" in the environment. Rena Palloff and Keith Pratt (2007) call this phenomenon a mutual sense of interaction. We look to students and faculty to cocreate a sense of presence in the online environment (Anderson, Ashraf, Douther, & Jack, 2000) and we know that our students attribute significant cognitive, emotional, and behavioral change to such interactions. Simply put, co-presence is the experience that someone else is there with you, "co-present" in the classroom. Novelty and unpredictability are key precipitants of co-presence. The optimal mix of surprise, predictability, and drama is required. The exchange of small talk, metacommunication about the course, attempts to build culture through the discussion of group process and norms, offers of support, encouragement, humor, and perspective are all part of building co-presence through collaboration.

In an online course at Fielding, the facilitator might begin his or her post with a comment about the moonrise or the weather in his or her location. An administrator might be asked to make a "guest appearance" in a course to initiate a discussion of norms across courses. Students are encouraged to share their non-classroom experience and create a sense of narrative across their posts. The facilitator is expected to model appropriate use of emotional and experiential material for students, but is cautioned against too much input, making it easy for students to sit back and wait for knowledge to fill their heads. Co-presence, then, is founded in collaborative interaction that covers the intellectual, emotional and everyday practical domains.

Over time, the variety and depth of student-faculty and student-student participation build a sense of shared community. As Hudson (2002) describes it, such classrooms are composed of "distributed many-threaded dialogue constructed as a process of self-organized discovery" (p. 213). There is a shift from hierarchy to a flat, decentralized format that is more flexible and actually permits faster changes than the more traditional classroom despite research that suggests change is more difficult to accomplish in the online classroom (Rungtusandtham, Ellram, Siferd, & Salik, 2004). This demand for collaboration may seem daunting, especially to the beginning student or faculty member who may feel overwhelmed by the possibilities for interaction. It is here that a grasp of group process can make an important contribution to co-creating presence.

CO-PRESENCE AND GROUP PROCESS

Co-presence and community are most efficiently created when participants learn to attend to the life of the group rather than responding constantly at the individual level.

For this reason, another key element in the model we have adopted for online learning is the consideration of the group process literature, particularly the work of Wilfred Bion (1959). Using Bion, Stevens-Long (1994) has argued that most groups can be understood in terms of two dimensions: boundary and role structure. Boundary refers to the limits of membership and the degree to which information flows into the group from the outside while role refers to the extent to which member duties are specified and hierarchically arranged. In most traditional classroom settings, roles are hierarchically structured. The teacher "delivers" knowledge through lecture or the design of experiential exercises. He or she has "objectives" and students are to meet these objectives through changes in their verbal and/or nonverbal behavior. The boundary of the group is physical. One belongs because one is on the roster and no one else may enter without the permission of the instructor.

In the computer-mediated classroom, boundaries are defined by the structure and timing of participation rather than by physical space. Anyone might be present in class since no one monitors who uses the computer on which a student "logs in." Boundaries have to be negotiated—who is allowed, who is not, how to guard confidentiality and privacy for the group. Privacy and confidentiality are of particular concern to lifelong learners who want the opportunity to reflect on their own personal and professional development and the operation of their organization.

Because there is no physical venue, the space has to be consciously bounded through interaction of some kind between the instructor and the students. This presents an opportunity to cocreate presence since it is not only a novel situation but one that is well served by stories, examples, hypotheticals and personal touches such as addressing students by name or asking for their considerations. Since students are called upon to give feedback to one another, norms for feedback may also be discussed—again, an excellent opportunity for verbal immediacy, novelty, and informal verbal behavior, as well as the comparison of experiences they have had outside the classroom.

Students need to know that there is a place, a set of rules and a structure. Discussion of these rules and norms can set a model for co-presence in the online environment. It has been our experience that the more often the instructor sets the parameters for class participation up-front, the more likely that he or she will be able to back off from participation later in the class and allow the students to learn from each other. In the optimal virtual classroom, the role structure is flatter than the traditional classroom. We talk about facilitating discussion, asking questions, giving and receiving feedback rather than presenting a lecture.

An appreciation of the literature on the group-as-a-whole or the group mind is a useful guide to optimal instructor presence (Wells, 1985). In this approach, the online facilitator is expected to direct the efforts of the group toward understanding the materials.

Facilitators are encouraged not to respond to every posting or to give feedback on every assignment. The level of interaction can get overwhelming quickly if the instructor makes an attempt to respond to every posting or thread of discussion in the classroom. It is assumed that mature students are capable of recognizing outstanding work by their peers, and also of recognizing the errors and learning difficulties of others. The facilitator attends to the understanding that the group as a whole is developing. In each small group, the facilitator will post a commentary following each assignment and the responses of group members to one another's work. In this commentary, the facilitator may summarize where the group stands in regard to the content, point out the ways in which the group has mastered the ideas or where the group has missed a point. He or she may refer to points made by individual students (or points missed by individuals), ask for clarification from the group, help the group make a course correction in regard to its understanding or create a segue for the group from one assignment to the next. He or she may share an example or a case study that is brought to mind by the group discussion or point to additional resources that might be helpful in light of the work of the group.

It is difficult for facilitators to learn to stay at the level of the group. Groups typically exert great pressure on the leader to do the work of the group. In the group process literature there is much talk of role "suction" (Horowitz, 1985), and the facilitator will often experience this as an undertow pulling for responses to individual postings. In the long run, however, responding to the group rather than to individuals makes it possible to create co-presence and promote community while keeping the workload at a reasonable level. In national surveys, faculty often complain that the online work is onerous compared to the traditional classroom (Arbaugh & Stelzer, 2003; Rungtusandtham, Ellram, Siferd, & Salik, 2004). Responding at the group level is a way of doing what Marks, Sibley, and Arbaugh (2005) refer to as responding "holistically," rather than at the level of the individual student.

Responding to the group level has long been associated with learning in psychotherapeutic settings. There is every reason to believe it can be as effective in dealing with mature students as it is in psychotherapy. Beyond that, as a model of working with virtual teams and a dispersed work force, facilitation at the level of the group can create metalearning for any management student who is called upon to work across large geographical distance. In fact, the modeling of facilitation online constitutes an additional imperative for the shift to a less hierarchical, more empowered vision of online learning for management graduate students.

AN EMPIRICAL ASSESSMENT OF COLLABORATIVE LEARNING

At this point, we present data that explores the extent to which our efforts are successful at creating co-presence in online management education. As noted by Arbaugh and Stelzer (2003), there is relatively little empirical work on multicourse Web-based teaching in comparison to research on single courses. To address this gap, we present descriptive findings for two implementations of online multicourse graduate programs in organizational management and development subject matter and compare that to a national sample of adult graduate learners in Web-based programs. The national study is conducted by Noel-Levitz (2005) and consists of a self-administered survey "gap analysis" comparing importance and satisfaction ratings for students across a wide range of variables from educational process and outcome factors to perceptions of institutional support services.

Noel-Levitz materials indicate that negative numbers represent performance gaps in which satisfaction with a feature of the online program is less than its importance as rated here by the student. Positive numbers indicate particular program strengths in which program performance exceeds student importance ratings.

We are reporting on data that focus on the issue of satisfaction with collaborative learning activities and outcomes. As Arbaugh and Stelzer (2003, p. 24) note, collaborative pedagogy is likely to be important for learning in the online environment since it builds the sense of interpersonal community that ideally would be present in a classroom. As described earlier, Fielding's management-related education programs provide considerable ongoing orientation to collaborative online learning emphasizing peer interaction among students and faculty members. This orientation is offered to students as well as the faculty.

We divided the Fielding sample into courses with online interaction only versus those that added a telephone conference component. The telephone conference allowed students and faculty members to discuss issues and cases in synchronous time and added another means of making the Web-environment more interpersonal. We could not control for content in our comparisons. The national sample included a wide range of academic content. In our online-only group, the content consisted of master's degree courses on organizational management and development, while the telephone conference courses were focused in a management concentration on theory and research related to executive coaching. These phone calls were focused on student-to-student discussions of their own cases (in a coaching course). Faculty did not present, but facilitated student interaction and the data suggest that this type of group work can support the experience of co-presence.

Admittedly, these comparisons are not as crisp as one would like but they confirm an expected pattern of findings in relation to creating interpersonal presence in a Web-based graduate management program. As shown in Tables 2.1 and 2.2, on nearly every variable the gap analysis revealed greater satisfaction among the online plus telephone implementation versus on-line only and the national online only sample. Fielding's online plus telephone had program strengths (i.e., a positive gap) on 7 of the 12 variables shown, whereas the national sample had no positive gaps.

We would expect the Fielding sample to show greater satisfaction than a national sample since the former have self-selected collaborative pedagogy and have experienced extensive training and orientation for working online. In addition, the progressive homogeneity of content in the national, Fielding and telephone samples might account for the increasingly positive direction of the ratings on each of the dependent variables. We did not expect, however, to see such large differences between online versus online plus telephone conference. Some of these differences might be explained by the fact that this was a new concentration in coaching with the extra attention and enthusiasm that can accrue to such an effort. We think, however, that a great deal of the difference is accounted for by the combination of asynchronous (online) and synchronous (telephone) modes of interaction. Telephone interaction is enhanced when it is built on the group process and critical thinking norms that are already established in the online environment. This factor could account for the large process differences on items 5 and 6 in Table 2.1 as well as the learning outcome differences on items 3 and 4 in Table 2.1.

CONCLUSION

For the next decade or more, the Bureau of Labor Statistics (2006) predicts that competition for management jobs will increase. They predict only average growth in these jobs while any number of qualified individuals will seek them. They recommend that job seekers attain at least a master's level education with the emphasis on communication and administrative skills. Online learning of the kind used at Fielding offers the opportunity for lifelong learners to add virtual communication and team-building to their repertoire. At Fielding, we offer a certificate in

Table 2.1.   Satisfaction With Collaborative Learning Outcomes[1]

Satisfaction With Collaborative Learning Activities	National Online	Fielding Online	Fielding Online Plus Telephone
1. My instructors involve me in assessing my own learning.	−.57	−.21	+.32
2. My instructors respect student opinions and ideas that differ from their own.	−.48	−.25	−.04
3. My instructors encourage student-to-student interactions through a variety of techniques.	−.21	+.03	.+32
4. I receive timely responses to my requests for help and information.	−.86	−.46	+.19
5. This program initiates many opportunities for me to connect with other adult learners.	−.33	−.43	+.55
6. The frequency of interactions with my instructors is adequate.	−.74	−1.28	+.18
7. Instructors incorporate my life and work experiences in class activities and assignments.	−.41	−.48	−.09

1. Ratings in Tables 2.1 and 2.2 are on 7-point Likert scales. Negative numbers indicate that the satisfaction rating is less than the importance rating. Positive numbers indicate that the satisfaction rating is greater than the importance rating.

Table 2.2.   Satisfaction With Collaborative Learning Outcomes

Satisfaction With Collaborative Learning Outcomes	National Online	Fielding Online	Fielding Online Plus Telephone
1. I receive the help I need to stay on track with my program of study.	−.48	−.67	.00
2. I'm assessed on the knowledge and skills I'll need in my life and career.	−.86	−.68	−.23
3. I have many ways to demonstrate what I know.	−.53	+.27	.+41
4. The learning experiences within my program of study challenge me to reach beyond what I already know.	−.52	−.44	+.09
5. I have a clear understanding of what I'm expected to learn in my course.	.−76	.−64	.−27

virtual team management as well as lifelong learning courses in online facilitation and coaching. In these courses, students not only learn course content through instructor facilitation and collaborative work with their peers, but they learn about how to do these things online.

There is a fair degree of support for the proposition that a sense of community built on student-to-student interactions can contribute to the success of the learning experience (Shea, Swan, & Pickett, 2003). However, the importance of student to student interactions has been more difficult to assess since the demand for and structuring of these interactions varies wildly from one course to another.

At Fielding, the virtual classroom is built around student-to-student interaction, and it appears to pay off in terms of student perceptions of learning and satisfaction with the experience. What is interesting is that even small changes in structure, like the addition of weekly conference calls, can also make important differences in student experience, contributing, we believe, to a sense of co-presence.

Co-presence reflects "the always unique, hopefully authentic, and frequently transient chemistry of each group's moment" (B. Hudson, personal communication, June 2006). Being a phenomenon of groups, it is more than the sum of its parts, but we believe that there are a number of practical ways to create the potential for it, including:

- The requirement that students interact with each other in substantive ways
- The use of collaborative, student-centered learning techniques, and activities
- The integration of inquiry into the student's own experience
- The use of novelty, humor, and drama
- Attention to and appreciation of the life of the group
- Holistic responses at the level of the group

Here we have made a beginning attempt to assess the efficacy of a fairly radical, student-based model and, even within that model, we find that one needs to know more about strategies and techniques particular to a course, especially the ways in which faculty coconstruct a sense of presence with students, in order to understand outcomes Clearly, more research on specific components of online communication will be of great use to those of us trying to construct effective, efficient, and satisfying online learning environments.

REFERENCES

Anderson, J., Ashraf, N., Douther, C., & Jack, M. (2000, March). *A participatory design study of user requirements for a shard virtual space.* Paper presented at the Third International Workshop on Presence, Deflt, Netherlands.

Anderson, T., Rourke, L., Garrison, D. R., & Archer, W. (2001). Assessing teaching presence in a computer conferencing context. *Journal of asynchronous learning networks, 5*(2), 1-17.

Arbaugh, J. B., & Stelzer, L. (2003) Learning and teaching on the Web: What do we know? In C. Wankel & R. De Fillippi (Eds), *Educating managers with tomorrow's technologies. A volume in: Research in management education and development.* Greenwich, CT: Information Age.

Bureau of Labor Statistics. (Spring, 2006). The 2004-14 job outlook in brief. *Occupational Outlook Quarterly, 50*(2), Retrieved January 15, 2008, from http://www.bls.gov/opub/ooq/2006/spring/art01.htm

Bion, W. F. (1959). *Experiences in groups.* New York: Basic Books.

Cervero, R., Wilson, A. L., & Associates. (Eds.). (2001). *Power in practice: Adult education and the struggle for knowledge and power in society.* San Francisco: Jossey-Bass.

Childs, G. B. (1949). *A comparison of supervised correspondence study pupils and classroom pupils in achievement in school subjects.* Doctoral dissertation, University of Nebraska.

Fontaine, G. (2002). Presence in "teleland." In K. E. Rudestam & J. Schoenholtz-Read (Eds.) *Handbook of online learning* (pp. 31-52). Thousand Oaks, CA: SAGE.

Freire, P. (1970). *Pedagogy of the oppressed.* New York: Seabury.

Freire, P. (1973). *Education for critical consciousness.* New York: Seabury.

Habermas, J. (1970). Toward a theory of communicative experience. In H. P. Dreitzel (Ed.), *Recent sociology #2* (pp. 114-148). New York: Macmillan.

Habermas, J. (1990). *Moral consciousness and communicative action* (S. W. Nicholsen, trans.). Cambridge, MA: MIT Press.

Habermas, J. (1994). Three normative models of democracy. *Constellations, 1*(1), 1-10.

Horowitz, L. (1985). Projective identification in dyads and groups. In A. D. Coleman & M. H. Geller (Eds.), *Group Relations Reader 2.* Washington, DC: A. K. Rice.

Hudson, B. (2002). Critical dialogue online: Personas, covenants, and candlepower. In K. E. Rudestam & J. Schoenholtz-Read (Eds.), *Handbook of online learning* (pp. 29-53). Thousand Oaks, CA: SAGE.

Knowles, M. (1984). *The adult learner: A neglected species* (3rd ed.) Houston, TX: Gulf.

Lombard, M., & Ditton, T. (1997). At the heart of it all: The concept of telepresence. *Journal of Computer-Mediated Communication, 3*(2), 1-39.

Marks, R. B., Sibley, S. D., & Arbaugh, J. B. (2005). A structural equation of predictors for effective online learning. *Journal of Management Education, 29*(4), 531-563.

Mehrabian, A. (1971). *Silent messages.* Belmont, CA: Wadsworth.

Mezirow, J. (1991). *Transformative dimensions of adult learning.* San Francisco: Jossey-Bass.

Mezirow, J., & Associates. (2000). *Learning as transformation: Critical perspectives on a theory in progress.* San Francisco: Jossey-Bass.

McClintock, C., & Stevens-Long, J. (2002, June). *Assessing the ineffable in graduate education.* Paper presented at the Association for the Advancement of Higher Education, Boston.

Maehl, W.H. (2000). *Life long learning at its best.* San Francisco: Jossey-Bass.

Nicol, D. J., Minty, I., & Sinclar, C. (2003). The social dimensions of online learning. *Innovations in education and teaching international, 40*(3), 270-280.

Noel-Levitz. (2005). *National Online Learners Priorities Report.* Retrieved January 15, 2008, from http://www.eric.ed.gov/ERICDocs/data/ericdocs2sql/content_storage_01/0000019b/80/1b/be/ec.pdf

Palloff, R. M., & Pratt, K. (2007). *Building virtual learning communities.* San Francisco: Jossey-Bass.

Parsons, T. S. (1957). A comparison of instruction by kinescope, correspondence study and customary classroom procedures. *Journal of Educational Psychology, 48*, 27-40.

Porush, D. (2005). Toward a universal learning environment: A vignette from the future. In J. C. Moore (Ed.), *Elements of a quality online education: Engaging communities: Wisdom from the Sloan Consortium* (pp. 191-202). Needham, MA: The Sloan Consortium.

Raelin, J. A. (2000). *Work-based learning: The new frontier of management development.* New Jersey: Prentice Hall.

Richardson, J. C., & Newby, T. (2006). The role of students' cognitive engagement in online learning. *American Journal of Distance Education, 20*(1), 23-37.

Roberts, T. S., & Jones, D. T. (2000, April). Four models of online teaching. In TEND 2000: *Proceedings of the technological education and national development conference, "Crossroads of the new Millennium,"* Abu Dhabi: United Emirates.

Rudestam, K. E., & Schoenholtz-Read, J. (2002). Overview: The coming age of adult online education. In *Handbook of online learning* (pp. 3-28). Thousand Oaks, CA: SAGE.

Rungtusandtham, M., Ellram, L. M., Siferd, S. P., & Salik, S. (2004). Toward a typology of business education in the Internet Age. *Decision sciences journal of innovative education, 2*(2), 101-120.

Schapiro, S. A. (2003). From andragogy to collaborative critical pedagogy. *Journal of Transformative Education, 1*(2), 150-166.

Shapiro, J., & Hughes, S. K. (2002). The case of the inflammatory email: Building culture and community in online environments. In K. E. Rudestam & J. Schoenholtz-Read (Eds.), *Handbook of online learning* (pp. 91-124). Thousand Oaks, CA: SAGE.

Shea, P., Swan, K., & Pickett, A. (2003). Teaching presence and the establishment of community in online learning environments. In J. C. Moore (Ed.), *Elements of quality online education: Engaging communities. Wisdom from the Sloan Consortium.* (pp. 33-66). Needham, MA: The Sloan Consortium.

Short, J., Williams, E., & Christie, B. (1976). *The social psychology of telecommunications.* New York: Wiley.

Stevens-Long, J. (1994, June). *The application of decision-making theory and theories of adult development to diagnosis and intervention in group process.* Paper presented at the meeting of the International Society for the Psychoanalytic Study of Organizations, Chicago.

Stevens-Long, J., & Crowell, C. (2002). The design and delivery of interactive online graduate education. In K. Rudestam & J. Schoenholz-Read (Eds.). *The Handbook of Online Learning.* Thousand Oaks, CA: SAGE.

Swan, K. (2002). Building learning communities in online courses: The importance of interaction. *Education Communication and Information, 2*(1), 23-49.

Wankel, C., & De Fillippi, R. (Eds). (2003). *Educating managers with tomorrow's technologies. A volume in: Research in management education and development.* Greenwich, CT: Information Age.

Wells, L., Jr. (1985). The groups-as-a-whole perspective and its theoretical roots. In A. D. Coleman & M. H. Geller (Eds.), *Group Relations Reader* (Vol. 2, pp. 248-285). Washington, DC: A. K. Rice.

Witmer, B. G., & Singer, M. J. (1998). Measureing presence in virtual environments: A presence questionnaire. *Presence: Teleoperators and Virtual Environments, 7,* 225-240.

CHAPTER 3

DEVELOPING LEARNING COMMUNITIES IN EXECUTIVE EDUCATION

A Case Study of a Global Senior Executive Program

Schon Beechler, Lyle Yorks, and Rachel Ciporen

This chapter introduces an integrative learning framework that represents key aspects of highly functional learning communities. In doing so, we draw on the findings from a case study that examines the impact of a senior executive program at a top-tier U.S. university as well as literatures from adult learning theory and management education. The chapter begins with a description of The Executive Program (a pseudonym) and its evolution over a 10-year period. We then present our integrative learning community framework to capture the connections between the unfolding program design and its links to learning theory. We describe a number of findings from our longitudinal case study and show that creating diverse learning communities facilitates learning in ways that challenge participants' existing mindsets and supports leaders in developing broader and more complex perspectives, a powerful outcome that supports individuals' and organiza-

University and Corporate Innovations in Lifelong Learning, pp. 33–57

tions' abilities to thrive in today's complex environment. We conclude the chapter with our lessons learned in designing a learning community in executive education programs.

I. INTRODUCTION

Business schools are perhaps more cognizant of the relative effectiveness of their teaching than at any time in recent history. For example, the Association of Advanced Collegiate Schools of Business (2002) is sponsoring an ongoing study of effective practices in MBA education and the Academy of Management has recently inaugurated a new journal, *Academy of Management Learning and Education*, raising the profile of teaching and learning in the United States. In the United Kingdom the Association of Business Schools has commissioned a research project into the teaching activities of business schools in that country and their relationship to individual, organizational, and, by extension, national performance.

In part, this growing interest in the effectiveness of management education is a response to increased pressures from students and their potential employers for programs that provide the best preparation for the challenges of today's business world where the rapid rate of technological advances, intense competition and globalization impact organizations across cultural and industry lines. This interest has also been fueled by widespread awareness of the importance of continuous learning as a critical element in individual and organizational success. Pressures are also being felt in the executive education departments of business schools. Traditionally treated as a source of revenue for the schools (and faculty who are generously compensated for teaching in them), executive education programs are increasingly finding themselves confronted with a more competitive market and a client base demanding accountability. Executive education is no longer a reward for a job well done (Conger & Xin, 2000). Participants are sent to these expensive programs to acquire new knowledge, skills, and increasingly mindsets needed by their organizations to succeed and to help advance their own careers. Consequently, the effectiveness of competing executive education programs has come under public scrutiny (see for the example the rankings of various publications such as *Business Week*, *U.S. News* and *World Report*, and the *Financial Times*). Learning new information and tools are critical components of successful executive education programs but, particularly at the senior executive level, the most important outcome is developing a higher level of leadership capacity with a focus on the learning mindset needed in a rapidly changing and complex world. A learning mindset is critical because the rapid pace of technological change, coupled with globalization requires leaders to make meaning in a way that acknowledges complexity and also allows them to adapt and act with greater flexibility in response to changes in their operating environment.

While challenging, there is opportunity embedded in this changing landscape. Executive education programs are potential laboratories for pioneering innovative curriculum designs that integrate adult learning theory with professional development. In this chapter we will share our experience in designing executive education programs which explicitly create learning communities designed to develop learning mindsets among global senior executives.

Learning community is a concept used to describe various ways of structuring educational contexts (Smith, MacGregor, Matthews, & Gabelinick, 2004). Common to most of these contexts is the idea of structuring the learning setting for a group of learners in a way that takes a multidisciplinary approach to challenges or themes through active engagement and reflection. Emphasis is placed on building connections among the participants, faculty, and disciplines. In this chapter we introduce an integrative learning framework that represents key aspects of highly functional learning communities. In doing so, we draw on the findings from a case study that examines the impact of a senior executive program (The Executive Program, a pseudonym) at a top-tier U.S. university, as well as literatures from adult learning theory and management education. As we elaborate below, our research shows that creating diverse learning communities facilitates learning in ways that challenge participants' existing mindsets and supports leaders in developing broader and more complex perspectives, a powerful outcome that supports individuals' and organizations' abilities to thrive in today's complex environment.

Following the presentation of the framework we describe the research project to show the connections between the unfolding program design and its links to learning theory, as well as illustrate the impact of the learning community on the participants. First, however, we begin with a description of The Executive Program and its evolving redesign over a 10-year period in order to contextualize the program and the framework for the reader.

II. DESCRIPTION OF THE PROGRAM

The Executive Program described in this chapter is a 4-week general management course that runs twice a year for a highly international group of 40 senior executives, 85% of whom are male, from a variety of industries and countries. A typical program class is comprised of participants from more than 12 countries with 32% coming from North America, 31% from Europe, 24%, from Asia, 9% from South America, 3% from Africa, and 1% from the Middle East. Participants from service firms make up 37% of the participant population while 32% come from manufacturing and 11% come from government. The final 20% of participants describe their industry as "other."

The program begins with an introduction to the course and staff roles and responsibilities. During this introduction, the faculty directors describe the program content in brief and then describe the process designed to achieve the vision of the program team: "Our vision is to make this four-week [senior executive] program a peak learning experience that will ultimately enhance both individual and organizational performance for every single person in this room." Then, the objectives of The Executive Program are described:

- Develop insights into changing environments and translate these insights into effective strategies
- Understand key levers of the business system and align them to implement effective strategies and lead change
- Build core capabilities for global leadership and management
- Increase self-knowledge, team and personal leadership effectiveness
- Apply program concepts and tools to professional and personal challenges by generating specific actions plans
- Facilitate lifelong learning by building and maintaining a global network of colleagues and friends

While the program offers new information, in addition to conceptual models and frameworks, the kind of learning envisioned in these objectives is not limited to increasing the participants' knowledge of facts or to learning specific rote behaviors or skills, but also involves challenging and testing the assumptions underlying existing frames of reference, gaining insight and developing a capability to continue the learning processes associated with these outcomes after completion of the executive program. It is an executive leadership program driven by the underlying assumption that the value executive leaders add to any organization is enhanced or limited by how they think and learn. Consequently, the first piece of data that the participants receive about themselves and about the class as a whole is how they prefer to learn and the implications of these learning styles for individual behavior, team work, and organizational effectiveness.

On the second day of the program, participants are challenged to think about the world in which they live and work, their assumptions about economic, political, and social history, as well as likely future trends. Using the past 1,000 years of history as a starting point, the participants' perceptions and views are challenged and debated with a leading faculty member and in small group discussions.

On day 3, the focus returns to building the learning community and diverse teams are formed on the basis of participant learning styles, national background, industry, and functional experience, as well as gender. The teams engage in a day of team building activities where the focus is to (1) build the learning community, (2) enable participants to get to know their group quickly and (3) to practice effective team leadership and followership behaviors in a safe and fun context. The remainder of week 1 focuses on strategic thinking and strategy development processes using specific tools and real life application opportunities to make the material practical and relevant to participants' own situations and to cement the learning.

In the second week of the program, the emphasis shifts to functional levers of excellence and different perspectives on leadership, while continuing to build the learning community. Frameworks in the areas of finance, accounting, marketing, operations, and human resource management are introduced and applied both to case studies and to participants' own work situations.

Throughout the program, participants are given the opportunity to learn new material, test their assumptions and conclusions, apply their knowledge to actual and case-based business situations, and integrate concepts and frameworks across the various disciplines in discussions with faculty and their peers. These cross-disciplinary and cross-industry discussions are foundational for creating the learning mindsets necessary for innovative strategic thinking and change management leadership. In fact, in postprogram interviews, alumni report that the opportunity of working, living, and building relationships with such a diverse network of people is one of the most important aspects of participants' learning. It is in conversations with peers across industries and cultures that core and previously unarticulated assumptions are discussed and challenged.

In weeks 3 and 4 of the program, the focus turns to individual leadership, personal development and the leadership and management of change. Participants are exposed to a number of different perspectives on leadership from both academic faculty and practitioners and experience a number of practice opportunities. Participants also receive 360 feedback reports which allow them to compare their self perceptions with perceptions of their manager, peers, and direct reports. In addition, peer groups spend a full day on an action learning component, working on a personal case project, and, with the help of their peers, devise an action plan for achieving their objectives after the program has concluded.

In its totality, the intent of The Executive Program is to expand executives' perspectives and ways of seeing the world and to give them frameworks, theories and tools for formulating and implementing strategies to improve their own, others, and their organizations' effectiveness. The program emphasizes enhancing self-awareness and core leadership skills such as listening and spoken communication; exposure to leading concepts and frameworks in a variety of functional areas—not to make functional experts out of participants, but to enable executives to ask the right questions of experts in their organizations; and helps increase leadership capabilities through 360 assessment and feedback, leadership coaching, values elicitation and values coaching.

Finally, in the two application projects at the end of the course, participants work on a personal case project with a group of their peers and present their leadership message which outlines their vision for their organization, the key values and behaviors needed to achieve that vision, and what the participant him- or herself believes in as a leader. Both application projects are designed to integrate and apply concepts and frameworks from the course, thus increasing the participants' ability to utilize their learnings after the program is over and to enhance their leadership effectiveness overall.

Throughout the program emphasis is placed on the learning process. Our experience demonstrates that creating a learning community with the intentional focus of developing learning mindsets is best served by putting explicit attention on four key knowledge domains: theory, utilization of participants' previous experience, and increasing knowledge of self and others. Further discussion of these dimensions follows in sections IV and V below.

In analyzing learning processes we draw on *experience*, *action*, and *reflection*, three interdependent concepts that are threaded throughout the adult learning literature. Kolb (1984; Kolb & Kolb, 2005) describes experiential learning as a cycle of concrete experience, reflective observation on the experience that leads to abstract conceptualization of experience, and active experimentation, which in turn produces additional concrete experience. A variation of Kolb's framework has been developed by the British specialist in executive and management development, Alan Mumford (1995), and his colleague Peter Honey, who describe the cycle as consisting of experience, reviewing, concluding, and planning components that evolve as a continuous spiral over time.

Additionally, these theorists call attention to the fact that while learning ideally involves the entire learning cycle, most people favor one or two aspects of the cycle over the others, giving rise to the notion of learning styles (activist, reflector, theorist, and pragmatist). Kolb postulates that in addition to reflecting preferred ways of learning, style preferences often produce defensive behavior when there is a mismatch between style and the press of a particular situation.

Our experience shows that providing executives with information about their own learning style decreases defensiveness and creates increased awareness of their own approach and those of other people on their teams who may have quite different learning styles. Learning groups are constructed specifically to include all four learning style preferences, as well as maximize diversity on other dimensions such as nationality, functional background, industry, and gender, and are used throughout the 4 weeks of the program. Participants are told about the criteria for creating the learning groups and are encouraged to discuss with one another how this diversity impacts their experience in working together as a group and how they can maximize their team and individual performance to achieve their objectives while at the executive program. While initially frustrating, the executives learn how to maximize their talents and approaches to team building and other tasks and explicitly use the language of learning styles throughout the program to understand and build a stronger learning community.

III. EVOLUTION OF THE PROGRAM

The Executive Program was born in 1995 out of the merger of two existing 4 week programs, one aimed at U.S.-based executives and the other targeting international executives. This change was precipitated by the increasing globalization of business and a participant body in each of the programs that had grown more and more similar over time. Nearly 8 weeks of largely nonoverlapping content was condensed into four weeks based on the track records of the teaching faculty and a relatively nonsystematic assessment of topic relevance and participants' interests. However, the teaching methodologies and the general underlying assumptions of the program remained relatively constant during this transition.

At the same time, this moment of consolidation proved to be a platform from which a process of continuous improvement emerged. Ironically, this process was not centered on decisions about academic content (although academic content was and remains an important priority), but rather grew out the personal curiosity of one of the faculty directors and co-investigator on this case study about the learning process. This curiosity was the basis for an emerging personal theory of program design that, not so ironically, parallels the learning process of adult learners in general—developing practical knowledge comprised of beliefs and values, content, process, and tacit knowledge.

The faculty director first became involved in executive education in 1992 as a junior faculty member and international specialist in the management department. When she became faculty director she was far outside of her "comfort zone," having been educated in a mainstream academic tradition and hired by the university in a typical tenure-track appointment in the management department.

After the merger of the two programs and the birth of the new Executive Program, she teamed up with two colleagues with many years of experience in the two former senior management programs. Both men mentored the faculty director. However, neither the faculty director nor her colleagues had any formal training in program design, adult learning theory, or even teaching effectiveness. According to the faculty director, "almost everything we did was out of gut feel, combined with our own real-life successes and failures on the job."

Probably because of her own steep learning curve, intensified by a strong fear of failure, it took the faculty director some time to realize that the participants' learning experiences were not being maximized during the program. After the first few programs, however, she began to see many missed opportunities and decided to do something about it. It was the faculty director's own personal quest to have a significant and meaningful impact that spurred her and her colleagues to begin to think about how they could more effectively integrate topics and learning across the program to help participants translate their learning into organizational and individual change and enhanced performance once the program was over.

The faculty director brought in an outside organization development consultant who had worked with executive education at the university in the past to help asses and improve the design of the program. Based on his analysis and advice, the faculty made a number of changes and the results of their efforts were well received by participants. Participant program satisfaction ratings rose from the 4.3-4.4 (on a 5-point scale) in the early 1990s to 4.5-4.6 on a regular basis by the mid-1990s. These successes gave the faculty director confidence that they were moving in the right direction and prompted her to go to the associate dean and director of executive education with a proposal to redesign the program.

One of the first major changes was introducing the idea of a learning community into The Executive Program, drawing on the work of Peter Senge and others. However, according to the faculty director, in the early stages, it was fairly superficial and we didn't design the program in a way where we could actually create a learning community effectively. In retrospect, I realize that this was because I didn't really understand the fundamental nature or implications of the concepts that I was standing up in front of the room and extolling. (author's interview with faculty director)

While they talked about the learning community and pitched it as a foundational concept guiding The Executive Program—trying to maximize learning through taking a learner-centered as opposed to a teacher-centered design while maintaining cutting edge content—the program directors did not design the program in a way where they could make this happen effectively. Realizing this disconnect through experience led to some very fundamental changes in the structure and administration of the program.

To begin this process, the faculty directors announced the redesign effort, the rationale, and its implications to all of the program faculty and staff. In addition, the faculty directors got much more involved in daily session design decisions, including domains such as material selection, teaching pedagogy, and so forth, that had been under the exclusive control of individual faculty members in the past.

To head off resistance, the faculty director met, face to face whenever possible, with each faculty member individually to explain her vision of the program as a learning community and to discuss the faculty member's motivations for participating in the program. While many faculty were unhappy with their relationship with executive education and the perceived lack of fairness in compensation, they nearly all participated because they wanted to make a difference in the participants' and their organizations' performance. Tapping into this shared objective, the faculty director described how, working together, the program could have much more of an impact collectively through collaboration and teamwork. Setting up the whole program as a learning community required faculty to present themselves as part of a team, as a unified whole which had a common mission, a common set of objectives, and which was working towards those objectives. Faculty were encouraged to talk together as a team, hold meetings before the program, discuss changes they were introducing into their material and identify linkages across sessions. Overall, this process worked effectively but there were two cases where the faculty director failed to motivate change and, in one instance she completely alienated the faculty member. To maintain integrity of what they were preaching at the front of the room and how they operated as a cohesive team, the faculty director had to make the difficult decision to take the faculty out of the program.

During this time the program team also realized that the administration of the program had to shift considerably to become more client-focused. In addition, they developed a flexible, action learning team-based approach with constant feedback and improvement and communication between faculty and staff in the office and on-site to create their own continual learning processes and to proactively handle change. For example, the program team conducted after action reviews (AARs) after each program and then, in recent years, added AARs after each week during the program and catalogued their insights to apply to the remaining weeks of the current program and to future programs.

This approach caries many costs, born by everyone on the program team as well as all of the program faculty, but the outcomes have been significant. In recent years the program as a whole has been consistently rated highly, with overall satisfaction ratings ranging between 4.65 and 4.95 since the redesign and averaging 4.95 for the last five programs—a level the program team and staff in executive education believed they would never be able to attain a few years ago. More importantly, research that we conducted concurrently with the program redesign (Yorks, Beechler, & Ciporen, 2007) shows the magnitude of the impact the program has had on participants and their organizations after they return home at the end of the program.

While they originally believed that the redesign would be a one-time event, once the learning process began, the faculty directors and staff realized that they needed to constantly innovate and change with every program. One insight which occurred approximately 2 years after the initial redesign was the realization that in order to keep everyone engaged and learning in an effective way, the program should be designed in such a way that every day, or at least over the course of every couple of days, participants had the time and the opportunity to act, to reflect, conclude, and plan (Mumford, 1995). Otherwise, much of the learning would be lost by the end of the four week program. Consequently, the learning cycle became a foundational concept for operationalizing the idea of a learning community in the program. The faculty directors even took the radical step (for them) of opening up dedicated time in the program schedule for reflection every day. The faculty directors experimented with different designs and, with feedback from program participants, settled on allocating a half-hour every day for reflection. In addition, learning groups, which meet regularly and help members both learn from each other and integrate the material, were established as a key component of the executive program. Participants were also encouraged to keep learning journals to facilitate both reflection and the integration of material. In addition, new components such as values elicitation, one-on-one coaching, and meditation were also introduced to help round-out the learning cycle and enhance the learning from the program.

IV. INTEGRATIVE LEARNING COMMUNITY FRAMEWORK

The section above describes a process of continuous improvement and creation of a learning community through first person experiential learning, which we believe is fundamental to the learning enterprise. This section looks more analytically at the process.

In developing our learning community framework, we reviewed existing theoretical and empirical work on adult learning theory and management education. Within those literatures, we summarize the existing work on learning communities along two primary dimensions; *knowledge domains* and *mechanisms to generate/transfer knowledge*. First, we summarize the *types of knowledge* that are generated and/or shared between members within the knowledge domains. Second, we summarize *mechanisms* for generating and sharing knowledge between members.

Knowledge Domains

Drawing on the adult and management learning literatures (Fox, 1997; Jarvis, 1992; Kolb, 1984; Kolb & Kolb, 2005; Mezirow, 2000; Mumford, 1995; Vaill, 1996) as well as conceptualizations from the intentions of The Executive Program faculty, we have identified four knowledge domains; theoretical concepts and practices, previous experience, self, and others. Bringing these domains together for the learner is the anchoring domain of the learning community. Within these four domains we can classify different types of knowledge: (1) Explicit rational knowledge that is rooted in the conceptual mode of a person's psyche and (2) implicit tacit knowing that is rooted in the affective mode of the psyche (Heron, 1992). The former provides the cognitive frames of reference through which we formally interpret and make sense of our experience. The latter is fundamental to how we take practical action in the world.

Explicit rational knowledge. Rational knowledge, whether derived from logical reason, empirical studies, or pragmatic action, has long been privileged in Western society. Broadly conceptualized, this kind of knowledge is cognitive and corresponds to what Heron and Reason (1997) call propositional knowing. In its most developed form, this kind of knowing is expressed in intellectual statements, both numeric and verbal, and is organized in ways that conform to the rules of logic and evidence. This form of knowing corresponds to what Quinn (1992) and Vaill (1996) describe as abstract knowledge involving *know what* and *know why*.

In executive education programs this kind of knowledge is conveyed by faculty in the form of theoretical frameworks and conceptual frameworks that are based on empirical studies and anecdotal evidence derived from experience. Because participants have considerable experience, they typically come to senior executive programs looking for content—cutting edge ideas, best practices, and new ways of approaching previously intractable problems. This is the domain of the theoretical conceptual frameworks. Additionally, participants are encouraged to develop and make explicit their own "practice theories" for guiding action. In developing these practice theories participants integrate formal theoretical knowledge with their own experience. This process is, of course, an exercise in cognitive rationality. However, it also draws on the participants' tacit experience, which also shapes how they interpret the meaning and usefulness of these theoretical frameworks for their own work contexts.

Implicit tacit knowing. Explicit knowledge can be expressed in words and numbers and easily communicated and shared in the form of hard data, scientific formulae, codified procedures or universal principles (Nonaka & Takeuchi, 1995). Tacit knowledge, on the other hand, is not easily visible and expressible. It is highly personal and hard to formalize, making it difficult to communicate or to share with others. Subjective insights, intuitions, and hunches fall into this category of knowledge. It is also deeply rooted in an individual's action and experience, as well as in the ideals, values, or emotions he/she embraces (Nonaka & Takeuchi, 1995, p. 8). Captured in the phrase "I know more than I can say" Polanyi (1967) argued that tacit knowledge is the foundation on which our explicit knowing is based. Accordingly, tacit knowledge is more holistic than explicit knowledge and critical to effective practice (Sternberg & Horvath, 1999). Rooted in the affective, this form of knowing is an important dimension to what Quinn (1992) and Vaill (1996) have termed knowing in practice, involving *know how*, and *care why*.

Drawing on the implicit tacit knowing that is embedded in executives' experiences adds richness to learning in a learning community. While by definition tacit knowing cannot be made entirely explicit, it can be drawn upon to enhance the understanding of self and the implications for translating theory into practice. This requires the use of expressive learning methods such as encouraging the use of metaphors and alternative mediums of learning, such as artistic engagement to tap into the affective dimensions of feeling and emotion. Theorists have long recognized that affect is an important dimension of learning (e.g., Bloom, 1956; Boud, Cohen, & Walker, 1993) because the whole person is involved with learning and feeling and emotions are integral to learning (Short & Yorks, 2002). Exposure to challenging content and the reactions it provokes in executives' thinking is both a rational and extrarational experience. However, this often comes as a surprise to most participants who have spent their working lives in a rational, economically-driven work environment.

The distinction between conceptual "know what/know why" and tapping into the more tacit "know how/care why" "makes it possible to differentiate 'talking about' from 'talking within' a practice: the former tends to be more descriptive, explanatory, and systematic, whereas the latter is more performative and *ad hoc*" (Fox, 1997, p. 30). *Know what and why* content knowledge is expressed formulaically in terms of propositions or heuristic guidelines for producing a result or solving a problem—what Revans (1982) has called programmed knowledge. *Know how and why* is the ability to perform and may or may not involve utilization of "know what" and "why." Know how does, however, require tacit knowledge and is marked by a feeling of caring on the part of the actor. Providing a learning experience that integrates the rational and extrarational dimensions of the learning process and explicit and tacit knowing is critical in terms of facilitating what Vaill (1996) describes as the "Changes a person makes in himself or herself that increase the know-why and/or know-what and/or the know-how the person possesses with respect to a given subject" (p. 21).

Tapping into the explicit and tacit knowledge of others. In a program like The Executive Program the advantage of diversity is the range of distinct experience that is brought into the learning community. At the same time, the more diverse the community, the more challenging it is for participants to establish the empathic field necessary to fully appreciate and understand the experience of others. Utilizing more expressive ways of learning that tap into the affective not only provides access to one's own tacit knowledge, it provides a pathway into the felt tacit experience of others. "Being told through words about experience is insufficient when there is little or no common experiential grounding" (Yorks & Kasl, 2002, p. 186). Maximizing the power of a learning community requires not only "know what" and "know how," but also *knowing who* the "other" is in terms of a felt sense of the other's experience.

Relevance of the domains. Learning communities are most powerful when they engage the whole learner. In order to accomplish this goal, learning communities must provide pertinent theory, opportunities for participants to reflect on prior experience, enhance self-knowledge, and increase knowledge of others. Without attention to these four domains learning is not maximized. These points are important because they are fundamental to realizing the purpose of executive education programs—

the development of practical knowledge that becomes part of the personal theories and behavioral repertoires of the participants.

Learning needs to be understood as a process involving cycles of sense making of reflecting on experience, not as a transfer of information, but as a process of integrating content into prior experience, and perhaps even arriving at new ways of framing one's experience. This involves the integration of the four domains of learning drawing on both the rational and affective capacity of the participants.

Mechanisms for Generating and Sharing Knowledge

Drawing on the work of Brown and Duguid (1991), Kasl, Marsick, and Dechant (1997), Huang, Newell, and Galliers (2002); and Marsick (2002), we can identify four mechanisms for creating and disseminating knowledge: the social, structural, intellectual, and technological dimensions which Huang et al. identify as relevant to understanding the effectiveness of learning communities. In the social dimension learning must be integrated, situated, collaborative, and socially constructed (Brown & Duguid, 1991), as well as marked by reflective capability and relationships that build trust. This dimension is enhanced through program designs that actively seek to foster and maintain a learning orientation across all aspects of the program, not just within the formal "classroom" and "class time" setting.

Fostering learning relationships is an all-inclusive aspect in such communities. Informal and incidental learning (Marsick & Watkins, 1990) are as important as formal learning activities. Structurally such communities can be thought of as containers or generative spaces (Nonaka, 1994) that provide for "outside-in" learning through cross-organizational contact. Hence the design and utilization of the formal learning activities sets the context for the learning experience, shaping the meaning that participants make of the experience. Intellectually such communities make it easier for participants to interpret "content" knowledge by gaining access to other's experience. Technology provides the possibility of virtual communication beyond the constraints of the physical community, assuming there has been sufficient face-to-face interaction that has developed trust, openness, and a foundation for constructive confrontation.

These mechanisms can all be used to both generate and communicate knowledge within the different knowledge domains of theoretical concepts and frameworks, past experience and practice, knowledge about the self, knowledge about others, and knowledge about the learning community itself. It should be noted that while it is useful to identify these as distinct mechanisms, in practice they are intertwined. The power of the integrative framework lies in the holistic synergies among the domains and the mechanisms—the learning community is more than the sum of its parts.

We assert that establishing an effective learning community requires treating the idea of a learning community as an anchoring domain that becomes a theme that must be understood as both an idea, a process, and a form of personal knowledge shared among participants. The learning community must be a set of dynamics that define the culture of the program.

The two dimensions of knowledge domains and learning mechanisms can be placed into a two dimensional table providing a model for an integrative learning community framework. In the next section we apply this integrative learning community framework to a number of the process and content elements of The Executive Program (see Table 3.1).

V. THE PROGRAM THROUGH THE LENS OF THE INTEGRATIVE LEARNING COMMUNITY FRAMEWORK

This chapter rests on the premise that through reflecting on the successful evolution of an executive education program, with the benefit of hindsight and a conceptual framework linking the components of high performance management education with the tenets of adult learning theory, we can provide a portal for understanding ways to enhance adult learning experiences through executive education. Table 3.1 summarizes the conceptual framework and relates it to the program design. Although described separately, we emphasize the importance of integrating both domains and mechanisms synergistically, rather than as independent components, with the goal of establishing a cultural superstructure of a learning community, which is the role of the anchoring domain.

Integration is a key dimension identified in the literature on learning communities and the faculty and staff in The Executive Program work hard to ensure that a high level of integration exists across the program content and processes. First, within the *social dimension* (Huang et al, 2002), there are a number of program components that help to ensure that the community is integrated, has reflective capability, and is situated. For example, in order to integrate the community, the program begins with a discussion of the concept of a learning community. As previously described, during this session the faculty directors present a summary of the academic and practitioner work on learning organizations, their own vision of The Executive Program learning community and the philosophy and values that drive that vision. There is also a strong emphasis on the

Table 3.1. Integrative Learning Community Framework Applied to The Executive Program

	Knowledge Domains				
Mechanisms to Generate/ Transfer Knowledge	Theoretical Concepts & Frameworks (Explicit, Rational)	Previous Experience (Explicit, Rational/ Affective)	Self (Implicit, Affective)	Others (Implicit/Explicit/ Affective)	Anchoring Domain: Learning Community (Implicit/ Explicit/ Rational/ Affective)
Social	Breakout groups to interpret and apply conceptual frameworks	Breakout groups to share experience and knowledge	Visioning exercise and Physical fitness	Collective visioning exercise to develop norms for community	Discussion of participants role in the program learning community
Structural	Breakout groups to interpret and apply conceptual frameworks; Personal Case Project	Breakout groups to share experience & knowledge; Team building activities; Personal Case Project, ½ hour in class reflection time each day	Visioning exercise; Informal activities; Maximizing diversity in breakout groups; Values elicitation; 360 Feedback and coaching; Leadership Message	Visioning exercise; Informal social activities; Maximizing diversity in breakout groups	Emphasis on "QUEST" as framework for behavior and cultural; program design with coordination and learning style implications
Intellectual	Readings and in class presentations by faculty; faculty coordination across content	Reflection time/Learning journal to apply concepts to past experiences and current business challenges	Currently not applicable in the program's design	Currently not applicable in the program's design	Definition and discussion of a learning community; learning styles
Technological	Program Web site postings of reference readings, Web sites, and discussion threads	Program Web site to share post program experiences and discuss applications of material and learning	Currently not applicable in the program's design	Currently not applicable in the program's design	Program Web site to link globally learning community members

role of the participants in the creation of their own experience and in cultivating a learning community. To facilitate this, diverse groups of 5-7 members are constructed and spend a day in team building exercises and a visioning session to articulate their collective vision for the program and the norms and behaviors that they will commit to in order to achieve their vision. These groups remain together as learning groups throughout the program and meet periodically to reflect on both the content and processes of the course, as well as to apply concepts to their own unique situations.

In addition, theoretical and tacit experiential knowledge are surfaced and addressed during the four-week program. At the practical level, theoretical knowledge, tacit knowledge, process capability and values, and beliefs are all leveraged and developed. For example, "know what" and "know how" of the participants are shared in both large and small group settings, a process that requires paying attention to "knowing who." Additionally, tacit knowledge and its role in decision making are explicitly addressed in a session on expert intuition.

Finally, individual values and beliefs are surfaced during team building sessions, one-on-one coaching for the values elicitation process, 360 leadership feedback and coaching, as well as in numerous small group discussions. In addition to identifying their own values, participants are asked to articulate their most important leadership values, as well as a story to exemplify those values, through the development and presentation of their leadership messages at the end of the program.

Turning now to the *structural dimension* of a learning community (Huang et al., 2002), the faculty directors emphasize the opportunities for seeing the world from a variety of vantage points and the need to develop a program culture based on openness, trust, and sharing. A large number of small group configurations are used throughout the 4 weeks with the goal that all members of the class have an opportunity to work with every other member in a small group setting during the program. In addition, in their opening presentation on The Executive Program as a learning community, the faculty directors identify five norms of behavior that they hope will characterize the course using the acronym of QUEST: Q is for questioning (oneself and others); U is for understanding (oneself and others); E is for experimentation (and the freedom to fail); S is for sharing (experiences, knowledge, and feelings); and T is for trusting (for without trust, none of the other four behaviors will occur).

To enhance the reflective capability of the community (Huang et al., 1992), the program ends each day with a half-hour of in-class reflection time and journaling to capture key insights, questions, and application ideas. In addition, at the end of every week, learning groups meet to discuss their key insights from the previous week, to surface questions, to reflect on the learning process and to articulate their own roles in achieving their objectives for the program. Groups report a summary of their discussions each Monday morning which are posted to the dedicated program Web site. The learning groups also serve as a key vehicle to integrate the formal learning from the course into experience, situating the program in the challenges of the participants' working lives.

In addition to the learning groups, the program directors form personal case groups of 5-6 members which function as a peer consulting team for a current business challenge faced by the participants. The personal case group members share their written case challenges and then discuss each case, in turn, during the final week of the program. Incorporating advice and feedback from their peers, participants are then asked to create an action plan to address their challenges once they return to the workplace and case groups are encouraged to meet virtually to follow up on the challenges after the program has ended.

The QUEST norms and the frequent use of small groups also enhance the *intellectual dimension* (Huang et al., 2002) of a learning community. Learning journals are used as part of the reflection time and participants are encouraged to share their experiences both formally in class and small groups, as well as informally. A number of class sessions use participants' own organizations as "cases" for the application of concepts and frameworks introduced in the program. In addition, when there is a great disparity of expertise in an area (such as finance) small groups are constructed to mix in participant "experts" with their less knowledgeable colleagues with experts explicitly taking on the role of advisor and teacher for their group.

While many of the executive program alumni classes have established regular e-mail communication and are extremely open and sharing in their communications with one another and the program faculty directors and staff, *technology* is the one area where the program can be significantly enhanced to provide the long-term benefits of a learning community before, during and after the program has ended. While the program does have a preprogram and on-site Web site and weekly e-mails between the participants, faculty and staff after the program, technology-enabled learning opportunities are still at an early stage of development. Feedback from alumni has emphasized how important this technologically driven lifelong learning opportunity is for the alumni but currently the lack of resources and infrastructure to achieve these objectives has hampered efforts in this area.

VI. ENHANCING THE
ONGOING REDESIGN WITH PRACTICAL RESEARCH

While it is beyond the scope of this chapter to present a full assessment of The Executive Program's outcomes, this section describes key findings from a comprehensive assessment effort that measures learning, application, and organizational results in order to measure the long-term impact of the program on participants' behaviors and business outcomes. Using qualitative and quantitative data the objectives of our research project were to assess the impact of the program and the value realized by participants and their organizations. The feedback guides ongoing redesign of the program to continue to enhance its long-term effectiveness for participants and their sponsoring organizations. Therefore our specific focus in this section will be on those results from the research that provide lessons regarding the connections between developing a robust learning community and a learning mindset.

Research Methodology

Very few assessments of training and development programs attempt to go beyond participant satisfaction questionnaires (Swanson & Holton, 2001). The reasons for this low level of assessment include the logistical costs and other expenses associated with conducting a thorough assessment, difficulty in obtaining responses from participants once they leave programs, political pressures, and the challenges of measuring both learning and results. These obstacles increase exponentially in open enrollment executive programs.

After careful study and consideration we decided to conduct pre- and postprogram interviews with participants using a critical incident methodology (Flanagan, 1954; McCormick, 1979; Wilson-Pessano, 1988) as a focal point for in-depth interviews to address the design challenges presented by the project—specifically, the infeasibility of control groups and reliance on self-report data. Using behavioral based interview methods, this approach is reasonably rigorous, producing qualitative data specific enough for assessing the "believability" of self-report data. Equally important, critical incidents are useful for producing data consistent with the action research aspect of our project. Critical incidents can provide insight into the linkages among what participants are learning and the settings into which they are applying their learning, along with the challenges and obstacles they confront in doing so.

Telephone interviews lasting approximately 60 minutes were conducted with each participant by trained research assistants before the program began and 6-8 months after the conclusion of the program. Data collected during the interviews included participant's description of the major business challenge or project for which they were responsible, its financial implications, and how, if at all, their approach to the challenge was influenced by their experience in the program; overall impact of the program on how they approached their jobs; and barriers and enablers to their ability to transfer their learning.

Additionally, we implemented a postprogram 360-degree feedback survey to supplement self-report data on the executive leadership competencies (a preprogram 360 for coaching purposes had been part of the program design) providing for pre- and postprogram 360 results. Data were collected from participants and their peers, direct reports, and superiors in the 360 leadership behavior assessments approximately 1 month prior to the program and approximately 1 year after the conclusion of the program. We ran t-tests to compare pre- versus postprogram 360 scores and found statistically significant positive changes in the majority of the leadership behavior dimensions. Because our analysis of the impact of the learning community was derived from the qualitative interviews, additional details on results from the 360 are beyond the scope of this article (see Yorks, Beechler, & Ciporen, 2007, for a summary of the 360 results).

Results From the Inductive Qualitative Analysis of the Postprogram Interviews

Our observations from the qualitative data are drawn from a random stratified sample of 30 participants from a total of 76 postprogram interviews conducted 6-8 months after the completion of the program with participants from two classes that ran in 2003. There was a 97% response rate on the postprogram interviews and those who were unable to participate stated lack of time and constant travel as the reasons for their nonparticipation. From these data we find that participants report a very strong impact of the program, with sessions focused on individual development and experiential sessions generating the most mentions. In addition, clear models and frameworks that are easy to remember seem to "stick" with the participants. Building on this finding, the faculty directors began to coach faculty teaching in subsequent programs to capture their ideas in simple models or frameworks and postprogram feedback from new classes confirmed that this enhanced the retention of the material after the conclusion of the program.

Overall, participants indicate that the biggest impact of the program on them has been on their mindset; their ability to reflect, become more self-aware, to appreciate diversity and to think broadly and globally. As one participant noted:

> I think ... the most beneficial thing over the course of the 30 days was the ability to spend time with yourself trying to figure out how does it all come together and not in terms of who am I and what do I change, but in terms of ok here I am at this particular stage and what can I take away that's better for me and that helps me kind of put everything into a better perspective.

Another respondent stated:

> So its been a real burden on the organization to figure out how you keep margins up, so we stepped back and said ok how do we question all the assumptions we've got, how do we think about things differently, what will we do to position ourselves to win.

Another participant observed:

> I think that I reflect more, that I listen more openly ... I'm more calm, I try to think globally.

As the quotes above suggest, realizing benefits from The Executive Program is dependent on whether it engages participants in reflective learning where they become more aware of patterns in their own thinking and recognize how these patterns are reflected in the workplace. Engaging in further reflection, discussion with peers coming from diverse business settings and coaching help to connect these insights to particular models and frameworks and, in totality, help participants to effectively transfer learning from the program to their organizations. Upon returning to the workplace, participants can make the connection between these patterns and the opportunities and downsides associated with the challenges confronting them. It triggers thoughtful action incorporating a specific set of "tools" learned in the program and consequently, there is often a change in the executives' approaches to challenges and, ultimately, to the outcome of their efforts.

VII. CONCLUSIONS ABOUT DESIGNING A LEARNING COMMUNITY IN EXECUTIVE EDUCATION PROGRAMS

This chapter has focused on the way the design of the learning community can aid in the development of a learning mindset among participants and the extent to which this influence impacts their continued growth following the program. This mindset is fundamental to sustaining lifelong learning. In addition, we have put forth an integrative framework of learning communities that draws on both the adult learning and management education literature and provides a foundation for the evolving design of the executive program. The framework is integrative not only of the literature, but of the experience-based learning of the faculty directors who continue to draw on experientially-based practical knowledge and the literature to innovate its design.

Although the components of the integrative learning community framework are presented analytically, their power, as suggested in our description, is in their interaction. Additionally, there is a temporal dimension to the experience that builds over time. The potential of both the interactive and temporal dimensions of the framework are evident in the assessments of participants. The program's initial sessions devoted to the learning community concept provide a "good introduction to the whole of the program" and aid in "quickly breaking down barriers and inhibitions, helping create a unified group conductive to information exchange" (verbatim quotes from participants). The learning tools that are subsequently introduced, particularly applications of the Learning Styles Questionnaire, are repeatedly mentioned as "very useful in pointing out how each of us approaches learning." Comments such as, "This opened my eyes and made me really think of my weakness and strengths. I have a journey ahead of me" were frequently made by participants in their postprogram interviews.

The value of the emphasis placed on the learning process by program faculty is apparent to the participants by the end of the program. As the program evolves, the idea of the learning community becomes practical, rather than theoretical, and "takes on more relevance in weeks two and three" (program participant). Participants come to appreciate the value of reflecting on the academic content with people who have diverse styles and professional experiences, constructing learning from the interaction with both the faculty "experts" and their peers, and relating content to personal business challenges. This is reflected in postprogram illustrative verbatim participant comments such as:

Interaction between team members was one of the most important learning experiences.

The mix of activities greatly facilitated the learning process particularly using the learning group idea.

Small groups (Learning, Personal Business Case) were very effective in driving home the power of teams and diversity.

High level content and structure.... Learning journal is very useful.

The ideal balance of know how transfer, training, and improving our skills, well-being and social skills.

The success of the program to date suggests that experienced senior executives not only accept, but also learn from and appreciate a learning experience that treats development as more than a transfer of information or one that relies on experiential gimmicks. What is interesting in looking through the messages, reflections, and inquiries of the continuing exchange of e-mails among The Executive Program alumni after the program is the extent to which program content is linked to language reflective of an enhanced awareness of learning, values, and personal leadership messages, program content, and new opportunities for leveraging learning opportunities over time.

The process of continual inquiry, learning from action, and developing practical knowledge comprised of content, process, values, and tacit knowledge (Jarvis, 1999) is the basis for executive effectiveness. Creating a learning experience that develops this capacity is one of the ultimate goals of The Executive Program and continuing to learn how to enhance this capacity is the ongoing challenge of providing meaningful executive education. In addition, understanding the learning process and how to enhance adult learning experiences in venues such as executive education can benefit not only executives but also university faculty and staff.

The Executive Program case study presented in this chapter highlights the fact that while pursuing learning experiences with greater impact for participants, faculty and staff also enhanced their own learning (and ultimately that of the participants) as they followed a new path of experimentation, reflection, conclusion and planning for each new program. The "program" became a process in which not only the participants, but each faculty member and staff member, were intimately engaged. We could only imagine what might happen should we follow a similar path with our doctoral students, our elementary school children and/or our communities.

REFERENCES

Advanced Collegiate Schools of Business. (2002). *Effective practices: MBA Career Services*. St. Louis, MO: Author.

Bloom, B. S. (1956). *Taxonomy of educational objectives. Handbook I: Cognitive domain*. New York: McKay.

Boud, D., Cohen, R., & Walker, D. (1993). Introduction: Understanding learning from experience. In D. Boud, R. Cohen, & D. Walker (Eds.), *Using experience for learning* (pp. 1-17). Buckingham, England: The Society for Research into Higher Education and Open University Press.

Brown, J. S., & Duguid, P. (1991). Organizational learning communities-of-practice: Toward a unified view of working, learning, and innovation. *Organization Science, 2,* 40-57.

Conger, J. A., & Xin, K. (2000). Executive education in the 21st century. *Journal of Management Education, 24,* 73-101.

Flanagan, J. C. (1954). The critical incident technique. *Psychological Bulletin, 51,* 327-358.

Fox, S. (1997). From management education and development to the study of management learning. In J. Burgoyne & M. Reynolds (Eds.), *Management learning: Integrating perspectives in theory and practice* (pp. 21-37). Thousand Oaks, CA: SAGE.

Heron, J. (1992). *Feeing and personhood: Psychology in another key.* Newbury Park, CA: SAGE.

Heron, J., & Reason, P. (1997). A participatory inquiry paradigm. *Qualitative Inquiry, 3,* 274-294.

Huang, J. C., Newell, S., & Galliers, R. D. (2002, April). *Inter-organizational communities of practice.* Paper presented at The Third European Conference on Organizational Knowledge, Learning, and Capabilities. Athens, Greece.

Jarvis, P. (1992). *Paradoxes of learning: On becoming an individual in society.* San Francisco: Jossey-Bass.

Jarvis, P. (1999). *The practitioner researcher: Developing theory from practice.* San Francisco: Jossey-Bass.

Kasl, E., Marsick, V. J., & Dechant, K. (1997). Teams as leaders: A research based framework of team learning. *Journal of Applied Behavioral Science, 33,* 227-246.

Kolb, D. A. (1984). *Experiential learning: Experience as the source of learning and development.* Englewood Cliffs, NJ: Prentice-Hall.

Kolb, D. A., & Kolb, A. Y. (2005). Learning styles and learning spaces: Enhancing experiential learning in higher education. *Academy of Management Learning and Education, 4*(2), 193-212.

Marsick, V. J., & Watkins, K. E. (1990). *Informal and incidental learning in the workplace.* New York: Rutledge.

Marsick, V. J. (2002, August). Building and sustaining networks using action learning. Symposium Presentation at the annual meeting of the Academy of Management, Denver, CO.

McCormick, E. J. (1979). *Job analysis: Methods and applications.* New York: AMACOM.

Mezirow, J. (2000). Learning to think like an adult. In J. Mezirow & Associates (Eds.), *Learning as transformation: Critical perspectives on a theory in progress* (pp. 3-33). San Francisco: Jossey-Bass.

Mumford, A. (1995). *Learning at the top.* New York: McGraw-Hill.

Nonaka, I. (1994). A dynamic theory of organizational knowledge creation. *Organizational Science, 5,* 14-37.

Nonaka, I., & Takeuchi, H. (1995). *The knowledge-creating company.* New York: Oxford University Press.

Polanyi, M. (1967). *The tacit dimension.* London: Rutledge and Kegan Paul.

Quinn, J. B. (1992). *Intelligent enterprise: A knowledge and service based paradigm for industry.* New York: Free Press.

Revans, R. (1982). *The origins and growth of action learning.* London: Chartwell-Bratt.

Short, D. C., & Yorks, L. (2002). Analyzing training from an emotions perspective. In J. L. Callahan (Ed.), *Perspectives of emotion and organizational change: Advances in developing human resources* (pp. 80-96). Thousand Oaks: CA: Jossey-Bass and the Academy of Human Resource Development.

Smith, B. L., MacGregor, J., Matthews, R. S., & Gabelnick, F. (2004). *Learning communities.* San Francisco: Josses-Bass.

Sternberg R. J., & Horvath, J. A. (Eds.). (1999). *Tacit knowledge in professional practice: Researcher and practitioner perspectives.* Mahwah, NJ: Erlbaum.

Swanson, R. A., & Holton, E. L., III. (2001). *Foundations of human resource development.* San Francisco: Berrett-Koehler.

Vaill, P. B. (1996). *Learning as a way of being.* San Francisco: Jossey-Bass.

Yorks, L., & Kasl, E. (2002). Toward a theory and practice for whole-person learning: Reconceptualizing experience and the role of affect. *Adult Education Quarterly, 52,* 176-192.

Wilson-Pessano, S. R. (1988, April). *Defining professional competence: The critical incident technique 40 years later.* Division I invited address presented at the annual meeting of The American Educational Research Association, New Orleans, LA.

Yorks, L., Beechler, S., & Ciporen, R. (2007). Enhancing the impact of an open enrollment executive program through assessment. *Academy of Management Learning and Education, 6,* 310-320.

Yorks, L., & Kasl, E. (2002) Toward a theory and practice for whole-person learning: Reconceptualizing experience and the role of affect. *Adult Education Quarterly, 52,* 176-192.

CHAPTER 4

REFLEXIVE CRITIQUE

An Innovation in
Lifelong Management Learning

Elena P. Antonacopoulou

This chapter advances the idea of reflexive critique and explores its contribution to lifelong management learning. Drawing on diverse literatures propounding a critical perspective, this chapter integrates the various propositions of "what it is to be critical" in advancing the notion of reflexive critique and proposes two additional forms of critique. It is argued that reflexive critique is supported by the critique of simplification and the critique of identity. These forms of critique have not been previously articulated in the relevant literature and they are presented here as a contribution to extending our understanding of what it means to be critical. These forms of critique derive from the experience of introducing an innovative course titled "Critical Thinking" (CT) offered to MBA students over a 5-year period. The chapter discusses the importance of critique in the business curriculum and explains the rationale for introducing the course and its objectives, as well as the learning and teaching techniques employed. The analysis considers how different forms of critique can instill a more reflexive approach to the analysis of management in relation to participants' experiences of managing. The chapter concludes with a review

University and Corporate Innovations in Lifelong Learning, pp. 59–89

59

of the main lessons learned from teaching this course and considers the implications that these lessons raise about lifelong management learning programs seeking to address management and the process of managing.

INTRODUCTION

While management studies continue to raise several key issues about the "lived" experience of "management" and the complexity of "managing," management education has been very slow to respond to such issues and to incorporate them within the business curriculum. One such issue concerns the role of *critique* towards analyzing management, which despite being widely discussed over the years, particularly in relation to "what it is to be critical," it still remains relatively unexplored in the graduate business curriculum. One possible explanation may be the fact that "being critical" underpins much of the existing work of *critical* theory (Habermas, 1978, 1984; Foucault, 1980), *critical* management studies (Alvesson & Willmott, 1992, 1996), *critical* systems (Flood & Jackson, 1991), *critical* pedagogy (Barnett, 1997; Dehler, Welsh, & Lewis, 2001; Giroux, 1997), *critical* thinking (Kurfiss, 1988; Paul, 1990). Each of these schools of thought propounds a different set of definitions about "what it is to be critical." For example, "being critical" is a form of questioning, reflective reasoning and a way of "disciplined" thinking. Moreover, being critical implies scepticism towards arguments, assumptions, practices, recognizing the impact of social and political dynamics, and the implications of the inequalities of power and control.

Despite the different epistemological, ontological, and methodological principles, that inform the interpretations of what it is to be critical across the various schools of thought, similarities do exist. At the most basic level, being critical in its broader sense encourages reflection and questioning of one's reason and practice so that one can be both informed and accountable of one's actions. This broader definition extends what it is to be critical beyond principles of emancipation, inequalities in power and control and the significance of systematic and insightful thinking. It does, however, elevate an important distinction between *being critical* and *critique*. The former often implies criticism and scepticism, whereas the latter, as this chapter will argue is about emphasizing *critique as reflexive praxis*.

This chapter focuses in particular in advancing the idea of *reflexive critique*. Reflexive critique seeks to integrate the various aspects of what it is to be critical to be found in the related literatures. It distinctively seeks to draw the emphasis on reflexive practice rather than criticism or scepticism. Critique therefore, propounds that being critical is not only about revealing inequalities or systematic reasoning. Instead, critique is also about reflecting and questioning one's practices when one is being critical. After all, to be critical one must start from being critical of the critical orientation one applies in assessing any situation including one's own reason and practice. It is important in analyzing further reflexive critique and the role it plays in the business curriculum, to also think about the forms of critique common across the various schools of what it is to be critical.

Mingers (1999) offers a good summary of the main forms of critique currently in the literature identifying: the *critique of rhetoric*, the *critique of tradition*, the *critique of authority*, and the *critique of objectivity*. In advancing the idea of reflexive critique, this chapter will argue that two additional forms of critique are necessary to any process of being critical. These are: the *critique of simplification* and the *critique of identity*. Each of these forms of critique will be developed and discussed in more detail drawing on the experience of teaching an innovative course as part of the MBA curriculum. Therefore, both forms of critique and the notion of reflexive critique are grounded in the empirical[1] praxis of the author. This point emphasizes that in reporting on the experience of introducing reflexive critique in the business curriculum this chapter also presents a reflexive critique of this particular teaching/learning practice (the introduction of a CT course). Moreover, the analysis will also aim to show how the critique of simplification and the critique of identity were exercised both in the context of the course in question, as well as, in the way the author practised them in the course of this specific set of activities.

Therefore, this chapter seeks to argue that reflexive critique can make a valuable contribution within the graduate business curriculum by integrating more closely the analysis of the nature of management with the experiences of managing. Considering that a common pedagogical feature in the curriculum of many MBA programs is that they tend to analyse management as a series of functions, currently there is limited evidence that the MBA curriculum encourages critique in exploring management in relation to experiences of managing. In other words, the functional model of curriculum design tends to be unquestioned and limits questioning personal practice (among practicing managers attending MBA programs and management faculty delivering them). MBA programs designed on functionally-based courses frequently leave participants with a set of disconnected knowledge and skills which bear little coherence and resemblance to the complexity of managing they experience. Moreover, the lack of a synthetic/integrative analysis of the cross-functional and multidisciplinary nature of management leaves little room for reflection and questioning of various social and political facets of managing in the context of organizational life. These observations are much in evidence in the ongoing criticisms about the lack of "relevance" and "applicability" leveled at management theory and research (see Pfeffer & Fong, 2002; Rynes, McNatt, & Bretz, 1999; Starkey & Madan, 2001).

There are therefore, several pedagogical issues about the educational experience that MBA programs offer. It is not sufficient that we provide ethics related courses to sensitize ourselves and MBA participants, that managing is complex and risky, flawed with traps that require informed judgement. This is hardly new, and perhaps we have much to think about the ethical practices in our profession (see Antonacopoulou, 2002, 2003a). What is perhaps more important is that we instill *reflexive critique* within the business curriculum so that critical reflection and a synthetic analysis of management in the light of participants' experiences of managing can be key elements on which our pedagogical practice rests. Moreover, reflexive critique in the business curriculum would emphasis that more attention be given to the learners' experiences and problems, and a more rigorous analysis of theoretical propositions and established wisdom, such that social and political dynamics can be revealed. Furthermore, what could be termed as reflexive critique in management education would also seek to create the space for management educators to be reflective and reflexive of their teaching and learning practices.

It is these issues that this chapter seeks to discuss in more detail, by reflecting on the development of the innovative CT course offered to MBA students. Drawing on over 5 years of work in developing and delivering this course, the analysis presents first some of the main characteristics of the course in the way it was designed and the way different theoretical frameworks emphasizing what it is to be critical were integrated in producing the distinctive emphasis of this course to advance reflexive critique and in particular the critique of simplification and critique of identity. Therefore, the first section of the chapter defines clearly the perspective on what it is to be critical that has informed the CT course. The structure of the course is reviewed and the three workshops, which constituted the course, are discussed in the section, which follows. The content of each workshop is discussed in relation to the teaching, learning, and evaluation techniques used. The chapter concludes with reflections on the lessons learned from the experience of introducing this course on the MBA curriculum and considers some of the implications of instilling reflexive critique in lifelong management learning.

REFLEXIVE CRITIQUE:
MULTIPLE PERSPECTIVES ON WHAT IT IS TO BE CRITICAL

The typical MBA curriculum consists of a range of functionally-based courses (such as accounting and finance, marketing, human resource management) and applies an economic logic in discussing the process of managing resources within organizations. The economic logic propounds corporate profitability as the core of effective management and a signal of efficient managers. This uncritical orientation to teaching and learning about management provides little space for experimenting with ideas that operate outside the dominant economic logic and hence, social and political aspects within management are frequently neglected. Moreover, it fails to provide the space for reflection and questioning of the practice of managing experienced by many of the participants on MBA programs.

There is clearly a need to support participants on MBA programs to experiment with other ideas and question the appropriateness of the economic logic to the analysis of management. Using personal experiences as a foundation, participants on MBA programs could be better supported in initiating and participating in debates that enable them to explore the relationships between the various aspects of management as currently presented in individual courses and to question the validity of the functionally-based model of management drawing on their personal experiences of managing. Moreover, there is a need to support participants in their learning and development throughout the MBA program, so that it can become an educational experience equipping them with the ability to reflect and to question theory as much as they need to question their practice.

It is these key considerations that shaped the development of the new CT course, which will form the basis of the subsequent discussion in this chapter. Before outlining the specific objectives and pedagogical approach adopted on this course, it is important to point out what is meant by critical thinking in the context of this course. Moreover, it is important to clarify the perspectives on "what it is to be critical" that has informed the *reflexive critique* that the course sought to instill.

As pointed out in the introduction, the CT course was an attempt to integrate different perspectives of what it is to be critical by incorporating the various forms of critique propounded by critical theory, critical management studies, critical pedagogy, and critical thinking in developing the distinctiveness of reflexive critique promoted by the CT course. Inadvertently, when considering how best to title this course so as to communicate more clearly to the participants on the MBA program the objectives of the course it was decided to give it a broader title. While critical thinking as a field of study[2] (Paul, 1993) informed the initial focus of the CT course, thinking and reasoning skills were not the only priority. The concern in the CT course was not only about *thinking* as: disciplined, self-monitored, self-directed, reflective, reasonable, questioning, creative, multilogical, intra- and interdisciplinary, metacognitive (Brown & Keely, 1986; Paul, 1990, 1993; Ruggiero, 1988). Nor was the course only about *reasoning* marked by intellectual standards on its: clarity, relevance, accuracy, fairness, completeness, precision, depth, breadth, and adequacy (Kurfiss, 1988; Norris & Ennis, 1989; Siegel, 1988; Paul, 1993). Moreover, central to critical thinking is the epistemology of thought and the promotion of standards by which thinking is assessed, and the way arguments are constructed, whether propositions are sound, whether conclusions draw from their premises, whether the premises themselves are justifiable, whether the language that is being used is appropriate, potentially misleading, emotive, ethical, and so forth (see Byrne, 1994; Chaffee, 1997; Gold, Holman, & Thorpe 2002; Hughes, 1996; McPeck, 1981; Weast, 1996).

Although the main principles of critical thinking have influenced the content and design of the CT course, *critical thinking* in the context of this course carried a different emphasis. Critical thinking in the way it was applied in the specific CT course encourages participants to unpack issues, to draw connections and explore the interrelationships between issues, to question, challenge, and reflect on their perceptions and assumptions, to more openly and inquisitively explore issues and their reactions to these issues. More fundamentally, in the light of the pedagogical objectives of the CT course, central to the idea of thinking critically was the importance of encouraging *critique*. Recognizing the distinction between the *power of critique* as opposed to the *power to critique* is essential in understanding how vital critique is in searching and *researching*[3] for new possibilities beyond reading issues in dualistic categorizations of good and bad, black or white, right or wrong (see Antonacopoulou, 1999).

As a process, critique can cause movement away from existing assumptions and practices and provide the strength and conviction to search for new meaning, to search for new understanding, to search for new ways of living. Critique maintains *egrigorsi* (mindfulness, alertness), and encourages change and progress by avoiding complacency. In its power to reveal both psychological and social needs, critique provides the power to exercise choice. Critique therefore, provides the power to think and to be responsible for one's own actions. The ultimate power of critique is to steer emotions—*to move*—by being moving. The affective orientation of critique encourages those who seek to engage with critique to explore its power to promote alternative ways of seeing created through a more integrative and synthetic approach which allows interconnections to be drawn that permit new possibilities to be explored where these previously may not have been thought possible. This process of interconnectivity and multiplicity is what underpins *reflexivity* (see Antonacopoulou, 2004). The ability to encounter the familiar as new (unfamiliar) is central to the capacity to reflect on ones reflections

(Antonacopoulou & Tsoukas, 2003; Gabriel, 2001; Steiner, 1991). Therefore, one can argue that reflexivity is central to critique as is critique central to reflexivity. Promoting *reflexive critique* therefore, encourages a critique of existing ways of seeing, a critique of prevailing perspectives, a critique of arguments and propositions (verbal and written), a critique of common sense as common (it rarely is), a critique of received wisdom and dominant assumptions, a critique of personal biases and partialities based on personal interests. Central to reflexive critique are the *critique of simplification* and the *critique of identity*.

The ***critique of simplification*** would seek to highlight the limitations of the assumed linearity of management (as reflected in the functionally-based model) and the reductionist analysis of the process of managing which fails to capture the full extent of the social and political dynamics. The critique of simplification would encourage recognition of the cross-functional/interdisciplinary complexity of management. It would support the search for understanding the working-net (network) of interconnections and interactions between social actors and social phenomena (activities and practices) and it is sensitive to the nature of the complexity in relation to the context, which nurtures and supports this complexity. Such critique would also encourage a careful examination of one's assumptions and interpretations of social phenomena and a reflection of one's responses and actions such that one does not get paralyzed by overelaborating complexity (Lynch, 2000). In the context of management learning, such critique would raise managers' level of "complicated understanding" (see Dehler et al., 2001) enabling me them to embrace rather than reduce the complexity of managing and organizing thus avoiding a false and misleading simplicity. Finally, this critique would support new modes of knowing and learning and would be closely connected with the critique of identity.

The ***critique of identity*** promotes the significance and reciprocity of the interaction between emotion and patterns of thought. Such critique takes as central the analysis of one's own subjectivity, the identity reflected in the lived reality, the significance of self-awareness both in relation to one's way of thinking, as well as in relation to the associated emotions that support the security sought. The critique of identity positions the self as a central element in the process of dealing with complexity, chance, and ambiguity. The critique of identity assists in tolerating ambiguity by providing the emotional support to overcome one's fears and anxieties, while identifying the opportunities available from which one can learn and continue to participate in the social construction of reality (Berger & Luckmann, 1967). Therefore, the critique of identity emphasizes that reflexivity and self-critique need to underpin all other forms of critique and must be conducted as much with intellectual rigor as with passion (if one truly believes in its significance). Essentially, it also reminds us that reflexive critique—disciplined reflexivity as Weick (2003) puts it—is also best pursued in community, rather than isolation. In the networked worlds of our professional practice, we do not work by ourselves, but with and through others. Critique (and the critique of identity in particular) therefore, serves to protect us from the narcissistic risks of self-reflexivity.

In the context of this course and in relation to the principles discussed above, reflexive critique is defined *as the cognitive and emotional process of demystifying the interrelationships between social actors and social practices in the specific context in which they occur.* This definition highlights only more clearly some of the basic pedagogical principles which have informed the design on the course and its intended contribution to management learning. These are discussed in more detail next.

INTRODUCING CT INTO THE MBA CURRICULUM

The CT course was first introduced in November 1996, as part of an MBA program designed to unfold over a three year period and comprising of a series of modules (Modular MBA[4] program (MMBA) of which the CT course was one. The course was a core element of the program, therefore it formed part of three critical stages in the program. CT was part of the induction, it was also part of the review of the second year once all core courses were completed and elective courses were about to begin and finally, it was also part of the third year before the final research project—dissertation was about to begin. Each of these interventions took the form of a two-day workshop where a series of interactive lectures and exercises were undertaken predominantly designed to create space for reflection and reflexivity in relation to one's learning on the MBA program and practices of managing based on their day-to-day experiences at work. Each of the three workshops was therefore, dedicated to a set of issues while as a whole the three workshops shared a common set of principles and objectives and employed a series of teaching and learning techniques to fulfil the learning outcomes sought.

The curriculum design of this course was heavily determined by the characteristics of the participants. A total of 60-65 participants are admitted on the MMBA program every year from various parts of the world and across a broad range of backgrounds (i.e., representing pretty much every industry—manufacturing, retailing, services), specialization (e.g. accountants, sales managers, personnel directors etc.) and sector (both public and private sectors of the economy) and both genders (approximately 20% were women and the remaining were men). The average age of participants on this program was 29 and typically they would have a minimum of 4 years of work experience before joining the program. What is perhaps more particular about participants on this MBA program by comparison to other MBA programs is that the far majority (85%) would tend to be funded by their employing organization. This also meant that participants would have the opportunity to continue to remain employed by their organization full-time and would tend to receive time-off to attend the week-long modules. In total, during the 3 years attending this MBA program participants would have attended 14 different modules.

In every attempt to be accommodating to the diaries of the busy executives, who formed the student body on this program, the CT course tended to be organized either before or at the end of a week-long (Monday to Friday) module. This implies that the CT workshops took place during weekends which also implies that while this course was an integral part of the MBA program, attendance was very much a matter of choice for the participants if they opted to give up their weekends to attend the workshops. Overall, over 500 students have experienced this course during the 5 years it was delivered by the author. The paragraphs, which follow discuss the main characteristics of the course as a whole and each of the three workshops, drawing attention to the learning and teaching principles, as well as the way in which the exercises developed sought to cultivate reflexive critique.

THE CT COURSE OBJECTIVES

The overriding principle of the course was to encourage participants to distil a more integrative analysis of the multifaceted nature of management and to critically reflect on their experiences of managing. Therefore, the aim of this course was to act as a space providing participants on the MBA program opportunities to reflexively critique their practice as managers and to be actively involved in directing their learning and development throughout the MBA program. From this aim the following three specific objectives also unfolded:

1. To gain a wider appreciation and understanding of the phenomenon of management by reflecting and reflexively critiquing personal experiences of managing.
2. To provide a space where the interrelationships and interconnections between the various modules on the MBA program can be explored.
3. To reflexively critique the functionalist-mode of management theory in relation to their experiences of managing and to develop

an integrative understanding of the contributing factors shaping the nature of management and managing in organizations.

The learning objectives and intended learning outcomes of the CT course indicate that the focus and orientation of the course fell primarily into the "cognitive" and "affective" domain on Bloom's (1972) taxonomy. In relation to the **cognitive** domain emphasis is placed on the participants' *comprehension* and *application* of the course materials and their *analysis*, *synthesis* and *evaluation*. For example in relation to the *analysis* and *synthesis* the objective is that students are able to unpack different ideas from the various modules, locate issues and problematic, and consider a range of alternatives in interpreting these issues, while exploring the interrelationships between the key components. Finally, the *evaluation* of the material is intended to enable participants to exercise reflexive critique in comparing management theory and practice to derive new insights and interpretations, as well as to review and improve personal management practices.

Clearly, in order to achieve these outcomes at the cognitive level it is imperative that students engage with the subject and have positive attitudes and feelings towards this process. The **affective** domain, indicates the importance of developing an awareness of the aesthetic factors of the subject so that one is actively immersed in the topic. In other words, one would value the different perspectives provided, as well as perceive that further understanding of the topic is significant for improving one's practice (see also Ellington, Percival, & Race, 1993).

The cognitive and affective learning outcomes reflect only more clearly the definition of reflexive critique offered in the previous section. In particular, it highlights that as a cognitive and emotional process reflexive critique is necessary for supporting the synthesis of the various issues on the MBA program in a way that provides space for self-reflection. These learning outcomes are central to the design and content of the three workshops and they also shape the type of teaching and learning techniques employed on the course. Each of these sets of issues is discussed next.

The Three CT Workshops: Content, Teaching, Learning, and Evaluation Techniques

The themes that the CT course sought to address necessitated a diversity of techniques to be employed. Considering the learning objectives and outcomes reviewed in the previous section, the approach to teaching and learning is governed by similar considerations. For example the philosophical model, which reflects the approach to teaching is a combination of the "insight model" and the "rule model" (Scheffler, 1973). This is because the approach to delivery on the CT course is to develop critique and reflexivity. In other words, the emphasis is on developing the ability to think analytically, beyond a "dualist" perspective, towards a "relativist" perspective (Perry, 1988). The relativist perspective encourages students to approach the analysis of issues with a "yes, and" mentality, rather than an approach which is based on "either, or." This point implies that polarized positions were to be avoided to allow room for multiple perspectives and realities in developing leadership capability (see Antonacopoulou & Bento, 2003).

These models of teaching reflect the approach of learning, which is also more relevant in this context; namely what Gibbs (1992) and Ramsden (1992) describe as "deep" approach to learning instead of "surface." The former approach to learning involves "thinking, seeking integration between components and between tasks" (Gibbs, 1992. p. 150). Moreover, as Ramsden (1992) points out, it is more concerned with "understanding, relating previous knowledge to new knowledge, relating theoretical ideas to everyday experience" (p. 52). This approach to learning is consistent with the objective of the CT course to support a critique of simplification—an integrative analysis of issues.

The CT course employed different teaching and learning methods alongside different techniques. The main methods employed were: interactive lectures, participative group exercises, and other flexible learning approaches which individuals on the course can employ to facilitate their learning, for example, self-directed learning resources such as reflective exercises and questionnaires, chapters and books which are more appropriate for adult learners (Brookfield, 1986; Knowles, 1984). Each of the three workshops is described in more detail next.

The First Workshop

The first workshop was designed to take place as part of the induction schedule inviting participants to reflect on their motives, expectations and aspirations from the MBA program. A questionnaire was circulated in advance, to all participants admitted on the program in order to establish a dialogue. Among the issues addressed in the questionnaire included: participants' perceptions of what is an MBA, their motives and expectations from the MBA and a series of other questions about their views in relation to the learning process, the factors facilitating or restricting their learning, and a self assessment of their familiarity of management theory and personal effectiveness as practicing managers.

During the first workshop the findings from the questionnaire were employed in an interactive lecture to discuss the expectations, assumptions and motives of different participants on the MBA program. This was followed by a series of individual and group exercises that encouraged participants, to focus on their learning preferences, their assumptions about management and their expectations from the MBA program. The tensions in balancing personal and collective priorities in relation to the groups in which they will be working in during the various modules on the MBA were also discussed. Particular attention was also given to the tensions between personal and organizational priorities in relation to development sensitizing students to the learning dilemmas they may be confronted with given that their employing organization was also their main MBA sponsor. For example one of the group exercises titled 'Creating a learning environment: Sharing experiences and developing together' sought to address the social and psychological aspects of the learning process. Working in small groups participants were asked individually first to identify and discuss the self-imposed and contextually imposed factors which may facilitate or restrict their learning. Then as a group they were asked to draw up a group learning strategy for overcoming the factors perceived to affect learning negatively, while laying out mechanisms for maximizing the use of factors helping individual and collective learning. A key objective in this approach was to draw attention to personal responsibility and choice in overcoming some of the personal and contextual factors affecting learning. Moreover, this and other exercises sought to highlight the support that the group (participants on the MBA) can provide in overcoming personal obstacles to learning, while the significance of developing a learning community among participants on the program was also highlighted.

Additional exercises were designed to support participants in building the foundations for developing critical thinking skills that would enable them in due course to exercise reflexive critique. It was considered important to provide support in recognizing the challenges they would face in dealing with the volume of information they will encounter during each course on the MBA program. They were also alerted to the importance of learning to assess information critically not accepting theories as taken-for-granted particularly when these are not consistent with their personal experiences of managing. Two exercises were developed both drawing attention to the process of argumentation and its analysis (in relation to the claims and warrants—Missimer, 1986; Moore, 1989; Toulmin, 1958). One exercise was titled "Learning to Read Critically" and the other was titled "Learning to Write Critically." These exercises were employed as means of encouraging participants to engage with the subject and to exercise critical reflection and analysis in their thinking and articulation of issues both during reading others' work (critique of theory, conventional wisdom) and in their writing (critique of their practice and the gaps in relation to the rhetoric often promoted in management theory). A key dimension in the whole process was the emphasis placed on the inseparability of theory and practice and the importance of exploring ways in which personal experiences may be integrated with ideas from management theory and research, while it could also help critique and inform management theory and research. Suspending judgements and personal bias in assessing the relevance or applicability of ideas to one's own practice was a key message that underpinned many of the exercises and activities of the first workshop. Therefore, the first workshop sought to lay the foundations for critique by presenting different aspects of being critical so that in turn they would support their subsequent critique of simplification and ultimately, critique of identity. The first workshop concluded by handing two booklets to each participant to be used in their own time and for their own purposes. The first booklet titled *The Personal Learning Experiences Log* aimed to encourage participants to remain focused on their learning and to identify specific learning goals that they may wish to pursue through different stages of the MBA. The second booklet titled *Personal Development Plan* was intended to be used by participants, if they so chose, as a mechanism for keeping track of their development throughout the program, by drawing closer experiences during the MBA program with experiences at work.

The Second Workshop

The second workshop was designed to take place 6 months into the MBA program at the stage where participants would have completed most of the core courses and would have begun to choose the elective courses. The purpose of this second workshop was to review and reflect on the modules covered on the MBA program thus far, and to explore the interconnections between the individual modules. A series of interactive exercises were designed to encourage participants to reflect on and critique their personal experiences of managing in relation to the perspectives on management promoted by the various MBA core modules.

One of the exercises designed to support this process was titled "Building a Bigger Picture: Reviewing the Interconnections Between Topics on the MBA: Issues of Application And Transferability." During this exercise participants were asked to discuss the main themes/lessons from the core modules and to explore their interconnections in building a bigger picture about management, while reflecting on their experience of managing. Participants were initially asked to reflect individually on the main issues that were significant to them personally from each of the modules that they have attended. In relation to their development and learning, participants were asked to consider any factors, which have facilitated or restricted the applicability and transferability of their learning experiences from the MBA so far, to their experiences in the workplace. Subsequently, as part of the group work, participants shared their personal experiences and collectively they discussed emerging issues and ways in which they could enhance the applicability and transferability of learning from the program to the workplace. This exercise also encouraged participants working in their groups, to explore the interconnections between the various topics covered on the MBA thus far and to represent these interrelationships diagrammatically. Participants drew pictures and diagrams representing the group's view of the way each topic relates to other topics and may inform, as well as, be informed by other topics as currently addressed in individual modules. The analysis and synthesis of the individual modules presented by participants raised some very interesting issues both about their understanding of management and managing, as well as the interconnections between the various modules.

For example, some of the pictures, participants drew depicted management and the process of managing as a human being drawing attention to the head (mind) and the heart. This picture sought to emphasizes participants' view of the human nature of management and the process of managing as a cognitive and emotional process. Another picture depicted management and managing as a snake eating its tail. This picture according to participants sought to depict the fluidity of managing and management as a cyclical process. Finally, a picture depicted management as a game of snooker (a game like Pool). In this picture participants sought to depict the various aspects of management as a series of balls that were strategically placed. The process of managing was depicted as the way individual managers play the game. In all these pictures participants also depicted the relationships and interactions between the various modules and topics experienced on the MBA program. One very interesting representation of the relationships between modules was captured in the snooker picture. Participants explained that each ball reflected each of the modules (core and electives) which captured different aspects of management. The process of exploring the interactions between the various balls could determine the nature of the game (i.e., the process of managing). Two participants from the group who presented this picture of management and managing, articulated in more detail the way their group explored the connections between modules. Their analysis is presented in the Appendix in full and in their own words. These examples, are the best illustration of how students exercised reflexive critique through their critique of simplification in exploring the interconnections between the various elements of management, as well as the interrelationships between management and managing.

In supporting the critique of their identity additional exercises, which were developed in the second workshop sought to expose both the common, as well as different issues emerging from the individual interpretations of the various modules. The impact of perceptions, assumptions and interpretations on learning were further addressed in an exercise titled "The Role of Stereotyping in Communicating, Listening, Giving and Receiving Feedback and Negotiating Understanding." This exercise sought to highlight the impact of personal subjectivity and to invite participants to reflect on their assumptions, particularly in relation to their self-perceptions and the way they perceive others. A role-play exercise enabled participants to confront stereotyping as they interacted with each other based on the label that each of them carried on their forehead. Individual group members were not aware initially of how they were "labeled" but the reactions of the participants to them was a good source for thinking about their self-image and identity. Typical labels included "insignificant" "dominant," "newcomer," "expert," "leader," "company-clown." This and other exercises supported students in reflecting and bringing into question their practices. The reflective comments that they offered during plenary sessions and informal interactions during coffee breaks revealed an increasing openness to reflexivity during the workshops.

The Third Workshop

The third workshop was scheduled to take place a year after the second workshop, when participants were preparing for the final part of the program, the dissertation. As part of the business curriculum on the MBA program graduates have to undertake a mini research project, which is intended to provide scope for a more in-depth examination of a specific topic, by collecting empirical findings, as well as by drawing on a variety of theoretical contributions to inform the analysis. As part of the preparation for the dissertation the third workshop was part of a 2-day event, which focused on research methods and other considerations in conducting research. Building on the themes of the previous two workshops the third workshop consisted of exercises, which encouraged reflection on learning and personal development however, it also extended its orientation to embrace the research process as a learning opportunity and one that emphasizes reflexive critique at its core.

Conducting research as a learning process, emphasized the importance of critically appraising existing theories and propositions in the literature, uncovering key assumptions, challenging the applicability of existing theories in different contexts of practice and critically understanding why things happen in particular ways in different settings. Moreover, by exercising a critical orientation to the collection and interpretation of data, as researchers, participants were encouraged to challenge their own assumptions and interpretations by consciously exercising their self-critique (critique of identity). This was pursued in exercises drawing on images of pictures and paintings (surrealistic themes), which prompted students to question what they think they can see. The discussions around the various images encouraged participants to reflect on how existing knowledge and previous learning, which forms the backbone to our repertoire of assumptions may in fact as much dictate what we see, as well as define what we perceive and therefore, are able (allowed) to see. By opening themselves to the possibility that any one picture may hold more than one possible images students were able to begin to apply different interpretations to the pictures and to engage in deeper conversation with themselves about what the pictures show, what they choose to see, why they would privilege one image over another. By reflecting on their view of the world and through that critiquing their identity (given that identities are often built on perceptions) students were beginning to embrace a wider openness to learn about possibilities instead of limiting themselves to only one possibility. This point is particularly central to the critique of simplification, which this workshop also sought to cultivate.

The third workshop sought to draw attention to the way the critique of simplification may support a reciprocal interaction between theory and practice, where theory informs practice, as well as practice informs theory. This reciprocity is central in exploring the multitude of possibilities that lie in the interaction and interconnection between management systems and processes. Through the critique of simplification one engages with complexity at the level where the space of possibility is unrestricted and where learning becomes a space of growth. In the case of this workshop in the context of the CT course, the interaction between theory and practice, was an attempt to align perceived dualisms so that the research process could both enlighten aspects of managing as well as aspects of management that students chose to study. A series of interactive group exercises, were designed for this purpose.

The exercise titled "Reflecting on the Applicability of Theory into Practice" sought to encourage participants to consider how far their understanding of their current practice as managers related to the way management theories depicted such practice. Moreover, in supporting a critique of their practice and their current ways of thinking, an exercise titled "Removing the Blinkers" invited participants individually to reflect on the factors shaping their perceptions of reality and the extent to which the perceived reality reflected the "whole" reality. In other words, to what extent there may be other dimensions of the current reality that the existing ways of perceiving the world could be limiting the multiple possibilities available. This sensitization into the wider space of multiplicity, was also supported by an exercise titled 'Silence as an act of Communication'. This exercise was designed to support students particularly in their role as active researchers during their research project. Through an interactive lecture approach this exercise highlighted some of the challenges presented to researchers searching for "truth." The analysis invited participants to critique frequently made assumptions in the process of communicating with others and to be sensitive to verbal as much as nonverbal signals particularly during the process of data collection. Finally, this last workshop sought to repeat again previous questions about the nature of learning on the program, the implications to their understanding, the conclusions that such understanding imposes on the nature of management and their practices as managers.

Evaluating Learning Outcomes Across the Three Workshops: Students' Reflections

The intention of this course, to support MBA participants in their learning and development raised the issue of assessment. Although the course itself was assessed both by formative and summative assessment techniques, participants on the course were not assessed. If assessment were to be introduced, this was felt that it would have removed the very essence of its purpose to support their development. Turning the focus of the course from personal development to assessment would have undermined the principle on which the course was built. Assessment would also be counterproductive, because it could potentially encourage superficiality and impression management. However, such a choice implied a responsibility on behalf of MBA participants to use this course in the supportive capacity that it was being offered. Particularly given that it was not offered as a compulsory course. It was rewarding to note that partly due to the strong emphasis placed by the MMBA program director on the CT course and the persistent encouragement to appreciate reflexive critique as a key capability to be developed on the MBA program, the large majority (over 90%) of students across all cohorts to which it was delivered attended voluntarily the CT course and the three workshops.

The evaluation techniques (formative and summative) employed on the CT course were intended to facilitate an active dialogue between the course coordinator and the participants. The formative assessment process adopted throughout the course included the various teaching and learning techniques employed to ensure that the workshop objectives were met and that participants' progress was consistent and in line with the learning outcomes sought. Summative assessment took the form of feedback questionnaires, which were completed by participants at the end of each workshop. The ongoing evaluation of the workshops and the course as a whole provided the opportunity for faculty and participants alike to learn and as Ramsden (1992) points out, to be in control of their learning.

The feedback received from the various formative and summative evaluation techniques suggest that the three workshops, and the CT course as a whole, were positively received by the far majority of the participants. A basic statistical analysis of the feedback forms across the various cohorts, which experienced this course (providing over 1,500 completed questionnaires) shows that consistently the course mean (from a scale of 1-5 excellent signalled by a mark of 5 out of 5) was 4.6-4.9. More detailed examination of the comments offered by students suggest that again the far majority (89%) across the sample (taking into account the various demographic characteristics typical of this group) valued greatly this course for the following two reasons: First, they felt that the course provided them the opportunity to reflect and think about the way they think and secondly, the course enabled them to explore the interconnections between topics on the MBA and issues in management that informed their practice of managing. These two factors reflect clearly that the objectives of the course have been met and that the critique of simplification and critique of identity were appreciated by students as part of exercising reflexive critique. Typical of the comments participants made in their feedback forms were the following:

Critical thinking is a useful area. It reminds us that we need to think critically. It has made me wonder if I am doing enough with the MBA learning back at the workplace.

Its excellent. It's more than "critical thinking." It's bringing home to me that interrogation of my learning experiences to-date is essential to refocus on priorities and objectives in the future.

A useful day of reflection. A reminder to be wary of perceptions and recognizing mind-sets. That was useful. Also the reassurance that complexity and hence state of mind—confusion—should not be worrying!!! I need to be more demanding at work in terms of requesting time to share ideas, debrief people. That was a helpful idea.

The course content explored was generally an insight into my and my course members' perceptions of how management and work interaction is accomplished.... The course caused me to think how I go about learning.

I was a little concerned about giving up a Sunday to come to a course on critical thinking, however, the course content to myself was invaluable and the structure was excellent.

This course teaches us about ourselves, others teach us about "stuff."

A small proportion (11%) of managers did raise concerns about the course. They expressed indifference about the need to think critically. They found the course "too abstract" and "vague" to deal with. These students appeared to be less willing to take responsibility for their learning and development. Instead, they were more comfortable and keen to be instructed on how to learn and how to think. They were not ready or willing to engage in critique. It seems that for these students this course was a threat to their identity and self-image, which they are very protective off and hence, unwilling to challenge or indeed allow others to challenge. Typical of the comments made by participants who were less receptive to this course were the following:

I don't think I have discovered anything about myself or the learning process from this day.

Is this necessary? On a Sunday?

Critical thinking feels "disconnected" rather than a potentially "linking" segment.

Finding this course confusing or unsatisfactory should not suggest an inability on the students' part to engage in reflexive critique. As Argyris (2004) has shown over many years supporting people in overcoming their defensive routines, need not lead to stereotyping them as uncritical. Instead, it challenges us as educators to work with them to help them overcome their defences. These responses are reflective of reactions to be expected when the "un-discussable" is being moved to the realm of the "discussable" (Argyris, 1994). That said, it is also acknowledged that not all participants wish to develop themselves or be developed, nor do they all wish to support others in their development. For some participants the choice of doing an MBA remains purely a means to some specific career end. This is particularly the case for participants who given that they were funded by their employing organizations they felt that the MBA was a signal of the organizations' investment in their future career. Consequently the MBA was a signal that they were being placed on a fast-track to promotion to a senior position. Therefore, what mattered to some participants was not the learning experience that the MBA program could offer, but the qualification and the three letters (MBA), which would signal their level of competence. It was also notable that these participants tended to be more self-centred and competitive on the program, thus less inclined to engage in the spirit of a learning community that the program and the CT course advocated. At any rate, students admitted on MBA programs with these sets of attitudes cannot be transformed through simply one course, particularly when other courses (functionally based courses) would be most likely to encourage these kinds of attitudes rather than reinforce the message of reflexivity and critique. These issues reflect some of the wider challenges in introducing reflexive critique in the business curriculum. The last section of this chapter presents my personal assessment of the course and reflections on the lessons learned.

The Challenges of Reflexive Critique in the Business Curriculum: Personal Assessment and Reflections on the Lessons Learned

The premise of introducing a critique into the business curriculum, was to provide the opportunity to think about one's learning and development, to create a space for reflection and consolidation of experiences seeking to explore the interconnections between courses on the MBA program. The CT course however, was also an attempt to develop a learning methodology for supporting the study of interconnectivity and through the critique of identity and the critique of simplification to practice reflexive critique. Moreover, the intention was to enhance confidence in the ability to learn and encourage learning as a lifelong process that extends well beyond the MBA. Perhaps what reflexive critique suggests above all is that, if management learning is to make a difference to our understanding of management and the process of managing, then learning programs, which are meant to be educational must reflect life, and the struggles to "manage" our lives to better ends, that have no end (i.e., are continuous). This is a view supported by critical pedagogists like Barnett (1997) arguing for the challenge presented to Universities in supporting the development of "critical beings." However, reflexive critique in and by itself does not create critical beings, nor does it overcome the multiplicity of contradictions and pressures within higher education. If nothing else, chances are it exacerbates them, by exposing and critiquing the pedagogical approach they promote which removes the reflective quality of learning that education ought to provide. If indeed, critical pedagogy is about developing "critical beings" then, perhaps reflexive critique ought be practiced before it can be preached.

The CT course curriculum was guided by the course objectives as stated however, the emphasis was not on the outcomes themselves, but the *process* (Kelly, 1989; Taylor & Richards, 1985). This issue suggests that apart from the stated objectives there are some implied objectives within the CT course curriculum, which place more emphasis on the process of developing the ability to critique reflexively. In light of this, it must be acknowledged that on its own a course on critical thinking is not sufficient for developing reflexive critique. Pedagogically, such abilities can only be developed if critique lies at the core of the curriculum of the entire MBA program and is reenforced in each course and acts as a key component of the holistic education that such a program ought to provide. It is therefore, justifiable why some students did find the CT "disconnected." The current course design (perhaps more so that the course content) of the CT course did not allow for the necessary integration of critique as an integral part of all courses. The three workshops may well have been placed strategically at different points in the duration of the program but they were by no means sufficient in enabling participants to practice reflexive critique on an ongoing basis.

In other words, it is easy to forget and lapse into old habits if one does not practice[5] what one learns systematically. Repetition may be the daughter of learning, however, *practicing* is the mother of all learning. It needs to be acknowledged therefore, that when students receive potentially contradicting messages across the various courses they experience on the MBA program they will undoubtedly be confused.

Although the reactions of other colleagues to the course overall were positive, partly because of the positive reputation the course enjoyed, the course itself did very little in influencing their practices in the way they delivered their courses. Therefore, the CT course to a large extent was a sole voice/call for reflexive critique in the business curriculum. The CT course did not overcome the functionalistic/positivistic nature of the MBA curriculum nor did it address the wider issues, such as the economic logic in the current business curriculum. Introducing reflexive critique in the MBA curriculum may have helped draw a lot more attention to the significance of reflection and questioning of theory and personal practice. However, a much more in-depth analysis of the assumptions that currently inform the business curriculum and a willingness on the part of management educators to engage in critical reflexivity about their practices in educating and supporting the development of managers certainly remains an ongoing challenge.

On a more personal level, designing and delivering the CT course has been a profound experience which has prompted me as an educator to see the bigger picture in my role as educator. Moreover, by stepping out of my frame of reference and reflecting on my practice I can see more clearly the relationship between my thought processes (Dewey, 1962) and my existing knowledge with the actions that I take (Schön, 1983). Applying critique in reflecting and questioning my own practice as a teacher and learner, on the CT course I would have to first acknowledge the subjectivity embedded in the curriculum design of the CT course. What essentially forms the body of the course content is to a large part shaped by the assumptions and values of the course coordinator (in this case myself). The familiarity with one's subject may often shape the issues which one considers relevant or appropriate to be taught during a course. In the case of the CT course clearly my familiarity with the ongoing debates in this area shape the themes, which I consider to be relevant and important to address during the course. It must be noted however, that the students' feedback is a valuable source of information about the validity of these assumptions in terms of their perceived reality. Reflecting-in-action (Schön, 1987) enables me to recognize the significance of the interconnection between learning and teaching as a key issue determining the quality of the CT course curriculum. From the analysis developed in this chapter one issue which I recognize needs to be considered further is to continue to question the relevance of my assumptions to the curriculum planning and to experiment with other teaching and learning methods so that the curriculum design of this and other courses that I manage bring me (the teacher) closer to the needs of the course participants (the learners) by being a lifelong learner myself.

Moreover, as a learner, I would have to acknowledge that the experience of designing and delivering the CT course was both rewarding and frustrating. It was rewarding, because one comes very close to the way participants on the course contemplate issues in their minds, raise questions about themselves and those around them, and seek meaning and justification from what they are doing and why they are doing what they are doing. While this process provides valuable insights and invites one as an ethnographer to explore others' worlds, it can also become frustrating at times when one is not always able to interpret fully issues nor to provide sufficient explanations for the multiplicity of realities encountered. Even more so, it becomes frustrating when there are not always sufficient ways for supporting or overcoming the obstacles identified. Therefore, supporting others to engage in reflexive critique necessitates a personal commitment to critique—self-critique—the critique of identity. This form of critique implies as much intellectual as emotional commitment. Perseverance, passion and patience are important elements if one is willing to remain committed to critique. These are also key elements in dealing with the constraints imposed by the University system and the resources available. For example, timetable constraints implied that the CT course would have to be a separate component on the MBA curriculum instead of an integral part of all courses and that the three workshops would tend to be organized during the weekends, something that some participants were understandably, not particularly happy about. This is where critique of simplification encouraged me to explore ways of linking this course with other courses. I could perhaps have done more to join forces with other colleagues in introducing critical reflexivity as an element on their courses.

Finally, from the perspective of the teacher introducing critique into the business curriculum on the one hand, provides the opportunity to become a learner as well, exploring one's ideas in the process of teaching, learning from the ideas participants bring to a learning event. However, on the other hand, it is difficult and at times risky to present ones' self as a learner particularly when students expect that in the role of a teacher, one ought to know it all (have the answers to their questions—never admitting one does not know!). Becoming a learner teacher, is not an image frequently encouraged in the academic profession and it is certainly not so in the light of the current emphasis on "competence" or indeed the language of "students as customers" which encourages more passive attitudes towards learning and a drive towards what Antonacopoulou (2003b) refers to as the commercialization of management education.

IMPLICATIONS FOR LIFELONG MANAGEMENT LEARNING

The issues raised in the previous paragraphs highlight some of the contradicting priorities one is confronted with in relation to management learning in the context of Higher Education. Such contradictions cannot be alleviated by just introducing an isolated course into an MBA curriculum. Reflexive critique calls for a holistic, interdisciplinary, integrative analysis of issues—a critique of simplification—a willingness and readiness to engage with others' reality to discover one's own reality. Reflexive critique also calls for self-critique and reflexivity—a critique of identity—an openness to explore *the other* and to rediscover new dimensions of one's self. These principles call for a renewed orientation towards management learning particularly if this is to form the basis for a more engaged lifelong process.

Adopting this perspective would call for rethinking MBA programs as learning spaces for rediscovering managing. This could be achieved by integrating participants' experiences of managing with further experiences of managing revealed by the research course contributors undertake. For one, such a possibility would transform the role of the teacher as much as it would transform the role of the learner.

One of the contributions of reflexive critique to management learning is that it could support a learning partnership between faculty and students which would make distinctions between learning and teaching unnecessary when the space for learning is so vast. This view is consistent with calls made already by Sotto (1994) and would be also be in line with much of the effort of action research to provide a better integration between theory and practice (see Dehler, 2006; McNiff, 2000).

Perhaps this is an "idealist" view and it does no doubt collide with the "reality" of what we tend to do. However, it is perhaps here that lies the challenge, because it is when the ideal and the real collide that exploration begins! And this perhaps is the main challenge in introducing reflexive critique in the business curriculum; namely encouraging management educators to explore, learn, critique, and reflect on their own identities and practices and to explore a more integrative approach to their teaching and learning about managers, managing, and management.

Equally, reflexive critique encourages practicing managers to problematize management and explore the intricacies of managing as a source of revealing new connections and possibilities in multiple perspectives. Managing and organizing cannot afford a linear representation. Reflexive critique celebrates complexity and encourages the multiplicity of perspectives to continuously enrich the emerging understanding that is itself pursued as a lifelong endeavor.

CONCLUSIONS

In this chapter I have reviewed and discussed the various perspectives on what it is to be critical and in synthesizing them I have proposed reflexive critique as an integrative form of being critical. In developing the notion of reflexive critique two new forms of critique were put forward; the critique of simplification and the critique of identity. The analysis illustrated both the way reflexive critique was applied in designing and delivering a CT course as part of an MBA curriculum and the way the critique of identity and the critique of simplification were developed in the three workshops which were part of the CT course. Perhaps more critically what this chapter has sought to do was both make the case for reflexive critique as well as practice it in the ongoing reflections that are presented both in the evaluations of the course by the students as well as the personal lessons learned. By reflecting on the dilemmas and challenges of introducing reflexive critique in the business curriculum a central conclusion that can be distilled from the analysis is that overcoming the functionalistic representation of management cannot be achieved if the lived experience of managing is not engaged with, reflected on, questioned, and more fundamentally *critiqued*. Encouraging participants on management education programs to think more about the way they think, and to draw their own conclusions about the complexity of managing while encouraging a more rigorous approach in defining their role as a manager may be a starting point. Maybe if we apply the same process in higher education, perhaps a reflection of the way we think, and a critical reflection on our role as educators may lead to other conclusions about the way we currently manage resources and the standards that we feel ought to reflect the quality of education that we seek to reach. Perhaps the realization that we have as much to learn from those we teach could be a good starting point.

ACKNOWLEDGMENTS

The author would like to acknowledge the support of the ESRC/EPSRC Advanced Institute of Management Research under grant number RES-331-25-0024 for this research. The useful comments of Professors Regina Bento and Gordon Dehler are also gratefully acknowledged.

APPENDIX

OUR MBA IS A LOAD OF BALLS (and we can't stop playing with them)

The aim in snooker is to deposit a series of different coloured balls into pockets. Each ball pocketed scores points. There are basic colours, reds, which once pocketed, allow you then to play the coloured balls which are of greater points value. However there is an element of competition. One has to play an opponent who is also trying to score more points with the same balls on the same table.

Consider the balls now to be elements of an MBA program. The reds are the core modules, the coloured are the electives or more specialised elements. One can consider that table characteristics speed, level, and lighting to be the external business environment. You have no control over them, but they are the basis on which you play the game. Your opponent is your business competitor. Your cue represents your level in the company to affect change. A good cue means you have direct influence, a damaged cue adds an element of luck and chance as you are not in direct control.

Each module mastered, or pocketed, adds value to you and your organization. The more you add the greater value you are in comparison to your competition.

Now snooker could be played in a totally random fashion. Hit the balls, see where they go, hope they go in the pocket. Hope that you add more value than you loose through penalties. As such you will always loose out to a more proficient competitor, and the time taken to add overall value would be far too lengthy. A very inefficient way to add value, if value is added at all.

As one becomes more proficient, one learns to understand the run of the balls, the interactions between each of them, how to use them to add value through a series of strategic options. How to leave the balls in a position to build further, how to play safe.

As one adds elements to the MBA, one starts to understand the links between all the differing elements of business administration. How the marketing strategy can affect the financial position. How the quantitative techniques can be used to understand and measure the success of the marketing strategy. How organizational behaviour helps us understand the effects of the strategy and how the financial performance affects the organization. It can enable us to determine if we have the right organizational culture to realise the strategy. In essence, we strike the marketing ball and predict the effects on all the other balls on the table. The greater the understanding of these interactions, the better position you are in to play another shot and continue to add value.

A thorough understanding of all the elements allows us to adopt either a defensive or offensive strategy. A snooker player will devise a game plan. This will be based upon his analysis of relative competitive strengths, the table, form etc. His ability to deploy that plan will be relative to his ability to control the balls in a range of differing situations.

This compares directly to the business plan where knowledge of the business position, competitive strengths and weaknesses allows a strategy to be developed. Successful deployment of this plan will depend on a thorough understanding of how all the elements interact.

However, nothing is completely predictable, you may not always be at the table playing the balls. You may be sat in the chair whilst your competitor is in control. Your ability to change plan and re-plan from a slightly different and often unexpected situation will again be dependent on your skill in understanding the interactions. You will learn how to play safe and leave your competitor in a hopeless position.

At the start of the MBA you know the table exists and that there are different coloured balls. Module by module you get more balls to play with. Slowly you start to understand how these interact, you see how they can be used to develop plans and strategy. You realise it is not a totally random process. You understand that by understanding the elements, their interactions, their relevance in certain conditions you can add greater value in a controlled manner.

Steve Davies never made it seem so interesting.

Dave & Peter

NOTES

1. Empirical here is used in the true sense of the word from the Greek *Εμπειρια*, (empiria) meaning experience. I am not seeking in this chapter to present so much a piece of empirical research, although this inadvertently I am doing by taking care in presenting sufficient information about the findings of introducing the CT course. What is more fundamental, however, is my effort to reflect on the experience itself and from that to propose new theory in relation to what reflexive critique may be and why the new forms of critique (critique of simplification and critique of identity) would add value to our understanding and efforts in management education to bring closer management practice and theory. Research is frequently assumed to take place by and among a research community, thus neglecting the possibility that research is an integral part of practice and practising. Research is not a profession it is a practice. Research viewed in this way responds directly to criticisms of rigor and relevance. It responds to rigor by reminding us that research is in fact research—the ongoing search. Even when we feel we know something research is what keeps us on our toes reminding us that there is always a possibility to be surprised by the unknown. This view of research also responds to criticisms of relevance by emphasizing that in management education we ought to be committed in a joint search of practice (both our own and that of others). Therefore, relevant research is the collective search of practice by practising ways our praxis can be improved. Research therefore, as verb and noun, provides room for theory to be seen as the intellectualization of good practices in a reflective mode where lessons learned from practice and which are relevant and particular to that practice can also inform other practices when practised.

2. CT is a well established movement supported and feed by the research undertaken at the Center for Critical Thinking at Sonoma State University, the Foundation for Critical Thinking, the International Center for the Assessment of Higher Order Thinking, the National Council for Excellence in Critical Thinking, the World Center for New Thinking in Indiana, the School of Thinking in Australia. There is also an annual International Conference on Critical Thinking, National Academies in the United States, professional development workshops, video resources, books and other publications. Further information about all these organizations and activities can be found at: http://www.sonoma.edu/cthink, and at http://www.montclair.edu/Pages/CRC/Bibliographis/Critical. For a brief history of the idea of critical thinking see: http://www.sonoma.edu/cthink/University/univlibrary/cthistory.hcilk

3. This is an attempt to further exemplify the points raised in the first endnote.

4. Along with the full-time, part-time (evening study) and distance learning programs, the modular program provides further flexibility to participants (learners). Similar to the other MBA variants, the modular MBA (MMBA) program is a response to the changing needs of organizations and

managers. The MMBA program enables participants to attend week-long residential courses and is therefore, best suited to those who wish to combine postgraduate study with full-time employment. The MMBA program consists of 14 intensive week-long residential modules, 5 of which are core modules and are compulsory within the first year of study, while the remaining 9 are optional modules that participants elect during their second and third year of study. The final part of the program involves a project undertaken in the participant's own employing organization and assessed by means of a dissertation based on a project.

5. The Oxford Dictionary (2001) defines *practice* as "the action of doing of something" or "a way of doing something that is common, habitual or expected" such as the work of a doctor working in general practice. *Practice* on the other hand, is defined as "to do something repeatedly or regularly in order to improve one's skill" or "to do something regularly as part of one's normal behavior" for example, to work as a doctor is to be in practise. The dictionary cautions the possible confusion between practice and practise and clearly points out that the former should be used when referring to the noun and the latter should be used when referring to the verb. It should be noted that in the U.S. language there is no distinction between the *c* and *s* hence, making the distinction more difficult.

Note: All exercises and materials developed for this course are available from the author. Please contact the author directly if you wish to obtain copies of the materials. Professor Elena Antonacopoulou, GNOSIS, University of Liverpool Management School, Chatham Building, Liverpool, L69 7ZH, United Kingdom.

REFERENCES

Alvesson, M., & Willmott, H. (1992). (Eds.). *Critical management studies*. London: SAGE.

Alvesson, M., & Willmott, H. (1996). *Making sense of management: A critical introduction*. London: SAGE.

Antonacopoulou, E. P. (1999, July 14-16). *The power of critique: Revisiting critical theory at the end of the century*. Proceedings of the 1st International Critical Management Studies Conference, UMIST, Manchester, England.

Antonacopoulou, E. P. (2002). Positive professional practice: A response to ethical dilemmas in our profession. *Academy of Management Newsletter, 33*(4), 1-3.

Antonacopoulou, E. P. (2003a). Ethical dilemmas in our profession: Critical self-reflection on our practices. *Academy of Management Newsletter, 34*(1), 4-6.

Antonacopoulou, E. P. (2003b). Corporate universities: The domestication of management education. In R. DePhillippi & C. Wankel (Eds.), *Rethinking management education* (pp. 185-207). New York: Information Age.

Antonacopoulou, E. P., & Bento R. (2003). Methods of "Learning Leadership": Taught and experiential. In J. Storey (Ed.), *Current issues in leadership and management development* (pp. 81-102). Oxford, England: Blackwell.

Antonacopoulou, E. P., & Tsoukas, H. (2003). Time and reflexivity in organization studies: An introduction. *Organization Studies* (Special Issue on "Time and Reflexivity in Organization Studies"), *26*(3), 857-862.

Antonacopoulou, E. P. (2004). The dynamics of reflexive practice: The relationship between learning and changing. In M. Reynolds & R. Vince (Eds.), *Organizing reflection* (pp. 47-64). Aldershot, England: Ashgate.

Argyris, C. (1994, July-August). Good communication that blocks learning. *Harvard Business Review, 72*(4), 77-85.

Argyris, C. (2004). *Reasons and rationalizations: The limits to organizational knowledge.* Oxford, England: Oxford University Press

Barnett, R. (1997). *Higher education: A critical business.* Bristol, PA: The Society for Research into Higher Education and Open University Press.

Berger, P. L., & Luckmann, T. (1967). *The social construction of reality.* Penguin: London.

Bloom, B. (1972). *Taxonomy of educational objectives.* New York: Longman Green.

Brookfield, S. (1986). *Understanding and facilitating adult learning: A comprehensive analysis of principles and effective practices.* Milton Keynes, England: Open University Press.

Brown, N., & Keely, S. (1986). *Asking the right questions: A guide to critical thinking* (2nd ed.). Englewood Cliffs, NJ: Prentice-Hall.

Byrne, M. (1994). *Learning to be critical.* Marcet, England: University of Northumbria at Newcastle.

Chaffee, J. (1997). *Thinking critically* (5th ed.). Boston: Houghton Mifflin.

Dehler, G. E. (2006). Using action research to connect practice to learning: A course project for working management students. *Journal of Management Education, 30*(5), 636-669.

Dehler, G. E., Welsh, M. A., & Lewis, M. W. (2001). Critical pedagogy in the "new paradigm": Raising complicated understanding in management learning. *Management Learning, 32*(4), 493-511.

Dewey, J. (1962). *The relation of theory to practice in education.* Cedar Falls, IA: Association for Student Teaching.

Ellington, H, Percival, F., & Race, P. (1993). *Handbook of Educational Technology.* London: Kogan Page.

Flood, R., & Jackson, M. (1991). *Creative problem solving.* London: Wiley.

Foucault, M. (1980). *Power/knowledge: Selected interviews and other writings 1972-1977.* Brighton, England: Harvester Press.

Gabriel, Y. (2001). The state of critique in organization theory. *Human Relations, 54*(1), 23-31.

Gibbs, G. (1992). Improving the quality of student learning through course design. In R. Barnett (Ed.), *Learning to effect* (pp. 149-168). Buckingham, England: Society for Research into Higher Education & Open University Press.

Giroux, H. A. (1997). *Pedagogy and the politics of hope: Theory, culture and schooling.* Boulder. CO: Westview Press.

Gold, J., Holman, D., & Thorpe, R. (2002). The role of argument analysis and story telling in facilitating critical thinking. *Management Learning, 33*(3), 371-388.

Habermas, J. (1978). *Knowledge and human interests.* London: Heinemann.

Habermas, J. (1984). *The theory of communicative action: Reason and the rationalization of society* (Vol. 1). London: Heinemann.

Hughes, W. (1996). *Critical thinking.* Ontario, Canada: Broadview Press.

Kelly, A. V. (1989). *The curriculum theory and practice* (3rd ed.). London: Paul Chapman.

Knowles, M. S., & Associates. (1984). *Andragogy in action: Applying modern principles of adult learning.* San Francisco: Jossey-Bass.

Kurfiss, J. (1988). *Critical thinking: Theory, research, practice and possibilities.* Washington DC: Association for the Study of Higher Education.

Lynch, M. (2000). Against reflexivity as an academic virtue and source of privileged knowledge. *Theory, Culture and Society, 17*(3), 26-54.

McNiff, J. (2000). *Action research in organizations.* London: Routledge.

McPeck, J. (1981). *Critical thinking and education.* Oxford, England: Martin Robertson.

Mingers, J. (1999). What is it to be critical? Teaching a critical approach to management undergraduates. *Management Learning, 31*(2), 219-237.

Missimer, C. (1986). *Good arguments: An introduction to critical thinking* (2nd ed.). Englewood Cliffs, NJ: Prentice Hall.

Moore, B. N. (1989). *Critical thinking: Evaluating claims and arguments in everyday life* (2nd ed.). Palo Alto, CA: Mayfield.

Norris, S. P., & Ennis, R. H. (1989). *Evaluating critical thinking.* Pacific Grove, CA: Midwest.

Paul, R. (1990). *Critical thinking.* Santa Rosa, CA: Foundation for Critical Thinking.

Paul, R. (1993). *Critical thinking: What every person needs to survive in a rapidly changing world.* Santa Rosa, CA: Foundation for Critical Thinking.

Perry, W. G. (1988). Different worlds in the same classroom. In P. Ramsden (Ed.), *Improving learning: New perspectives.* London: Kogan Page. Retrieved January 15, 2008, from http://isites.harvard.edu/fs/html/icb.topic58474/perry.html

Pfeffer, J., & Fong, C. T. (2002). The end of business schools? Less success than meets the eye. *Academy of Management Learning and Education Journal, 1*(1), 78-95

Ramsden, P. (1992). *Learning to teach in higher education.* London: Routledge.

Ruggiero, V. (1988). *Teaching thinking across the curriculum.* New York: Harper Row.

Rynes, S. L., McNatt, B., & Bretz, R. D. (1999). Academic research inside organizations: Inputs, processes and outcomes. *Personnel Psychology, 52*, 869-898.

Scheffler, I. (1973). *Reason and teaching.* London: Routledge & Kegan Paul.

Schön, D. (1983). *The reflective practitioner.* New York: Basic Books.

Schön, D. (1987). *Educating the reflective practitioner* New York: Basic Books.

Siegel, H. (1988). *Educating reason: Rationality, critical thinking and education.* New York: Routledge Chapman & Hall.

Sotto, E. (1994). *When teaching becomes learning.* London: Cassell.

Starkey, K., & Madan, P. (2001). Bridging the relevance gap: Aligning stakeholders in the future of management research. *British Journal of Management, 12*, 3-26.

Steiner, F. (1991). *Research and reflexivity.* London: SAGE

Taylor, R. W., & Richards, C. M. (1985). *An introduction to curriculum studies.* London: NFER-Nelson.

Toulmin, S. E. (1958). *The uses of argument.* New York: Cambridge University Press.

Weast, D. (1996). Alternative teaching strategies: The case for critical thinking. *Teaching Sociology, 24*, 189-194.

Weick, K. E. (2003). Real time reflexivity: Prods to reflection. *Organization Studies* (Special Issue on "Time and Reflexivity in Organization Studies"), *26*(3), 893-898.

CHAPTER 5

CHALLENGES OF EDUCATING EUROPEAN MANAGERS OF LIFELONG LEARNING

**Steven J. Armstrong, Denise Thursfield,
Paolo Landri, and Giuseppe Ponzini**

It is an ambition of the European Council to become one of the world's most competitive and dynamic economies. Lifelong learning is seen as a focal point for realizing that ambition. This chapter reports on the efforts of a group of European partners to construct an innovative education course for managers of lifelong learning across Europe. The aim was to construct a course to help managers develop the knowledge and skills needed to promote lifelong learning in their organizations. This aim was to be achieved through fusion of the diverse understandings of various partners. We show how, through negotiation between team members, the project culminated in a final course that provided participants with a toolbox of ideas, concepts, models and methods that can be usefully used to promote lifelong learning.

University and Corporate Innovations in Lifelong Learning, pp. 91–131
Copyright © 2008 by Information Age Publishing
All rights of reproduction in any form reserved.

INTRODUCTION AND BACKGROUND

The concept of "lifelong learning" has witnessed burgeoning interests over the past decade on a global scale (e.g., Kuhn, 2007; Oduaran, 2000). The concept is now at the center of many national and international policies for fostering economic competitiveness and for improving social participation and inclusion. The term seems to have become a mantra for societies attempting to deal with ever increasing complexities and technological, demographic and societal changes confronting our contemporary age (Field, 2002). Some scholars argue that the concept has become part of a dominant discourse about society that is difficult to disagree with, because it refers to a set of common understandings that appear to be "undeniable truths" of our times (Coffield, 2002; Contu, Grey, & Ortenlad, 2003). The concept has global currency and travels through the circuits of key agencies such as the European Union (EU), the Organization for Economic Co-operation and Development (OECD), World Bank (2003), and the United Nations Educational, Scientific and Cultural Organization (UNESCO). Those transnational agencies support and feed the discourse and policies of lifelong learning as effective solutions to the globalization of societies and economies. The term "lifelong learning" is believed to have derived from the former concept of "lifelong education" which was at the center of a debate promoted by UNESCO and OECD among scholars and practitioners in the 1960s and 1970s as a way of reframing educational systems in order to devise a more just and better society following World War II (Aspin & Chapman, 2000; Crowther, 2004). The concept of lifelong learning was slowly substituted for that of lifelong education during the 1990s in many of the documents emerging from within the EU, and including OECD (OECD, 1996). In particular, the advent of Jacques Delors's (1996) white paper on competitiveness and economic growth and the European Year of Lifelong Learning in 1996 led to the concept of lifelong learning becoming a cornerstone for many national and international political agendas.

Between 1999 and 2004 OECD initiated a thematic review of lifelong learning across 17 countries including the United States (OECD, 2005) and, importantly, many of the member states of the European Community (OECD, 2006). This review focused on understanding adults' access to, and participation in learning activities, and on enhancing incentives for them to undertake such activities. These themes were taken forward in a recent UNESCO report which argued that the capacity of nations, society and individuals to adjust to the new global economy is dependent on improving competencies through continuous adult learning. Adult learning has been argued to serve a number of purposes.

It counteracts socioeconomic divisions and the marginalization of excluded groups. It can also improve productivity and labor market participation, and promote active citizenship (Desjardins, Rubenson, & Milana, 2006). With specific reference to Europe, it is argued that lifelong learning is important for the promotion of social justice and development in the context of increasing economic and social globalization (Sussmuth, 2003; UNESCO, 2003). The Lisbon European Council of 2000, for example, set out a strategic goal for 2010: "to become the most competitive and dynamic knowledge-based economy in the world, capable of sustainable economic growth with more and better jobs and greater social cohesion" (Lisbon Agenda, 2007). In this context the aims of lifelong learning set out by the EU are to promote active citizenship; personal fulfilment; social inclusion and employability and flexibility (European Commission, 2001). To achieve this the commission calls on member governments to target efforts at disadvantaged groups and to tailor education and training to their needs (European Commission, 2003a). However, participation in lifelong learning in Europe is low, with fewer than 10% of adults participating in further learning (European Commission, 2003a).

It could be argued that the EU is sending out confused messages with regard to the direction of lifelong learning. The rhetoric on lifelong learning described above clearly encapsulates three themes: to overcome social division and promote social cohesion, to enhance personal development, and to improve competencies amongst the labor force to support the productivity and competitiveness of companies and the EU as a whole. Thus, on the one hand, lifelong learning is about social cohesion and social justice, and is to be targeted at disadvantaged groups. On the other hand, lifelong learning is about the development of higher level, technical skills needed if the EU is to compete in a globalized economy. It is also argued that this latter theme has become the overarching hegemony in the discourse of lifelong learning. Moreover, the majority of adults who participate in lifelong learning in Europe do so for job related reasons (Desjardins, Rubenson, & Milana, 2006; Gouthro, 2002). These divergent messages are, we will demonstrate later in this chapter, reflected in the perceptions of academics and practitioners involved in the development and delivery of lifelong learning programmes. We will also argue, however, that a pluralist approach can facilitate diversity of provision that meets the needs of different groups.

Our aim in this chapter is to describe how a course for managers of lifelong learning was developed in the context of the wider European discourse described above. We show how the plurality of meanings held by members of the project team shaped and became embedded in the course. The chapter begins with a description of the main features of the project and the methodologies employed. We will then chart the journey of the project in relation to the development and delivery of the final training course that provided a lens through which both course participants' and course designers' perceptions and meanings of lifelong learning could be elicited. Finally, we will discuss how providing a toolbox of ideas, concepts, models, and methods can be usefully used by managers to feed into their own intersubjective sensemaking processes and provide a variety of techniques for mapping out new territories and helping them envision a future that can be shared by others.

EUROPEAN SUPPORT INITIATIVES

The EU supports a number of education programs designed to support the needs of managers responsible for implementing lifelong learning initiatives by providing funding opportunities for research and training projects. One such initiative is called "Socrates" which supports European cooperation on a range of educational projects, initiatives, and professional development, providing opportunities for all sectors, including higher education and lifelong learning. Socrates spans the entire breadth of the education system and is broken into eight priorities which aim to improve quality and strengthen the European dimension in education. One priority, known as "Grunvtvig," is concerned with adult education and places particular emphasis on lifelong learning. It aims to improve the availability, accessibility, and quality of adult teaching and learning through supporting European cooperation projects, learning partnerships, staff training, and the development of networks.

A European Cooperation Project

In October 2004, a group of European partners were granted Grundtvig funding of almost 250,000 euro to develop an education and training course that would help satisfy the needs of managers of lifelong learning initiatives in Europe. The project can be contextualized by considering the statement that "professional development of vocational teachers and trainers also remains a challenge for most countries" (European Council, 2006). The partners involved in this project are listed below:

- Estonia Business School Executive Training Centre, Tallin, Estonia.
- Centre for Management and Organizational Learning, University of Hull, United Kingdom.
- IVLOS Institute of Education, Utrecht University, the Netherlands.
- Schouten & Nelissen Training Agency, the Netherlands
- Foundation for Local Government Reform, Bulgaria.
- Ed-Lab Education Laboratory, Germany.
- Institute of Research on Population and Social Policies, National Research Council, Italy.

The set of partners includes organizations working in academic, research and further vocational training fields, belonging to the public (United Kingdom and Italy), private (the Netherlands, Germany, and Estonia) as well as semipublic realms (Bulgaria). As a consequence, the project encompassed a plurality of complementary professional competencies and experiences. The project duration was 2 years, and ended on September 30, 2006. In the early stages of the project, a detailed comparative analysis was carried out to generate an understanding of the core dynamics associated with lifelong learning initiatives being embraced by a variety of European countries. Data were collected using open ended questionnaires concerned with eliciting information associated with various aspects of lifelong learning in the various European countries including: policies of adult learner education and training; settings of the organizational field of adult learner education and training; profiles of the various managers of learning; and controversies and emerging debates.

The results of these analyses (discussed in more detail below) helped pave the way to designing a framework for the education and training course being developed on this project. Data that emerged from this stage of the project included demographic information on population, wealth, social expenditure, labor market situation, educational level, educational expenditure, and national welfare models for each of the different countries. Other useful information emerged on policies associated with adult education; training, and lifelong learning; plurality of provision of the different countries; range of providers; coordinating policies; partnership details; certification of learning and quality assurance; funding of lifelong learning; managers of learning; debates and future challenges; and best practices.

Following this initial empirical stage, a series of developmental meetings and workshops were held in the various partner institutions in order that the project partners could begin to design and develop the course. A number of aims, objectives and learning outcomes were identified for the course.

Project Aims and Objectives

The agreed aims and objectives of the course were to provide managers of lifelong learning initiatives in Europe with the concepts and tools necessary for successful promotion and implementation of those initiatives, irrespective of their institutional type or affiliation. These were:

- To understand and assess socioeconomic, political, and cultural factors that may constrain or enable lifelong learning in particular national contexts.
- To identify a set of needs associated with a range of different target groups.
- To motivate potential learners to become engaged in lifelong learning initiatives.
- To develop an increased awareness of the variety of tools and methods for assessing learning needs.
- To use a range of tools associated with strategic management and the management of change.
- To develop and promote the use of the information and communication technologies (ICT) in the field of lifelong learning.
- To conduct an evaluation of existing lifelong learning programs.
- To manage individual differences in preferred approaches to learning and instruction.
- Evaluate the relevance and appropriateness of both formal (credit based) and informal (work-based) approaches to lifelong learning.
- Develop an implementation plan.

A number of modules were then developed in order to meet these learning outcomes and a prototype of the training course was tested in each of the partner nations in the early part of 2006 and involved a wide variety of managers of lifelong learning initiatives. The final training course (see Appendix) was delivered at two sites. The first was in Gremmelin, Germany, between June 26 and June 30, and the second was in Talin, Estonia between August 28 and September 1, 2006.

Methodology

The sample of countries involved in the project offers a good summary of the EU context and of its recent developments. The six nations are representatives of the different "worlds of welfare" (European Commission, 1993, 1995, 1998; Esping-Andersen, 1990; Ferrera, 1998; Flora, 1986; Flora & Heidenheimer, 1981) and of the new European social dimension emerging with the enlargement process (European Commission, 2003b). Germany and the Netherlands can be included in the core model of the European welfare system (the well developed "corporatist" model). The United Kingdom represents an intermediate case between universalistic and corporatist models. Italy is an example of the Mediterranean model, that is, a low developed corporatist welfare model. Bulgaria and Estonia represent experiences from the new European member states facing the transition from an egalitarian ("communist welfare regime") to a more market-oriented welfare model.

The methodology of our project was largely characterized by a qualitative approach, and was aimed at producing "usable knowledge" for designing an education and training course for managers of lifelong learning. That was the primary expected outcome of the funded project. At the same time, the authors of this chapter were interested in studying the process of knowing among the two sets of actors engaged in designing the course and participating in the course. The usable knowledge for designing the course drew on a comparative analysis of several characteristics associated with the interorganizational fields of adult education and training in the six European countries included in the project (Bulgaria, Estonia Germany, Italy, the Netherlands, United Kingdom). The purpose was to clarify mutual understanding of the "core dynamics" of the interorganizational field of adult education in a variety of different countries faced with the challenge of implementing lifelong learning initiatives.

Our study of the process of knowing among actors engaged in designing and participating in the course was based on tape recorded data of various meetings throughout the duration of the project, documentation produced by the various partners, 14 tape recorded interviews carried out with members of the project team and with course participants. Semistructured interview questions were used for soliciting data from the course participants to gain a deeper understanding of issues such as understanding of the concepts of lifelong learning, challenges faced when attempting to manage lifelong learning initiatives in their home country, opportunities for lifelong learning, and experiences and problems associated with implementation. Questionnaires were also completed by some course participants who were unavailable for interview. Feedback data were also collected from participants using questionnaires completed at end of delivery of each of the course modules, and again at the end of the entire course.

Interviews with the various projects partners were initially aimed at soliciting information concerning their initial expectations of the course, changes in those expectations, and the extent to which the project aims were met. These interviews then took on a more open ended approach in order to accommodate feedback about wider issues and perspectives associated with the lifelong learning agenda.

The country reports were integrated with statistical data from Eurostat. Feedback data were also collected from discussions and analyses conducted during various project meetings and prototype courses held in partner countries. An online groupware facility also allowed us to both reinforce mutual understandings and express ongoing critical remarks.

These different approaches to collecting data provided us the empirical materials needed for this chapter. These data were analyzed with the intention of mapping out the many ways of interpreting the concept of lifelong learning according to the views of both course participants and project partners, and for tracking managers various processes of sense making.

In the next section, the chapter will present the main results of the comparative analysis, and a provisional typology based on the different interpretations of lifelong learning emerging from the analysis. Here, the validity of our findings should not be considered in terms of generalizability, but of transferability of knowledge in a situated context of use (Lincoln & Guba, 1985). It is hoped that these results will lead to a better understanding of key dynamics associated with implementing policies of lifelong learning in Europe.

COMPARATIVE ANALYSIS OF
LIFELONG LEARNING INITIATIVES

The concept of "lifelong learning" is a key word in most of the debates about the future of contemporary societies as well as in many of the strategies suggested for individuals and organizations for dealing with the accelerating pace of socioeconomic change. However, the policies for implementing lifelong learning have a "local dimension" in the sense that they imply a set of processes to be translated in current organizational and individual practices. These processes concern the scope, the resources, the agenda setting, the overall means, and suitable training program for developing the relevant professional competencies needed to translate policy into practice.

In paying attention to the "local dimension," it is suggested that there is a need to map the different trajectories of diverse countries that have tried to implement lifelong learning, and also to identify the common threads that persist regardless of the situated nature of particular policies. In this project, a comparative review was undertaken to help clarify and develop mutual understandings of the core dynamics associated with the field of adult education from the variety of perspectives of different European countries trying to implement policies associated with lifelong learning initiatives. The comparative review was constrained to the countries of our particular consortium. Its primary purpose was to determine the social embeddedness of our training target group ("Managers of lifelong learning"—with a modernist accent) and to identify the issues they are charged with addressing. The sample comprised six European countries as follows:

- Bulgaria
- Estonia
- Germany
- Italy
- Netherlands
- United Kingdom

It is believed that these six nations represent a useful milieu for acknowledging the diversity of European nation states. Open ended questionnaires were used with the various project partners in order to solicit information regarding:

- Policies of adult learner education and training
- Organizational perspectives of adult learner education and training
- Profiles of managers of lifelong learning
- Controversies and emerging debates.

Our review revealed that adult education and training in a European context tends not to be a specialized domain in an educational system, but is viewed more comprehensively as learning through a lifecycle. It is inculcated by a process of de-differentiation that leads to a continuing process of shifting boundaries of "traditional" institutional domains (Edwards, 1997; Kuhn & Sultana, 2006; Ragatt, Edwards, Small, 1996. This de-differentiation is driven by the widening of scope of national adult education policies, and the broadening of the adult education provision. This concept of de-differentiation within these European countries leads to emerging issues related to new modes of governance and the restructuring of regulations in order to:

- Overcome difficulties of establishing sustainable partnership among organizations with different and sometimes conflicting institutional goals.
- Deal with the certification of learning and the policies of guidance.
- Develop new strategies for funding lifelong learning.

Process of De-differentiation

From Education to Learning

Despite the widespread diffusion of the idea of lifelong learning inside the international agenda of different nation states, and its inclusion in many national and local policies, there are few examples of successful implementation (Field, 2002). One notable difficulty is that it seems impossible to find a unique definition of the term (Aspin & Chapman, 2000). This is thought to be because the concept appears to present many dimensions and includes different practices and activities, as well as involving many institutional sectors at the same time (Alheit, 1999; Griffin, 1999a, 1999b). The concept, born in the notion of adult education that emerged as a provision oriented towards liberal education at the end of the 1960's discussed above, now encapsulates a wider range of learning contexts and practices occurring along the entire life span of individuals (Tuijnman, 2002). In EU documents, for example, the concept is said to include:

- Formal learning—defined as intentional education provided by traditional educational organizations and training colleges.
- Informal learning—defined as intentional learning activities not leading to certification or any form of assessment
- Nonformal learning—defined as learning that occurs in everyday practices.

The concept is expanding to include forms of learning considered as objects of policy—that is "the provision of education." It is difficult to understand how human practices such as these can be viewed as "objects" of any policy, because learning often emerges in an unpredictable way and follows trajectories with high levels of individuality (Griffin, 1999a, 1999b). The present concept, therefore, seems to be a "catch all" term to encapsulate different political alternatives. These include the social democrats approach, with its focus on the traditional educational provision, or the neo-liberal approach where reference to lifelong learning sustains a rhetoric of reform of welfare state arrangements emphasizing the role and the responsibilities of individuals in facing the challenges of the new globalized economy.

Lifelong learning is also a contested terrain, since according to a humanistic approach it focuses attention on a new vocationalism in education, and tends to blame nonparticipants of lifelong learning by placing on them the responsibility to align with ongoing learning trajectories, while at the same time it imagines a dark future for the nations and individuals not embracing this policy in practice (Coffield, 2002; Tight, 1998). In this view, lifelong learning and its advocates favor initiatives and policies almost exclusively concentrated on work related learning and suggest the development of a "learning market" rather than a renovation or an expansion of the state-provided education (Edwards, 1997; Field, 2002). According to Field promoting lifelong learning does not only require new government measures, but rather a new approach to government and Rhodes (1996) argues for less government (or rowing) and more governance (or steering). This simple perspective, however, should not hide the difficulties of the task. While it is now evident that lifelong learning initiatives have become policy in many European countries, ways of creating learning cultures in order to achieve the "learning age" that is being widely espoused remains a significant challenge.

Our review demonstrated that this shift from education to learning, reflected in the shift from formal to informal learning, is occurring across many institutional domains as revealed in Table 5.1. Reference to lifelong learning appears in policy documents associated not only with traditional educational policies, but also social policies, economic policies, labor market policies, elder policies, health policies, migrants' policies, and policies supporting enterprises. As a consequence, the new focus signals an increasing homogenization of discourses and policies in the EU.

This shift is away from the traditional model of education and training that relied on formal methods, from primary through to higher education, where there were clear boundaries between both level of education, and between education and noneducation. These changes have been sustained by discourses about the need to increase "skills" in order to improve competitiveness of both regions and nations. The need to develop opportunities to encourage participation and integration in society has also been highlighted by extending these arguments to classic issues of citizenship and democracy. Consequently, policies of adult education are no longer regarded as specialized subdomains of education

Table 5.1.   Policies Referring to Lifelong Learning

Bulgaria	• Law on Higher Education (1997, 1999) • National plan for economic development 2001 • National action plan on employment 2001; • The Labor Code (2001) • National strategy on human resources development 2006; • National and regional projects and program on employment and professional qualification
Estonia	• Adult Education Act (1993) • Basic Schools and Upper Secondary Schools Act (1993) • The Universities Act (1995) • The Vocational Education Institutions Act (1998, 2001) • The Applied Higher Education Institutions Act (1998) • The Private Education Institutions Act (1998) • The Social Protection of the Unemployed Act (2000) • The Employment Service Act (2000) • The Rural Development and Agricultural Market Regulation Act (2000)
Germany	• Reform Project for Vocational Training—Flexible Structures and Modern Occupations (1997) • Lifelong Learning for Everyone (2001) • Jointly agree strategy on L3 (2004)
Italy	• Enterprise Training Plan, 1993 • Agreement for Occupation, 1996 • Act n. 196/1997 ("Pacchetto Treu") • School Autonomy (Act 59/1997) • [1]Legislative Decree N. 112/98 (Decentralization) • Reform of University (2000) • Reform of Social Assistance (Act 328/2000) • Training leaves for workers and nonworkers (Act 53/2000) • Reform of Education and Training (Act 53/2003)
The Netherlands	• Adult and Vocational Education Act (WEB, 1996) • Skills Recognition (EVC, 2003) • Taskforce lifelong learning (2004)
U.K.	• Supply-side policies (past 2 decades) • Investors in People (early 1990s) • ILA (Individual Learning Account, 1998) • Skills Strategy Whitepaper of 2003 • Trades Union Learning Representatives' (2002) • Workforce Development (2002)

1. In 2006, this reform is still under debate. In autumn, the new minister decided to suspend its implementation.

Sources: Landri & Ponzini (2005).

policies, because they are increasingly recognized as being relevant to a wide variety of institutional environments.

The notion of a shift from education to learning is criticized on a number of points. First, it can be argued that formal education is, in theory at least, a cognitive activity that requires critical thinking and questioning on the part of the learner. At its heart are questions of "why?" Learning, in the sense of nonformal learning, is about the development of job-related skills. It is about "know how" rather than "know why." Although acquisition of job-related skills may improve an individual's employability, it is questionable as to whether nonformal and informal learning can address the issues of socioeconomic divisions and social exclusion. Second, the notion of "learnerism" shifts responsibility for learning from the state to the individual. Third, learnerism is argued to undermine welfare by:

> Disguising the reduction of the democratic public sphere, and working on people as objects of policy to ensure their compliance with the brave new world of flexible capitalism. (Crowther, 2004, p. 130)

These issues and critiques are, we demonstrate shortly, woven into the conceptualizations of learning held by project team members.

Broadening the Provision

The passage from education to learning leads to a widening of the provision and concomitant increases in the number of providers of adult education. The typology of provision now includes compensatory education, general education, vocational training, continuing vocational training, tertiary education, special programs, and distance education. The need to raise skills to improve the competitiveness of nations leads to an increased emphasis on vocational training and a need to strengthen the supply of that type of learning. In the United Kingdom there is explicit evidence of a move towards "economic instrumentalism." There is also some evidence of this in reports from other countries such as the Netherlands, and Italy, albeit implicit.

Flexibility in the design and delivery of courses was a key word in the discourse of all of the nations sampled which implies a need for a type of provision that can match the needs and the time constraints of both individuals and institutions prepared to engage in educational and training initiatives.

Throughout the various policy documents, "flexibility" was used to imply modularization of courses and scheduling of educational activities in a way that suits a wide variety of adult learners. Provision identified included part-day and single day courses, evening courses, and a combination of day courses and self learning. Distance learning approaches are also attracting growing interest in the field of lifelong learning. These types of flexibility are attracting substantial economic investments in all of the countries in our sample. Our questionnaire survey revealed that the most notable examples of where e-learning is being heavily promoted include Bulgaria, and the United Kingdom through initiatives such as "Learn Direct." Similar initiatives were identified to a lesser extent in all other countries in our sample.

Table 5.2.   Providers of Adult Education and Training

Bulgaria	• Professional schools • Universities—departments for further education • NGOs • Private firms for training and human resource development • Licensed centers for vocational education
Estonia	• 32 evening schools and adults' public schools • 80 vocational education institutions with departments for adults • 62 Folk High Schools • 56 High school adult education departments and Open Universities • 320 others, incl. private and municipal training centers
Germany	• University • Technical university (Fachhochschule) • Evening school (Volkshochschule) • Chambers of industry and commerce (IHK) • Chambers of crafts (Handwerkskammer) • Vocational schools • Educational services of unions or charity organizations • Municipal adult education centres • Private organizations
Italy	• CTPs (Public Local Units for adult education) • Secondary Schools • CFPs (Public Regional Units for Vocational and Educational Training) • Universities • Chambers of Commerce • Public Administrations • Private companies
The Netherlands	• 49 regional training centers (ROCs) • Private training institutes
U.K.	• Further education colleges • Learn Direct • Open University • Private sector trainers

Sources: Landri & Ponzini (2005).

This plurality of provision has resulted in a diverse range of providers working in the field of lifelong learning as shown in Table 5.2. It can be seen that the provision of learning is no longer constrained to formal educational institutions but that organizations embedded in other fields such as the private sector, social services, cultural sectors, and voluntary associations are also active. There is organizational heterogeneity according to size, institutional domains (public and private), and geographical area (national, regional, local). Three broad types of provision can be identified within the context of lifelong learning as follows:

- Providers whose exclusive and dominant organizational mission is "education and training" (for example, the 62 folk high schools of Estonia);
- Providers who are frequently involved in educational and training activities, but whose mission includes social policies (educational services of unions or charity organizations in Germany, for example),
- Providers whose organizational mission is focused on other areas of activity but depend on learning at both the individual and organizational level in order to remain competitive (private companies within all of the countries sampled).

Modes of Governance and Regulatory Bodies

The widening scope of education and training policies, plurality of provision, and expansion of providers raises issues of governance at both the macro-level involving relationships between institutions at national level, and the meso-level at the point of implementation of lifelong learning programs. Our research suggests the possible need for establishing a "new system of governance" in order to counterbalance the increasing risk of fragmentation. This would require careful coordination between the line ministries in central government and the various linkages between education and training providers and training and development within workplace settings.

Our review of the various regulative bodies in Table 5.3 identified three different settings. The first refers to the case of Italy and Bulgaria who each have two ministries responsible for adult learning. The second refers to the cases of the Netherlands, United Kingdom, and Estonia, where there is a single ministry at national level responsible for adult learning. The third refers to Germany, where governance develops within a federal model composed of a diversity of states (Länder). Consequently, there is a complex relationship within and between the local and the national levels.

Table 5.3.   Regulatory Bodies

Bulgaria	Ministry of Education and Science (MES)
	National Agency for Vocational Education and Training (NAVET)
	Ministry of Labor and Social Policy
	The Employment Agency (EA)
	National Consultative Council for Vocational Qualification of the Work Force
	The Regional Employment Committees
	9 regional and 122 local labor offices
Estonia	Ministry of Education and Research
	Council of Adult Education
	The Education and Culture Departments of the County Governments
	The Education Departments of the City Governments
	Estonian Adult Educators Association "Andras"
	Estonian Nonformal Adult Education Association
	Estonian Open Education Association
	Estonian Association of Andragogy
Germany	Federal Ministry of Education and Research
	Ministries of Education and Cultural Affairs of the Länder
	Standing Conference of Ministers of Education and Cultural Affairs
	The Federal Institute for Vocational Training
	German Institute for Adult Education
	Local Chambers of Industry and Commerce
	Local Chambers of Crafts
Italy	Ministry of Education,
	Ministry of University and Research
	Ministry of Work and Social Policies
	Standing Conference State-Regions
	Regional Commission
	Local Commissions for Adult Education
The Netherlands	Ministry of Education, Culture, and Science
	Central Register of Vocational Courses
	Examination Quality Centre
	Inspection of education
	Local government (contracts adult education)
U.K.	Department for Education and Skills
	The Learning and Skills Councils
	National Institute for Adult Continuing Education (nongovernment agency)

Sources: Landri & Ponzini (2005).

For the first setting involving Bulgaria and Italy, two ministries work in the fields of work and social policies and education and science. They share a point of coordination in a national commission and in the standing conference state-regions (in the case of Italy) as well as in an agency the National Agency for Vocational Education and Training (NAVET) that supports the ministry for vocational education and training (in Bulgaria). Along the vertical dimension of governance there is regional deployment with local bodies responsible for the coordination, design, and monitoring of policies.

The second setting identified is characterized by the responsibility of one ministry or one point of national reference. Estonia has the Ministry of Education and Research, The Netherlands has the Ministry of Education, Culture, and Science, and the United Kingdom has the Department for Education and Skills resulting from a recent process of integration. Similar levels of complexity exist in the first setting for the concrete delivery of educational policies as well as for the management of those initiatives at the regional and at the local levels.

The third setting represented in Germany is characterized by a federal model of the state. This leads to additional levels of coordination with the Federal Ministry of Education and Research at one level, the Ministries of Education and Cultural Affairs of the Länder at a second level, and the Standing Conference of Ministers of Education and Cultural Affairs at the Länder level.

The Problem of Partnership

The need to establish effective modes of alignment among partners at the meso-level also represents a key component for ensuring successful implementation of lifelong learning policies, for overcoming possible closure associated with adult education and training initiatives, and for dealing with differentiated forms of schooling. This need was identified in some way or other in all of the countries in our European sample and below are some exerts from the various reports which illustrate this.

Estonia. "Cooperation between state and local authorities must be reinforced. Until now local authorities have not been sufficiently involved in adult education and lifelong learning. In order to create an educational environment and make lifelong learning a reality, all essential institutions—local authorities, employers, employment offices, social partners, trade unions and learning providers—have to be actively involved in the networking process."

United Kingdom. "Because the system of lifelong learning is fragmented, a high degree of partnership is required. Research suggests, however, that partnership and collaboration are not easily achieved."

Italy. "There is a lot of emphasis about the importance of partnership between the organizations in order to successfully carry out the respective policies. The myth of the "network" is the dominant representation both in private (where the idea is the "system building") and in public sector even if it is not always clear if it is a claim or an effective description of the situation"

We do, of course, already have successful practices of collaboration both within and among various European partners. Examples include Roc's in The Netherlands who collaborate widely in a national council for defending common interests, or many private organizations that enter into networks aimed at generating a more organized learning market. There are also several examples of horizontal collaborations between institutions at national level in various countries in order to enhance the success of implementing Lifelong Learning policies that leads to the establishment of local agreements at regional and local levels (examples can be found between Germany and Italy. These relatively new practices are somewhat episodical, and confirm the difficulties associated with working together among different organizations.

The Certification of Learning

Certification of learning is an area where collaboration and agreement is urgently required. Transition to a system of demand-driven learning reinforces the need for policies of guidance.[1] Some organizations in both public and private sectors do provide guidance for various target groups but vertical and horizontal coordination problems are evident at national and trans-national levels. In the United Kingdom, Estonia, and Italy there are no national systems of guidance, but there are various services where adult learners can receive some form of guidance. In United Kingdom, for example, the Jobcentre Plus is an important provider for individuals in long-term employment. In contrast, adults in Estonia seeking guidance are extremely limited. In Italy, policies designed to activate the labor market have led to new local public units being formed (*Servizi per l'impiego*) that offer guidance to many target groups.

The most important examples of certification for learning can be found in the national frameworks of qualification: for example, Kwalificatiestructuur Educatie (KSE) in Netherlands; National Vocation Qualification (NVQ) in United Kingdom; the qualifications structure of the dual system of Germany. However, these frameworks are often limited to the recognition of skills and competencies acquired beyond formal schooling. A variety of arrangements for recognizing individual skills and accrediting them were identified in our review but there is very little cohesion between them. In the United Kingdom the ultimate responsibility for evaluation of policies of lifelong learning lies with the Department of Learning and Skills, although there are some specific program of assessment at the local level carried out by regional bodies. In Estonia, there is the Adult Education Council and the Department of Vocational and Adult Education of the Ministry of Education and Research. In Bulgaria the responsibility for formal education lies initially with schools and universities, but ultimately with the Ministry of Education and Science. A stark omission in all of the nations sampled is that there is no official system of evaluation for informal adult learning, education and training.

Funding Lifelong Learning

A key question facing providers of national and transnational levels of lifelong learning initiatives is how they should be financed. In our survey, we found little or no commonality in the responses received. We failed to obtain consistent information about whether it is the adult learner, the private sector, or the state which funds providers.

In some cases the state represents one important source. In Bulgaria for example, financial resources for public schools and for the employed and unemployed come from the state budget and from the municipalities but schools in vocation and education training collect part of their resources from sponsorship, and part from national and international programmes. In the Netherlands, the government funds adult education via direct and indirect sources. The state funds vocational education directly, whereas central adult education is funded via the municipalities according various parameters. The municipalities then draw up contracts with the various regional training centers (ROCs) for more concrete course deliveries. In Italy, the state plays a major role in financing the lifelong learning strategy by means of a plurality of policies. Where relevant, there is also cofinancing from EU structural funds, particularly for disadvantaged regions. In some cases, the learner contributes to expenses by paying a fee. In the Netherlands, for example, adult learners pay fees for taking full- or part-time courses. In other cases, adult learners can be eligible for student loans and in the United Kingdom this is in the form of a carrier development loan. In Estonia, financing learners takes several forms. Sometimes a portion of the fees is paid by employers who then receive a partial refund from the state. Some states also offer tax benefits to those employers who can demonstrate specific activity in education and training initiatives. The Act 383/01 in Italy is one example of this.

Finance for adult education and training is increasingly coming from a combination of sources across Europe which means that opportunities for flexible solutions to lifelong learning initiatives are likely to become less standardized. To address this problem, the federal government of Germany has organized a commission of experts for deepening our understanding of the financial constraints and alternatives available for putting lifelong learning initiatives into practice.

Conclusions of the Comparative Analysis

Findings of our comparative review highlight a trend of de-differentiation among our sample of European countries. The review identified consistent national policies that reflect the shift from education to learning, and underlined the immediate effect of this uniformity in terms of increasing the typology of provision, as well as the increasing diversity of providers. This trend of de-differentiation is having the effect of completely redefining adult education and training which raises serious concerns over issues relating to governance regarding the regulative framework, the structure of authorities, collaboration issues at both the macro- and meso-levels, and the question of funding lifelong learning strategies. The review revealed a complex social milieu in which managers of lifelong learning have to operate. This inevitably leads to severe difficulties when attempting to implement the concepts in organizations, institutions or society.

INTERPRETATIONS OF THE CONCEPT OF LIFELONG LEARNING

Lifelong Learning Defined by Project Team Members

It is clear from the previous section that a plurality of approaches to lifelong learning exists across Europe, albeit within a context of de-differentiation between countries. The context for the design and development of the course in question is therefore ambiguous. This ambiguity is reflected in differing conceptualizations of lifelong learning held by project team members. These plural conceptualizations are not necessarily oppositional. Rather, they can be placed on a continuum between hard economic instrumentalism and social egalitarianism. In the context of de-differentiation, it is worth pointing out that the national background of team members does not necessarily determine their approach to lifelong learning. For example, the "lifelong learning as social justice" approach is taken by one team member from the United Kingdom, despite the fact that U.K. policies on lifelong learning are more closely associated with the "lifelong learning as competitive advantage" perspective, as stated earlier.

Three conceptualizations of lifelong learning emerged from a range of semistructured interviews conducted with participant team members. These are lifelong learning as competitive advantage; lifelong learning as personal, organizational and societal development; and lifelong learning as social justice. A common thread running through each perspective is that the need for learning is embedded in profound economic and social change.

Lifelong Learning as Competitive Advantage

The competitive advantage perspective emphasizes hard economic instrumentalism. Lifelong learning is conceptualized as the means through which nations of the EU can compete with developing economies such as china and India. It is the tool through which the West must deal with the problems of globalization. For example:

> If the EU does not change its ways of making money and organizing its economy, in the end there will be no future for Europe. We cannot compete with 2 billion in china and 1 billion in India. We cannot compete when you know that in India each year thousands of people of top ICT programmes leave the universities and we do not have huge numbers of people. So there is a knowledge gap.

From this perspective lifelong learning is indistinguishable from human resource (HR) development in that it occurs exclusively within organizations. It is delivered by "expert" trainers and consists of discrete packages of knowledge that are transferred from the expert to the trainee. Employees have little or no input into the process except as passive recipients of expert knowledge. For one participant the current project is about:

> Training and development for managers and education managers here in Europe so that they will be able to develop a lifelong learning programme in their own organization … my interest is about how to help enterprises become more competitive, and what we can do so that employees will continue learning. And not just as something it is nice to talk about, but as something which the company's top management considers is an urgent need.

For this team member the target group for the course is "top managers" who have responsibility for ensuring the company's competitiveness. Moreover, lifelong learning is concerned exclusively with developing the skills and competencies required by business organizations:

> It is all about business and business needs. If people see the business needs they will realize the kinds of lifelong learning programmes that are needed.... My expectation for this course is that I have made a next step in how we can realize, in concrete terms, lifelong learning in companies and organizations.

The competitive advantage approach is also characterized by a belief that policymakers give too much attention to improving the basic skills of poorly educated groups and individuals. Although this is important, it is even more vital that European economies are able to enhance existing competencies and develop new ones at the higher end of the skills spectrum. Thus:

> You see the policy papers on lifelong learning, 80% of the text is focused on low educated people. It is not talking about how we become competitive in the economy. The situation that is coming up in the economy is competition from China and India.

This perspective is summarized as one that privileges economic instrumentalism and the needs of business. Issues such as personal development, social justice and social cohesion are disregarded in the search for competitive advantage. The target group for the course are managers of organizations and HR managers. The aim of the course is to pass "expertise" from trainers to managers in order that managers can use these tools to encourage learning in their organizations.

Lifelong Learning as Personal, Organizational, and Societal Development

Lifelong learning as personal, organizational, and societal development takes a Unitarian approach based on notions of mutuality and shared benefits. Learning is seen as vital to individuals, organizations and society as a whole. Individuals benefit from learning because it enables them to "keep up" with others in the twenty-first century economy. Organizations become more competitive if staff is involved in continuous learning. Similarly, nations are more able to compete in the global economy if the workplace is well trained and developed. According to one team member:

This is an important project because lifelong learning is very important for individuals as well as organizations and society as a whole, because if you want to keep up in the twenty-first century you have to learn. And this needs to be stimulated from a number of points so that individuals as well as groups and organizations, can learn continuously.

The emphasis on organizational and societal development appears similar to lifelong learning as competitive advantage. There is, however, one important difference in that this perspective places equal emphasis on the needs of the economy and company, and on individuals' needs for personal and professional development. Thus:

> People learn everyday and in every way - from experience and from working with other people. My interest is in lifelong education and how people manage their education and learning.

From the lifelong learning as personal, organizational. and societal development perspective, lifelong learning is a means of ensuring that individuals and groups do not fall behind and suffer social exclusion. It is also a means of ensuring that companies can compete in the global economy.

> Lifelong learning for adults is about giving opportunities to people who have lower education for instance.... Also, how to acknowledge and certify informally acquired knowledge.... Then we could use that for the company, for business.

From this perspective, the aim of the course is to create an awareness of the importance of lifelong learning. It is about developing a course that can be delivered across Europe to assist managers of adult educational institutions and HR managers promote and develop lifelong learning.

Lifelong Learning for Social Justice

The lifelong learning for social justice approach emphasizes the reduction of inequality in society through learning and education. The purpose of lifelong learning is to provide opportunities to those individuals and groups who have traditionally been marginalized through formal education. Examples would be unemployed adults with low educational attainment and individuals in low skilled, poorly paid employment. The aim of lifelong learning is to open up access to education and increase the social mobility of certain groups. For example:

> Learning is significantly related to equality—for example, education for all. So learning is important because all people have to be educated.

In terms of the importance of economic instrumentalism, there are two strands of thought from within this perspective. First is the view that learning is inextricably linked to change, both at the level of the individual and in relation to economic changes:

> I think it is important to understand that individuals are always changing and for me there is equivalence between learning and change. Lifelong learning is the same. We can also make the observation that recently there is this stress on the life course of individuals, so it seems like learning is a matter for individuals. But sometimes this is a misleading point of view.... I think at the European level the idea of policy makers is to make Europe the most competitive economy in the world. So basically the idea is to compete with Asia and China, and it is the same for Asia and America, because if you look at the USA debate it is the same, they want to be the most competitive economy. How to be more competitive, to change, and to change means to learn.

This approach to social justice does not exclude instrumentalist notions. Rather, the approach is about improving competitiveness through learning, and ensuring the fruits of competitiveness are shared equally in terms of opportunity and life chances. The following quote encapsulates this view:

> I think there is a problem linked to the context for our ideas. For example, we need economic development and social equity. This idea was always present in European documents—and in the USA too if you look at it. The line of social equity is strong even if there is a practical orientation to the market. Now the idea of learning as a way to social equity and economic development has become a need. This is because we live in a quickly changing world.

The extent to which lifelong learning can increase the competitiveness of the EU is, nonetheless, questioned from the second strand of thought within the social justice perspective. One team member rejected the notion that HRD within organizations (as proposed by the economic competitiveness perspective) can overcome the effects of neo-liberal economics and globalization. Increased access to learning may serve a number of purposes such as improving the employability and life chances of individuals; improving the competitiveness of companies because a better trained workforce may well be more productive; and promote social inclusively amongst marginalized groups. It cannot, however, counter the effects of globalization. Such a project requires political action on the part of governments. Thus:

This idea that if so called "experts" teach a few "top managers" some techniques in training and development, companies and nations will then have the tools to overcome the effects of neo-liberalism and globalization is ludicrous. Dealing with the economic threat posed by developing countries will take far more than anything we can do—it needs action by governments.

The social justice perspective defines managers of lifelong learning as anyone managing in a lifelong learning context. This might include managers of schools, colleges, and training agencies. It might also include HR development managers in business organizations. The course developed in this project is seen as a means by which such managers might come together to share ideas, knowledge and good practice. The aim would be to construct new ways of opening up access to learning for all members of society.

The various perspectives on lifelong learning described above are emergent from the contradictory discourses of lifelong learning that exist at the global and European levels and which were described at the start of this chapter. They are, moreover, broadly similar to the triadic model of lifelong learning proposed by Aspin and Chapman (2000). They suggest that lifelong learning contains three elements: economic progress and development; personal development and fulfilment; and social inclusiveness and democratic activity. Each element is equally important to the achievement of a learning society. Responses from our project team members suggest very different approaches to the management of lifelong learning and, in fact, to the question of how managers of lifelong learning should be defined. These differences have implications for the development of the course. The plurality of views articulated by team members is not, moreover, surprising in the context of the ambiguity surrounding national policies on lifelong learning. Before we attempt to make sense of the complexity described thus far, we consider the different views on lifelong learning expressed by some course participants.

Lifelong Learning Defined by Course Participants

As expected, course participants came from a diverse range of backgrounds, both culturally and professionally. Nationalities of course participants included British, Portuguese, Estonian, German, Bulgarian, and Slovakian. Their professions were also diverse and a selection of these included:

- Lecturers from universities and colleges of further education.
- A senior manager from a vocational training institution.
- A president of a private University for Leisure and Tourism with more than 500 students.
- A manager of international projects in a technical University.
- Trainers working in private consultancy firms.
- Employees from nongovernment charitable organizations.
- A Learning Coordinator at a recording studio, a nonprofit making community learning organization.
- Staff from a ministry of foreign affairs.
- A middle line manager and training specialist from a company producing doors and door frames.
- An online tutor and instructional designer for an e-learning company for adult education.

They also had a diverse range of responsibilities with respect to managing lifelong learning initiatives in their own institutions and organizations as follows:

- Responsibility for teacher development and training of nearly 200 staff.
- Responsibility for vocational training, especially for women in rural regions of various state municipalities
- Responsibility for the provision of education in the fields of music and recording to help long-term unemployed people become motivated to learn.
- Responsibility for organizing in-service training at a ministry of foreign affairs
- Responsibility for developing training systems for 750 employees at various levels of a manufacturing organization using both internal and external trainers.
- Responsibility for managing the education of minority groups including refugees and gypsies, for managing short training courses, and motivating people to learn.

As might be expected, participants shared a wide variation of views on their own understanding of lifelong learning and once again, these can be broadly categorized into the three conceptualizations expressed in the previous section. For example, with regard to lifelong learning as competitive advantage, one participant expressed the following view:

> We have 750 employees at various levels and my job is to find the best training systems for our company by organizing inside and outside training. My expectations of training are to find out new and modern solutions of how to reorganize my work and make it more effective.

And with regards to lifelong learning as personal, organizational, and societal development, others reported that:

> Our vocational training institutions put the focus on self management and self development rather than on being dependant on someone else. And I think that part of lifelong learning is to be responsible for your development for yourself—this is very important.

> In my opinion, lifelong learning is a capacity and readiness to acquire new knowledge and/or skills by either formal or informal learning. I think that lifelong learning and personal development are essential both in the person's working life and personal development. The need to acquire new (academic or vocational) skills is important for your career whereas learning as a hobby makes your life (and yourself as a person!) much more interesting.

With regard to lifelong learning for social justice, one participant had the following to say:

> We work with people working and living in rural communities and it is very difficult for them to get further education, in a sense, or requalification courses. So that is why we are one of those NGO sector organizations who are trying to supplement state institutions. Lifelong learning means literally, for me, that you are learning your whole life, be it languages, or accountancy, or whatever. So each time you need a new skill, you learn through the life and you learn theory and you learn practical things,—and people need to be helped with that.

During interviews with participants, a wide variety of challenges and problems associated with implementing lifelong learning initiatives were expressed. These were not only associated with the complexities and ambiguities expressed so far in terms of a lack of common understanding of lifelong learning, but were also to do with

> national educational policies being weak (to put it mildly) and surrounded by shady political bargaining. While the lifelong learning agenda has been prioritized, a lot has remained largely just on paper, with the possible

exception of free ICT training (computer skills) and enhanced programmes for unemployed people.

Recapitulating, we have so far reported on a comparative review undertaken to help clarify the situation regarding national policies on implementing lifelong learning initiatives. The review revealed a plurality of approaches to lifelong learning across Europe and a complex social milieu in which managers of lifelong learning have to operate. This leads to difficulties when attempting to implement the concepts and, furthermore, makes the design and development of training course such as the one required by this particular project to be highly onerous. Problems were exacerbated when ambiguities were found to be reflected in the differing conceptualizations of lifelong learning held by team members, and also course participants. We will now attempt to make sense of these complexities and ambiguities.

SENSEMAKING

Acknowledging the ambiguity of the concept of lifelong learning is important because it draws attention to the practical problems faced by managers of lifelong learning initiatives. Recognizing ambiguity is certainly not new in the field of policy studies, organizations, or the world of management. In these domains, ingredients of the process of organizing are less about clarity of goals and the rationality of choices, and more about the uncertainties of change, the presence of competing, and sometimes conflicting issues, the necessity for generating new knowledge in the face of unknown futures, and difficulties associated with making future predictions (Brunsson & Olsen, 1993; March & Olsen, 1989; Powell & Di Maggio, 1991; Weick, 1995). In many cases, the drive for organizational agency is often more of a generic claim to act, rather than a definitive move toward well structured goals.

According to March (1994) (cited by Weick, 1995): "ambiguity refers to a lack of clarity or consistency in reality, causality, or intentionality. Ambiguous situations cannot be coded precisely into exhaustive or mutually or exclusive categories" (p. 178). They are said to represent an "ongoing stream that supports several different interpretations at the same time" (Weick, 1995, p. 92). Ambiguity is virtually synonymous with organizations where scenarios with multiple interpretations of the form that present significant difficulties when trying to find ways of handling them are commonplace. In the field of organization studies it is argued that such situations give rise to possibilities for managers to enter a process of sensemaking. In the same way, ambiguity of the concept of lifelong learning needs to be regarded as an opportunity for both managers and organizations alike to engage in key processes of sensemaking in order to successfully translate the various initiatives and policies into practice. Such processes might involve managers developing conceptual maps of both internal and external environments facing the organization, and establishing ways of creating mutual understanding through social activity within their organizations. In this respect, according to Weick (1995), organizing can be considered as lying at the top of that movement between the intersubjective and the generically subjective. "By that I mean that organizing is a mixture of vivid, unique intersubjective understandings and understandings that can be picked up and perpetuated by people who did not participate in the original intersubjective construction" (p. 72). Particularly relevant are the transitions from intersubjectivity to the generic subjectivity, and the management of these transitions which can be regarded as a balancing act between the innovation (intersubjectivity) and control and coordination (generic subjectivity).

The concept of lifelong learning with all the ambiguity it conveys can be used to trigger the development of "openings" in management thinking that lead to attempts at elaborating organizational forms for dealing with increases in intersubjectivity in the process of sensemaking. In this respect, the project described in this chapter led to the culmination of a toolbox of ideas, concepts, models and methods (refer to the Appendix) that can be usefully used by managers to feed into these intersubjective sensemaking processes, irrespective of their particular lifelong learning initiatives or agendas. It provides a variety of tools and techniques for mapping out new territories and helping managers envision a future that can be shared by others. Additionally the project served as a useful vehicle for those members whose role was to design and deliver the course to engage in a sensemaking process of their own. This helped us to arrive at a (relative) position of shared understanding with respect to what began as widely differing views about various interpretations and practices associated with the rather nebulous term—lifelong learning. Throughout the project, a major difficulty was with how we could provide managers with a conceptual map of lifelong learning when the providers themselves were experiencing alternative (and sometimes competing) views on how that map could be usefully represented. In that respect, the project itself evolved into an organizational sensemaking arrangement for dealing with the tensions associated with different conceptions of educational management as well as between different understandings of the concepts of lifelong learning.

EDUCATING MANAGERS OF LIFELONG LEARNING:
THE FINAL COURSE

Managers responsible for implementing lifelong learning initiatives at all levels of our knowledge based societies (e.g., education establishments, private sector training departments, governmental departments) clearly require a firm grounding and understanding of a range of complex issues in order to succeed in delivering those initiatives. Several previous studies have identified the need for management training that will equip these people with the necessary skills. Such skills might include ways of stimulating demand, creating culture change, generating ownership and inclusion, building effective partnerships, implementing both nonaccredited learning and credit based qualification frameworks, and so on.

The course for managers of lifelong learning developed in this particular project emerged out of the plural perspectives on lifelong learning held by project team members and was to some extent shaped by the professional concerns of those individuals. The professional backgrounds of team members were described earlier in the chapter.

The final course therefore incorporated the competing perspectives held by team members and its development was characterized by disagreement and arguments over fundamental issues. Disagreement over the meaning of lifelong learning led to an inability initially to agree on the contents of the course or its likely participants. The result is a course that contains ideas from all members, but which does not fully meet with the approval of any one individual. This failure to agree on a clear direction for the course might be regarded as a failure. However, reviewing the course at the end of the project led the team to conclude that the variety of perspectives built into the course is its strength rather than a weakness. Added value arising from this variety of perspectives also became apparent during national pilot tests carried out in each country before the final course was delivered. Paradoxically, the variety in the course helped participants with different views to find an appropriate map for dealing with the ambiguity, and to build a common understanding for reducing complexities

Referring to the course outline (see Appendix), some might argue that the course is divided into what may appear to be a set of disparate modules. We would suggest, however, that these modules are complementary and that the course as a unified whole provides a comprehensive understanding of the complex, and sometimes competing issues that face managers of lifelong learning across Europe. This section of the chapter will continue with a short description of each module followed by a discussion of the contribution to management education made by the course. The course lasted 5 days.

Module 0: E-Learning

According to Arbaugh (2005) use of the Internet to deliver management education has increased dramatically over the past 10 to 15 years (Alavi & Leidner, 2001; Eastman & Swift, 2001) and is now regarded as an accepted tool in the development of a broad range of adult learning (Selwyn, Gorard, & Furlong, 2004; Sloman & Reynolds, 2003). It is particularly valuable when students are widely dispersed geographically like the ones in this project. Prior to beginning the taught element of our course, students were given the opportunity to undertake a number of e-learning activities. A Web site was developed by the project partner representing an e-learning training agency to serve the following four functions:

1. To provide a support and networking system for the groups of students. A project team member was designated the role of facilitator. They began by posting their individual profiles and expectations prior to beginning the course.

2. To provide a medium through which students could submit their reflective reports to course tutors (the reflective report will be discussed later).

3. To provide students with an opportunity to gain practical experience of using Web-based technology, and to learn how to integrate e-learning into daily work processes.

4. To enable students to undertake on-line preparatory activities prior to attendance on the taught course. Psychometric tests, for example, were used to prepare students for their third module on "Meta-cognitive learning."

Case studies of lifelong learning from each of the nations involved were also placed on the Web site. These were designed to provide contextual understanding in preparation for module one. Prior to delivery of the five main modules a series of ice breakers, discussions, and idea exchanges took place.

Module 1: Introduction to Lifelong Learning

This module was designed to encourage students to identify and think about the economic, social and political factors that impact on lifelong learning in their own organizations and in society as a whole. The module was developed by academics who espouse the social justice in the context of economic change perspective. Students were required to read the evidence from the survey of lifelong learning across Europe, and the case studies provided. Students were also asked to research lifelong learning policy in their own country before attending the course. The learning strategy then required students to use this information to reflect on their reasons for taking part in the course and to think about what they wished to gain from it. module one was also the foundation for module two. module 1 was delivered on day 1 together with an introduction to personal implementation plans and concepts of experiential learning, the use of learning logs, and reflective analyses which form important components of module 5 discussed below.

Module 2: Managing Learning: Networking Knowledge

Module 2 scheduled for day 2 of the course began by exploring aspects of stakeholder analysis, scenario planning, and strategic change associated with traditional planning models where a future is envisioned and mechanisms put into place in order to realize that vision. The fact that such approaches depend on shared culture and belief systems and paradigms of stable equilibrium (Kuhn, 1970) were then explored as a way of challenging the adequacy of conventional wisdom (Hurst, 1986) espoused by these approaches. This was followed by a consideration of ways in which organizations change and evolve through a process of organizational learning (Easterby-Smith, 1997) where knowledge is collectively constructed through social interaction and language (Gherardi & Nicolini, 2002; Lave & Wenger, 1991). Scenario planning (Fahey & Randall, 1997; Galer & van der Heijden, 2001; Ringland, 1997) was used as a vehicle to demonstrate the concept of collective learning. Students worked in small groups to identify an issue of common concern in relation to lifelong learning. The issues were then problematized and possible causes and consequences identified as a way of developing students' understanding of how economic, social and political factors influence the distribution of opportunities for learning. A further aim was to encourage students to consider how lifelong learning policies can be developed in order to overcome inequalities through improvements in access to learning. Much of this section of the module drew on critical, sociological texts on lifelong and workplace learning (Contu, Grey, & Ortenblad, 2003; Fenwick, 2005; Hamblett, Holden, & Thursfield, 2001).

Module 3: Implementing Lifelong Learning

This module was scheduled to run over days 3 and 4 of the course. The module sought to provide managers of lifelong learning with a deeper understanding of the implementation issues surrounding lifelong learning processes. It began by exploring how managers can identify a range of learning needs for the various target groups, and provided a range of tools and methods in order to help them properly assess those needs. The module also identified ways of motivating these target groups to engage in the process of lifelong learning, drawing on module 2 (managing learning) to demonstrate how effective learning can be facilitated in informal as well as formal learning environments. The last section of the module considered cognitive approaches to individual learning through the concept of metacognition which is an awareness of the process of learning or "learning to learn" (Winn & Snyder, 1996). A variety of metacognitive skills were explored such as taking conscious control of learning, planning, and selecting learning strategies (Riding & Rayner, 1998), considering cross-cultural learning styles (Armstrong, 2006), monitoring the progress of learning, correcting errors, and changing learning behaviors when necessary (Ridley, Schultz, Glanz, & Weinstein, 1992). Concepts of cognitive styles, thinking styles and learning styles (Armstrong, 2006) were also explored.

Module 4: Evaluating Lifelong Learning

Module four was scheduled for day 5 and aimed to provide managers with the tools needed to assess the impact of training. A number of elements of evaluation were considered including quantitative and qualitative aspects of evaluation. The former relates to cost-benefit analyses of training in organizations whereas the latter relates more to the impact of training on individuals and companies; in terms of personal development and motivation for example. The module also explored the impact of national and regional lifelong learning policies in terms of their ability to address social injustice. Students were encouraged to consider whether cost-benefit techniques can deliver hard financial evidence of the impact of training in the short-term. The overarching purpose of this module was to develop students understanding of the various approaches to evaluation, and to understand which approach is best suited to specific circumstances.

Module 5: Implementation Plans

Module five runs concurrently with other modules over the full 5 days of the course. The aim of reflective practice is to promote the use of reflection in personal learning. It is based on the work of Dewey (1933, 1938) who argued that human beings learn from active reflection on experience. Dewey rejected the cognitive view of learning as a one-way process consisting of facts passed from teacher to student in a noninteractive fashion. Rather, learning was believed by Dewey to emerge from the rational thought required to question assumptions and solve problems in specific situations. His theory was adapted to the workplace by Elkjaer (2003, 2004). She argues for a theory of workplace learning based on inquiry into organizational problems. Development of this particular module met with disagreements between project partners over whether the focus should be personal learning or organizational. Team members adopting an economic instrumentalist perspective argued that reflection should focus on the needs of the organization. Others argued that managers' own learning should be the focus, and that concentrating on the organization was oriented more towards "training needs analysis" not "reflection" The outcome was an instrumentalist module that was linked to the needs of the organization. Students were therefore instructed to bring a specific work-related problem to the course associated with implementing lifelong learning initiatives in their own workplace. At the end of each day, 2 hours were scheduled for students to work together, or alone, on the development of an implementation plan which they could take back to their workplace in order to begin to resolve their specific work-related problem. Students were encouraged to develop their implementation plan by integrating ideas and materials provided on the course. At the end of the week, students presented their implementation plan to the project team and other participants. Clearly there would also have been a degree of personal reflection on ones own learning as part of this process but in this case, that was not deemed to be the primary focus.

Module 6: Post E-Learning Activity

The final element in the course was an opportunity for participants to engage in post e-learning activities in order to provide coaching, mentoring and advice on the development and finalization of their personal implementation plans, and also to provide the project team with an evaluation of the course.

CONCLUSIONS

The plural perspectives on lifelong learning held by the team members' of this project are interpreted in relation to two contextual factors. First is the process of de-differentiation described at the start of this chapter. Each of the nations represented is characterized by a discourse of change in response to competition from developing economies. In each country adult education is a means of improving workforce skills to deal with this change. Moreover, each country is shifting its focus from formal education that ends at a specific age towards lifelong learning. Each of the three perspectives on lifelong learning identified in this chapter relate to this discourse in some way. "Economic instrumentalism" accepts that the needs of the economy, and thus organizations, must be paramount. This perspective accepts the discourse of change without question. Lifelong learning as personal, organizational, and societal development accepts the argument of learning and change, but incorporates notions of liberal education and development alongside hard instrumentalism. From the social justice perspective, one strand of thought views up-skilling in the context of economic change as vital to the achievement of social justice. From the second strand of thought, the idea that adult education can be used to defend nations from the economic threat from developing countries is rejected. This is a political issue and, it is suggested, arguments for change are used to control the adult education agenda.

The second contextual factor is the range and diversity of adult education and training providers across the participating nations. This diversity was described earlier in the chapter and was also reflected in the project team whose members variously represented each of the three conceptualizations of lifelong learning. Economic instrumentalism tended to be associated with members from private organizations and training agencies. The personal development and social justice perspective tended to be associated exclusively with academics, whereas the personal, organizational and societal perspective was favoured by trainers associated with private universities and the e-learning consultancy. These differing conceptualizations meant that the development of this particular training course seemed highly onerous and often led to disagreements among project partners on many issues.

Whilst it might be expected that this diversity of backgrounds and perspectives would hinder the quality of the final course, leading to ineffective and inappropriate methods of developing these managers of lifelong learning across Europe, this turned out not to be the case. As pointed out earlier, the fact that the overall concept represents a high level of ambiguity, and includes a variety of overlapping dimensions without being open to any precise interpretation, this is not necessarily a bad thing. By incorporating many possibilities it also becomes a virtue in the sense that it enables many possibilities and provides a vehicle for sets of agreements among a variety of differing perspectives. It is likely that the course was strengthened by the debates and arguments that took place. The project culminated in a final course that provided participants with a toolbox of ideas, concepts, models and methods that can be usefully used by managers to feed into their own intersubjective sensemaking processes, irrespective of their particular lifelong learning initiatives or agendas. It also provided a variety of techniques for mapping out new territories and helping managers envision a future that can be shared by others. These views would appear to be substantiated by formal feedback from the course participants themselves because they all responded by saying that their expectations had been either partly or fully met. One respondent reported that "my goals were totally achieved … I expected that by the end of the course my implementation plan would be ready, its not, but I now have great ideas to work with." Another said, "I now see a gap in my organisation between what we have, and what has to be." The average overall final rating of the course by participants was 5.8 on a 7-point Likert scale. Negative feedback was of the form, "This is too much information for one person," and "there was a lot of information to digest in such a short period."

Additionally the project served as a useful vehicle for engaging those members whose role was to design and deliver the course in a sensemaking process of their own.

APPENDIX: COURSE CONTENTS

Module 0:	**Preparatory e-learning activity**
	• implementation of e-learning
	• tools and skills for evaluating e-learning
	• online collaboration
	• integrating e-learning into daily work processes
Module 1:	**Introduction to lifelong learning**
	• approaches to lifelong learning
	• national systems of workplace learning
	• comparisons of European and non-European nations
	• personal implementation plans, learning logs, and reflective practice and analysis
Module 2:	**Managing learning: Networking knowledge**
	• Scenario planning
	• Strategic planning, stakeholder analysis, learning strategies
	• Managing and communicating change
	• Collective learning
	• communities of learning
	• formal versus informal learning
	• knowledge management
	• Organizational learning
Module 3:	**Implementing learning**
	• Identification of target groups and assessment of needs
	• Assessment tools, methods, and techniques
	• Metacognitive learning
	• learning to learn
	• thinking styles
	• learning and teaching strategies
	• Study trip
Module 4:	**Evaluating lifelong learning**
	• Evaluation models
	• Individual, team, and organizational evaluation
	• Evaluation tools and methods
	• Training needs analysis
Module 5:	**Implementation plans**
	• Reflective learning logs
	• Knowledge transfer to the work environment
	• Presentation of personal implementation plans
Module 6:	**Post e-learning activity**
	• Coaching and advice on Implementation Plan development
	• Finalization of Implementation Plan
	• Training course evaluation

NOTE

1.   This transition usually receives a lot of emphasis in the official documents of the EU and in most influential trans-national organizations on education and training such as OCDE, UNESCO, or the World Bank (see for example World Bank, 2003)

REFERENCES

Alavi, M., & Leidner, D. E. (2001). Research commentary: Technology-mediated learning: A call for greater depth and breadth of research. *Information Systems Research, 12*, 1-10.

Alheit P. (1999). On a contradictory way to the "Learning Society": A critical approach, *Studies in Adult Education, 31*(1), 66-82.

Arbaugh, J. B. (2005). Is there an optimal design for on-line MBA courses? *Academy of Management Learning and Education, 4*(2), 135-149.

Armstrong, S. J. (2006). Cognitive styles and learning styles: Origins and implications for teaching, learning and research in cross cultural contexts. In S. H. Ong, G. Apfelthaler, K. Hansen, & N. Tapachai (Eds.), *Intercultural communication competencies in higher education and management* (pp. vi-xviii). Singapore, Southeast Asia: Marshall Cavendish Academic.

Aspin, D. N., & Chapman, J. D. (2000). Lifelong learning: concepts and conceptions. *International Journal of Lifelong Education, 19*(1), 2-19.

Brunsson N., & Olsen, J. P. (1993). *The Reforming Organization.* London: Routledge.

Coffield, F. (2002). Breaking the consensus: Lifelong learning as social control. In R. Edwards, N. Miller, N. Small, & A. Tait (Eds.), *Supporting lifelong learning, making policy work* (Vol. 3, pp. 174-200). London: Routledge Falmer.

Contu, A., Grey, C., & Ortenblad, A. (2003). Against learning. *Human Relations, 56*(8) 931-952.

Crowther, J. (2004). In and against' lifelong learning: Flexibility and the corrosion of character. *International Journal of Lifelong Learning, 23*(2), 125-136.

Delors, J. (1996). *Learning: The Treasure Within—Report to UNESCO of the International Commission on Education for the twenty-first Century.* Paris: UNESCO.

Desjardins, R., Rubenson, K., & Milana, M. (2006). *Unequal chances to participate in adult learning: international perceptions,* Paris: UNESCO.

Dewey, J. (1933). *How we think: A restatement of the relation of reflective thinking in the educative process,* Boston: Heath.

Dewey, J. (1938). *Logic: The theory of inquiry.* New York: Henry Holt.

Easterby-Smith, M. (1997). Disciplines of organisational learning: Contributions and critiques, *Human Relations, 50*(9), 1085-1113.

Eastman, J. K., & Swift, C. O. (2001). New horizons in distance education: The on-line learner centred marketing class. *Journal of Marketing Education, 23*, 25-34.

Edwards, R. (1997). *Changing places? Flexibility, lifelong learning and a learning society*, London: Routledge.

Elkjaer, B. (2003). Social learning theory: Learning as participation in social process. In M. Easterby-Smith & M. Lyles (Eds.), *The Blackwell Handbook of Organizational Learning and Knowledge Management* (pp. 28-53). Oxford, England: Blackwell.

Elkjaer, B. (2004). Organizational learning: The "Third Way." *Management Learning, 35*(4), 419-434.

Esping-Andersen, G. (1990). *The three worlds of welfare capitalism.* Cambridge, England: Polity Press

European Commission. (1993). *Social protection in Europe.* Luxemburg.

European Commission. (1995). *Social protection in Europe.* Luxemburg.

European Commission. (1998). *Social protection in Europe.* Luxemburg.

European Commission. (2001). *Communication from the Commission: Making a European area of lifelong learning a reality.* Retrieved January 15, 2008, from http://ec.europa.eu/education/policies/lll/life/communication/com_en.pdf

European Commission. (2003a). *Education & Training 2010, The Success of the Lisbon Strategy Hinges On Urgent Reforms: Joint interim report of the Council and the Commission on the implementation of the detailed work programme on the follow-up of the objectives of education and training systems in Europe.* Retrieved January 15, 2008, from http://ec.europa.eu/education/policies/2010/doc/jir_council_final.pdf

European Commission. (2003b). *Space: A new European frontier for expanding union.* Retrieved January 15, 2008, from http://ec.europa.eu/comm/space/whitepaper/pdf/spwhpap_en.pdf

European Council. (2006). *Brussels 23 and 24 March 2006, Presidency conclusions 7775/06.* Retrieved January 15, 2008, from http://ec.europa.eu/information_society/eeurope/i2010/docs/interinstitutional/spring_council_conclusions_mar_06.pdf

Fahey, L., & Randall, R. (1997). *Future mapping: The art of gaining competitive advantage through scenario planning.* Chichester, England: Wiley.

Fenwick, T. (2005). Conceptions of critical HRD: Dilemmas for theory and practice. *Human Resource Development International, 8*(2), 225-238.

Ferrera, M. (1998). *Le trappole del welfare.* Bologna: Il Mulino.

Field, J. (2002). Governing the ungovernable: Why lifelong learning policies promise so much yet deliver so little. In R. Edwards, N. Miller, N. Small, & A. Tait (Eds.), *Supporting lifelong learning, making policy work* (Vol. 3, pp. 201-216). London: Routledge Falmer.

Flora, P., & Heidenheimer, A. J. (Eds.). (1981). *The development of welfare states in Europe and America.* New Brunswick, NJ: Transaction Books.

Flora, P. (1986). *Growth to limits: The Western European Welfare States since World War II.* Berlin, Germany: De Gruyter.

Galer, G. S., & van der Heijden, K. (2001). Scenarios and their contribution to organizational learning: From practice to theory. In M. Dierkes, A. Nerthoinantal, J. Child, & I. Nonaka (Eds.), *Handbook of Organizational Learning and Knowledge* (pp. 849-864). Oxford, England: Oxford University Press.

Gherardi, S., & Nicolini, D. (2002). Learning in a constellation of interconnected practices: Canon or dissonance. *Journal of Management Studies, 39*(4), 419-436.

Gouthro, P. A. (2002). Education for sale: At what cost? Lifelong learning and the marketplace. *International Journal of Lifelong Education, 21*(4), 334-346.

Griffin, C. M. (1999a). Lifelong learning and social democracy. *International Journal of Lifelong Education, 18*(5), 329-342.

Griffin, C. M. (1999b). Lifelong learning and welfare reform. *International Journal of Lifelong Education, 18*(6), 431-452.

Hamblett, J., Holden, R., & Thursfield, D. (2001). The tools of freedom and the sources of indignity. In J. McGoldrick, J. Stewart, & S. Watson (Eds.), *Understanding human resource development: A research based approach* (pp. 65-92). London, Routledge.

Hurst, D. K. (1986, Autumn). Why strategic management is bankrupt, *Organizational Dynamics*, 4-27.

Kuhn, T. S. (1970). *The structure of scientific revolutions.* Chicago: University of Chicago Press.

Kuhn, T. S., & Sultana, R. (2006). *Homo Sapiens Europeus?—Creating European learning citizens.* Frankfurt, Germany: Peter Lang.

Kuhn, M. (2007). *New society for a new millennium. The learning society in Europe and beyond.* Frankfurt, Germany: Peter Lang.

Landri, P., & Ponzini, G. (2005). Adults learners' education and training in six European countries (Bulgaria, Estonia, Germany, Italy, the Netherlands, and United Kingdom): *Towards a comparative analysis.* IRPPS-CNR, Report ILME Project.

Lave, J., & Wenger, E. (1991). *Situated learning: Legitimate peripheral participation.* London: Cambridge University Press.

Lincoln, Y. S., & E. G. Guba. (1985). *Naturalistic inquiry.* London: SAGE.

Lisbon Agenda. (2007). Retrieved January 15, 2008, from http://www.euractiv.com/en/future-eu/lisbon-agenda/article-117510

March, J., & Olsen, J. P. (1989). *Rediscovering institutions.* New York: The Free Press.

Organization for Economic Co-operation and Development. (1996). *Lifelong learning for all.* Paris: Author.

Organization for Economic Co-operation and Development. (2004). *Thematic Review on Adult Learning—United States.* January 15, 2008, from http://www.oecd.org/dataoecd/46/49/34467856.pdf

Organization for Economic Co-operation and Development. (2005). *Thematic Review on Adult Learning—United States.* Retrieved November 7, 2007, from http://www.oecd.org/dataoecd/60/23/35406014.pdf

Organization for Economic Co-operation and Development. (2006). *Thematic reviews on adult learning—Europe.* Retrieved January 15, 2008. from http://www.oecd.org/findDocument/0,3354,en_2649_37455_1_119663_1_13_37455,00.html

Oduaran, A. (2000) Globalization and lifelong education: Reflection on some challenges for Africa. *International Journal of Lifelong Education, 19*(3), 266-280.

Powell, W. W., & DiMaggio, P. J. (1991). *The New Institutionalism in Organizational Analysis*. Chicago: University of Chicago Press.

Ragatt, P., Edwards, R., & Small, N. (1996). *The learning society: Challenges and trends*. London: Routledge.

Rhodes, R. A. W. (1996). The new governance: Governing without government. *Political Studies, 44*(4), 265-267.

Riding, R., & Rayner, S. (1998). *Cognitive styles and learning strategies*. London: David Fulton.

Ridley, D. S., Schutz, P. A., Glanz, R. S., & Weinstein, C. E. (1992). Self-regulated learning: the interactive influence of meta-cognitive awareness and goal-setting. *Journal of Experimental Education, 60*(4), 293-306.

Ringland, G. (1997). *Scenario planning: Mapping for the future*. Chichester, England: Wiley.

Selwyn, N., Gorard, S., & Furlong, J. (2004). Adults Use of ICTs for learning: reducing or increasing educational inequalities? *Journal of Vocational Education and Training, 56*(2), 269-290.

Sloman, M., & Reynolds, J. (2003). Developing the e-learning community. *Human Resource Development International, 6*(2), 259-272.

Sussmuth, R. (2003). Meeting the challenges of lifelong learning. In C. Medel-Añonuevo (Ed.), *Lifelong learning: Discourses in Europe, Institute for Education* (pp. 17-26). Hambourg, Germany: UNESCO. Retrieved January 15, 2008, from http://unesdoc.unesco.org/images/0013/001364/136413e.pdf

Tight, M. (1998). Lifelong learning: Opportunity or compulsion? *British Journal of Educational Studies, 46*(3), 251-263.

Tuijnman, A. (2002). Themes and questions for a research agenda on lifelong learning. In R. Edwards, N. Miller, N. Small, & A. Tait (Eds.), *Supporting lifelong learning* (Vol. 3, pp. 6-29). London: Routledge.

UNESCO. (2003). *Lifelong learning discourses in Europe: Preface*. Hamburg: UIE.

Weick, K. E. (1995). *Sense making in organizations*. Thousand Oaks, CA: SAGE.

Winn, W., & Snyder D. (1996). Cognitive perspectives in psychology. In D. H. Jonassen (Ed.), *Handbook of research for educational communications and technology* (pp. 112-142). New York: Simon & Schuster Macmillan.

World Bank. (2003). *Lifelong learning in global knowledge economy: Challenges for developing countries*. Washington DC: Author. Retrieved January 15, 2008, from http://siteresources.worldbank.org/EDUCATION/Resources/278200-1099079877269/547664-1099079984605/lifelonglearning_GKE.pdf

CHAPTER 6

PREPARING MANAGEMENT STUDENTS FOR A LIFETIME OF LEARNING THROUGH INNOVATIVE ASSESSMENT

Maria Avdjieva

A capacity for a lifetime of management learning has become a critical attribute of business graduates. This paper presents an innovative assessment designed to develop students' capacity for lifelong learning. It uses participatory action research and a case study approach to look at the curriculum re-design and delivery of a first year undergraduate business course. I document students' enhanced self-awareness about careers and learning, increased ability to deal with the challenges of the higher education environment, as well as capacity for creative learning strategies. The design principles and steps for embedding assessments that create a life-changing management education experience establish a platform for self-directed lifelong learning.

University and Corporate Innovations in Lifelong Learning, pp. 133–159

INTRODUCTION

Do not try to satisfy your vanity by teaching a great many things. Awaken people's curiosity. It is enough to open minds; do not overload them. Put there a spark. If there is some good inflammable stuff, it will catch fire.

(Anatole France, in Gookin, 2003, p. 44)

We have entered "the knowledge era": our environment is characterized by increased complexity, uncertainty and global competition. Combined with the unprecedented global interconnectedness of societies and economies, we are challenged to identify new ways of thinking about learning and adapting to new environments (Candy, 2000; Drucker, 1993). Current and future employees are moving from guaranteed lifelong employment to self-managed lifelong employability (Samson & Daft, 2003). As Drucker (1993) emphasized more than 10 years ago, lifelong employability implies that "people have to learn how to learn ... subjects matter less than the student's capacity for continuous learning (p. 201). The challenge is not just to students—Salmi (2002) states that tertiary education sector must play a vital role in supporting the construction of knowledge societies:

> Tertiary education is indeed central to the creation of the intellectual capacity on which knowledge production and utilization depend and to the promotion of the lifelong-learning practices necessary for updating people's knowledge and skills. (p. 1)

The capacity for lifelong learning has emerged as a critical attribute of today's graduates who may face a series of careers over their lifetime (Pelsma & Arnett, 2002). As no curricula can ever teach students everything they will ever need to know in a particular discipline, the pressure for universities to enable students to keep on learning for the rest of their life is building up. This requires education to develop graduates' ability to adapt, both in anticipation of, and in response to, key environmental factors such as technological innovations. Although the majority of commencing students appear to be aware of the half-life of disciplinary knowledge and skills, research and practice show that many of them enter the university with little, if any, background in the principles and practice of "Learning How to Learn" (Glenn, 2000, p. 4A). This limits students' ability to take up the challenge of becoming lifelong learners. Furthermore, in the case of management education, Schein (1988) has suggested that graduates' inability to understand the nature of learning and development creates serious problems in the workplace.

This chapter presents an assessment pathway that engages business students with lifelong learning to prepare them to successfully enter and address the contemporary challenges they will face. First, the chapter provides an overview of management education from a lifelong learning perspective. Second, it establishes the need for embedding structures, including assessment pathways, into the curriculum to assist graduates to engage in lifelong learning. Third, the chapter introduces the development and refinement of an innovative assessment pathway that engages students with their career aspirations, goal setting, and strategizing for learning in an uncertain future. The development and evaluation of the pathway is illustrated through a case study featuring the assessment aspects of a core introductory business course in a new degree. This case study demonstrates how this pathway encourages students to make sense of a range of abstract learning concepts that underpin the development of their capacity for lifelong learning. The effectiveness of assessing for lifelong learning is discussed in terms of its immediate and longer-term impact on students' scholarly and personal growth. Finally, the chapter presents a set of guiding design principles and steps for embedding lifelong learning into the curriculum and makes some concluding remarks about the transferability of my approach to other courses.

MANAGEMENT EDUCATION AND LIFELONG LEARNING

Over the past 20 years management education has been challenged by the globalization of business and technology, as well as diversity in the workplace, and just-in-time learning (Boyatzis, Cowen, & Kolb, 1995). Contemporary managers need to be able to continuously develop their skills to respond quickly to the demands of fast-changing markets, as well as to seize emerging opportunities presented by new technologies. "Knowledge workers" have to learn to acquire knowledge, skills and attitudes in order to remain employable (Marsick & Watkins, 1999). Although the notion of graduates as self-directed learners has been widely promoted, we question whether general academic practice matches the rhetoric (Rothwell & Ghelipter, 2003). Over the past decade Boyatzis and others (see Boyatzis, 2000, 2004; Boyatzis & Kram, 1999; Boyatzis & McLeod, 2001) have been arguing that business schools traditionally focus on knowledge content and process even though there is growing evidence of the demand for lifelong employability skills and attitudes. In a similar vein Hawkins and Winter (1995, cited in Rothwell & Ghelipter, 2003, p. 243) suggest that "University teaching needs to move from a model of teaching knowledge to one of enabling learning" as people's careers do not plateau, their knowledge does.

Enabling learning is seen as a means of overcoming the challenges of continuing change and growth in bodies of knowledge (Cornford, 2002). The increasing importance of "learning how to learn" individually and collectively was also emphasized by Garratt (1999). To capture and reflect upon the multiple aspects and roles of this individual and organizational learning competency, he drew upon quotations from The 1998 Learning Declaration:

- "Learning is the most powerful, engaging, rewarding, and enjoyable aspect of our personal and collective experience. The ability to **learn about learning** [emphasis added] and become masters of the learning process is the critical issue for the next century."
- "The **capacity to learn** [emphasis added] is an asset which never becomes obsolete."
- "**Individual and collective learning** [emphasis added] reinforces the informed, conscious, and discriminating choices that underpin democracy" (Honey & Kandola, 1999 in Garratt, 1999, p. 202).

The above quotations strongly suggest that to become lifelong learners, people first need to gain a good understanding of learning per se and then develop their capacity to learn. Such a capacity appears to be a prerequisite for both individual and organizational liberation and growth. The latter view is strongly echoed by Antonacopoulou (2002). In critically reflecting on management education in the twenty-first century, she revisits the notion of *paideia*[1] to argue the "centrality of education in supporting individual development and social progress" (p. 187). She contends that it is the notion of education as a "pedagogy for freedom" (p. 186) and lifelong learning that is at the heart of management education programs, designed as vehicles for advancing learning organizations within learning societies. In practice this means that such programs need to explicitly facilitate the development of students' understanding of learning per se first and then build their capacity to learn.

The traditional priorities of management education in the United States, though, seemed primarily to lie in designing offerings that develop hands-on competencies to meet the immediate demands of the businesses: "U.S. businesses would like to recruit managers who are more broadly educated in business, are good communicators and team workers, understand the importance of process, and minimize competition with fellow workers" (Elliott, Goodwin, & Goodwin, 1994, p. 56). It is only towards the end of the twentieth century that management education ""became of age" when educators recognized that "the curriculum ought to address the development not only of knowledge and skills, but also of abilities and values" (Boyatzis, 2000, p. 14). At postgraduate level, attention is increasingly focused on leveraging self-directed learning processes that yield sustained behavioral change (Boyatzis, 2004). This shift suggests that embedding self-directed learning into the curriculum is seen as a powerful methodology for enabling management students to go beyond merely acquiring and applying predetermined knowledge.

Recent studies in Australia also highlight the necessity and means of continuing development after business students graduate. Four categories of postgraduation learning were discerned where self-directed learning is a category in its own right (Candy, 2000 p. 109):

1. Workplace-based learning
2. Continuing professional education
3. Further formal study
4. Self-directed learning.

This taxonomy reflects the "recognition that lifelong learning includes all aspects of education and training—formal, nonformal, and informal—at all ages and stages of life, irrespective of where it occurs or who organizes it" (Candy, 2000, p. 109). Identifying self-directed learning as a category in its own right though, may raise two important issues. First, this taxonomy appears to assume that a capacity for self-directed learning is not necessarily related to making informed and strategic decisions about the first three options for postgraduation learning. Second, it tends to suggest that graduates have already developed their capacity for self-directed learning and can confidently tap into the "huge—indeed virtually unlimited—sea of opportunities whereby people as adults and as citizens seek 'to be,' 'to become' and 'to belong'" (p. 109). Current university practices, however, do not appear to effectively develop students' capacity for lifelong learning. They tend to reflect a rather piecemeal approach to promoting lifelong learning and most importantly, lifelong learning does not appear to be genuinely valued and modeled by staff. As a result universities are producing graduates who are "not sufficiently attuned to the need for lifelong learning" (p. 106).

To address these issues, universities and other institutions of higher education need to recognize the importance of a capacity for self-directed learning within the total domain of lifelong learning. Similarly to their American counterparts, Australian universities need to reconsider their place regarding the first of the following two aspects of lifelong learning:

1. The steps they might take to "produce lifelong learners" (Candy, 2000, p. 101), that is assist students and graduates to develop the

    skills and attributes of lifelong learners, including capacity for self-directed learning;

2. The steps they can take—both administratively and pedagogically —"to support and encourage lifelong learning itself" (Candy, 2000, p. 101), for example, provide graduates with opportunities to further their education.

The above position leads me to conclude that both post- and undergraduate degrees do not appear to be designed to prepare students for a lifetime of learning. Drawing upon Antonacopoulou's (2002) insightful interpretation of education as "nurturing from young age, guiding one's development and providing opportunities for learning" (p. 187), I argue that the principles of education as a "pedagogy for freedom" should be applied from the very beginning of higher education degrees. Even though universities that begin to recognize that their students may face a series of careers over their lifetime are already mounting programs that teach students "how to learn" (Frank, 1996). Catts (2004) emphasizes that developing students' lifelong learning capacity is still a very challenging task for university educators. He points out that "often higher education is failing to provide the tools to sustain lifelong learning" (p. 1). To address this failure, he suggests that as "we cannot know the specific skills that will be required of future work" (p. 14), educators should see the way forward in developing students' capacity for responding to emerging needs, rather than just meeting content-based targets. As I detail below, this challenge to develop students' capacity for lifelong learning has lead me to an innovative pilot project in undergraduate business education.

THE CASE FOR
EMBEDDING LIFELONG LEARNING INTO THE CURRICULUM

I present my case for embedding lifelong learning into the curriculum by examining the issues that I faced as a coordinator of a core introductory business course in an innovative degree: Bachelor of Business and Information Management (BBIM). This highly structured double-major degree was introduced by the University of Auckland Business School (UABS) in 2001 in response to growing demand for graduates able to effectively bridge the worlds of business and information technology. Integrated design and delivery of the highly dynamic discipline of information management with the traditional business functions of accounting, marketing, or human resource management was crucial to the success of the degree. The introductory business course, however, appeared to be solely responsible for developing students' capacity for working across disciplines by fostering their higher order thinking skills, including integrative problem solving, and their ability to manage their learning needs in a rapidly changing and highly challenging environment.

One year after the double major was implemented, teaching staff raised concerns about the effectiveness of the formative assessment (Pellegrino, Chudowsky, & Glaser, 2001) used to support student learning through feedback to in-class activities on learning strategies that were not graded. Efforts to develop students' abilities to draw upon concepts of thinking and learning to help them engage with what Ramsden (1992) refers to as the deep learning aspects of their written assignments were not successful. On surveying sample assignments and interviewing students and staff, students' preconceptions of learning tended to reflect a cursory, or what Ramsden refers to as a surface approach to learning where students demonstrate a quantitative accumulation of facts rather than a change in the way they understand the world around them. The majority of students were not able to engage with their assessments in a timely and meaningful way as they expected their teachers to impart knowledge rather than facilitate their ability to construct knowledge as they learn.

These preconceptions were barriers to students appreciating the need for putting their approach to learning into perspective and committing to developing their capacity for self-directed lifelong learning. The initial constructive alignment approach (Biggs & Moore, 1993) of setting challenging assignments based on teachers assumptions about student learning characteristics, did not develop deep learning, which is essential to motivating and enabling students to appreciate and internalize the need for lifelong learning. Students had difficulties relating new concepts to previous knowledge in the context of their current learning experiences and future needs. To enable students with an ingrained surface approach to move into deep learning, the full potential of innovative course design and delivery had to be unleashed.

Instead of practicing single-loop learning by focusing on an error-detection-and-correction process within the existing curriculum (Argyris & Schön, 1978), I considered redeveloping it to engage me and my students in a double-loop learning cycle. Thus we could detect and address issues in ways that involved the modification of our underlying assumptions (Schein, 1999) about learning. We could share and assess our beliefs about why we value our approaches to learning and the intended outcomes, as well as why we assumed our previous learning strategies would still work. Moreover, we could create, evaluate, and generalize new strategies for learning from a lifelong learning perspective. For example, to leverage the interrelatedness of deep learning, self-directed learning and lifelong learning, I considered introducing assessment strategies that grew out of students' prior learning experiences. To further enhance the impact of authenticity, I also recognized the need to draw upon the management body of knowledge to engage students with the development and implementation of innovative learning strategies specific to their current and future learning needs. To achieve these challenging objectives though, I needed to take an interdisciplinary approach to curriculum innovation.

Innovating for a Lifetime of Management Learning

Future managers need to start developing their capacity for lifelong learning while learning to become managers at the undergraduate level of their management education. In this way, they have the unique opportunity to leverage their newly acquired management knowledge by applying a range of management theories to their own professional and personal development as lifelong learners. Yet, the assumption that learners automatically know how best to learn is unwarranted (Cornford, 2002). This assumption, then, must be addressed in teaching: teachers must assume responsibility for creating effective teaching strategies to help students "learn how to learn" because there are limits to the extent and types of self-knowledge that can be acquired through direct instruction. For example, according to Bar-Lavie (1987), Novak's and Gowin's "learning how to learn" strategies for enhancing and evaluating meaningful learning are very useful in this respect as they have a significant impact on moving students towards making new connections and new meanings. To become lifelong learners, though, students also need to "learn how to learn about themselves" (Schein, 1988, p. 5)—an important step in the process of developing the ability for self-insight, proactivity, and responsibility taking. While knowledge about sources of motivation and to some extent awareness of personal characteristics may be learned, many aspects of self-knowledge are in fact impossible to teach directly as they can only originate through self experiences and a willingness to be relatively brutal in self-judgment. For example, self-knowledge of desired approaches to learning involves personal judgments and can be acquired by applying management analytical frameworks to prior and current learning experiences.

Making learners aware of themselves as thinkers and how they process and create knowledge involves the development of both cognitive and metacognitive learning strategies as they are essential for effective lifelong learning to develop over the entire lifespan. For this to occur, the closely related components of metacognition: knowing about cognition, particularly one's own cognitive strategies, and monitoring, regulating, controlling and applying this knowledge to the planning and implementation of appropriate activities related to learning must be facilitated (Devlin, 2002). Cognitive learning strategies, according to Cornford (2002), are goal-directed, intentionally invoked, effortful and are not universally applicable, but situation specific. Metacognitive strategies, though, provide more universal application and develop students' ability to plan for lifelong learning in a dynamic and complex environment. Cornford, however, cautions that mastery of cognitive and metacognitive skills takes time to be fully achieved. Metacognitive skills in particular are only likely to reach fuller development through work experience. These findings have important implications for university educators as they challenge them to use their creativity to accelerate and sustain the process of developing students' cognitive and metacognitive skills.

To add appropriate depth, richness and authenticity to the process of developing students' capacity for lifelong learning, in 2003 the whole curriculum was critically reviewed and redesigned. The main focus was on developing an assessment pathway that enabled and rewarded self-directed learners who demonstrated deep, strategic approaches to learning and higher order thinking skills. As this process coincided with the development of a graduate profile for the degree, I was able to ensure that "students' capacity for self-directed learning throughout life" and "an ability to adapt to uncertainty, complexity, and ambiguity" (UABS, 2004, p. 17) were incorporated in the values, attitudes, and personal qualities section. In turn, the development of the new course learning objectives and assessments was informed by the newly created graduate profile. For example, to facilitate the paradigm shift towards "self-directed learning throughout life," a new motto—*"Learning to learn for the uncertain future"*—was introduced for the course. The course learning outcomes were also revised to demonstrate how they establish a sound platform for building towards fulfilling the BBIM graduate profile.

1. Learn independently and collaboratively, practice higher levels of thinking, and communicate strategically for learning.

2. Research and examine business and its interdependent relationship with the environment using appropriate theoretical frameworks; and

3. Correlate relationships between marketing, operations, and human resource management functions in the context of the broader business strategy and objectives. Examine the implications of these

relationships for strategic choices about structure, technology, and culture in a rapidly changing business environment.

To assist students in achieving the first learning outcome, assessments were focused on fostering a learning culture. Enabling students to take deep and strategic approaches to learning was essential for changing the way they view themselves and the world, including business, and thus facilitating the achievement of the other two learning outcomes.

My new course design is based on the premise that context is what is learned (Avdjieva, 2005). Hence, fostering a learner-centered learning culture (Weimer, 2003) is essential to engage students with lifelong learning by encouraging them to talk candidly about their aspirations and the learning capabilities that they would need to achieve those aspirations. My strategies for fostering such a culture draw upon organizational learning theories (Senge, 2000) and integrate them with an ecological education model that advances a holistic approach to curriculum design (Frielick, 2004). Practicing the learning organization disciplines (Senge, 2000), for example, is a vital strategy as it fosters what Candy (2000) found to be at the heart of facilitating the acquisition of the qualities and attributes of lifelong learners—"a climate of intellectual inquiry" (p. 115). The holistic approach is instrumental to creatively enacting the ecological configuration of the eight principles and practices for comprehensive curriculum design—teachers, students, intended outcomes, course design, content and workload, assessment, classroom, and evaluation (Frielick, 2004). This approach provides for iteratively conceptualizing, designing, planning, delivering, and learning from feedback by practicing both reflection-in-action and reflection-on-action (Schön, 1987). This comprehensive model also allows for addressing all the five facets of the undergraduate experience that Candy identified as "essential steps for producing lifelong learners" (p. 101). These five facets are: (1) the content of the curriculum, (2) the structure of the curriculum, (3) teaching methods, (4) assessment approaches, and (5) the place of student support services" (p. 101). As a whole, this integrated learning model is a powerful engine for empowering students to take more and more responsibility for their own learning (Weimer, 2003).

Embedding Authentic Assessment to Lifelong Learning Into the Curriculum

To effectively support the challenging process of developing students' capacity for lifelong learning, I took a strategic approach to engaging students in meaningful and authentic assessment tasks (Kolb, 1984). The carefully crafted assessment pathway shown in Table 6.1, aims to encourage, support, and assess students' capability to self-manage their learning needs and processes through practicing transformational learning. This pathway emphasizes connected and lifelong learning (Hanna, 2003). Connectedness of assessments underpins my spiral view of the learning process and is essential to developing students' systems thinking, as well as keeping them on track. When learning takes the shape of a spiraling process, it deepens understanding and expands a learner's perspective. By building upon previous and concurrent assessments, students are able to make meaningful connections to see how their achievements for each piece of work are interrelated and contribute to their final mark or grade.

The above assessment pathway is created by integrating pedagogical, career, and organizational learning theories and requires students to apply certain aspects of these theories to their personal and professional development. For example, this coherent mix of nongraded formative and graded summative assessments including interactive classroom activities, online assessments and discussions, and written assignments is informed by the "Nine Principles of Good Practice for Assessing Student Learning" (Astin et al., 1992). These nine principles are: (1) The assessment of student learning begins with educational values. Assessment is not an end in itself but a vehicle for educational improvement; (2) Assessment is most effective when it reflects an understanding of learning as multidimensional, integrated, and revealed in performance over time; (3) Assessment works best when the programs it seeks to improve have clear, explicitly stated purposes; (4) Assessment requires attention to outcomes but also and equally to the experiences that lead to those outcomes; (5) Assessment works best when it is ongoing, not episodic. Assessment is a process whose power is cumulative; (6) Assessment fosters wider improvement when representatives from across the educational community are involved; (7) Assessment makes a difference when it begins with issues of use and illuminates questions that people really care about; (8) Assessment is most likely to lead to improvement when it is part of a larger set of conditions that promote change; (9) Through assessment, educators meet responsibilities to students and to the public. The implementation of the first, third, fifth, and seventh principles in particular, is facilitated through Arthur, Inkson, and Pringle's (1999) career competency theory complemented by practicing the Learning Organization Disciplines of Personal Mastery (PM), Shared Vision (SV), Team Learning (TL), Mental Models (MM), and Systems Thinking (ST) Senge (2000). In transitioning into a productive learning environment, students are enabled to articulate their aspirations (PM) and gradually take over the responsibility for making their own choices and developing the learning aspects of their *knowing-why, knowing-how,* and *knowing-whom* career competencies (Arthur, Inkson, & Pringle, 1999). Students focus their energies on *why* to "learn how to learn" (MM and SV), *what* (the know-how) to learn and *how* to learn learning *together* (TL). The shift from recipients of information to actors of cognition is facilitated by dedicating the first two weeks of the business course to raising students' awareness of 'learning about thinking and learning' and 'learning about strategic communication' in the context of their current studies and future careers (ST).

Below I detail further each of the assessments featured in Table 6.1:

> **Formative Assessments:** To engage students more fully with non-graded in-class activities, the enriched teaching techniques range from teacher-led discussion with questioning, listening, and responding, to group activities involving brainstorming ideas, consolidating them, and then reporting to class. In this way, *all* learners—*both* students and teachers—are encouraged to provide formative nongraded feedback. These techniques are essential for re-defining students' approaches to learning.
>
> **Learning Contract**: The process of steering by values and culture towards learner-centered learning is initiated through brainstorming and negotiating a Learning Contract. This activity is designed to enable students to embrace lifelong learning by thinking about their underlying desires and intentions, or as Zohar (2004) puts it, connecting with their spiritual intelligence to build their spiritual capital. Once students have understood these powerful forces, they feel able to have more say in their choices, including learning strategies for developing their career competencies for twenty-first century. Aspirations and expectations about the course, key aspects of learning, and the role of learners are shared and shaped by *all* learners through a judicious balance between structure and freedom (Weimer, 2003).

To facilitate students' induction to their new environment, as well as to provide better opportunities for clarifying one's aspirations and expectations about the course and its relevance to their future careers, students conduct peer interviews and report on behalf of their interviewees. This process raises students' awareness of their learning needs, their responsibilities to themselves and to others, and establishes a baseline for creating a common identity, or shared vision. To encourage students to use their Learning Contract as a living document that frames their evolving views of learning, they are expected to continuously draw upon their newly acquired knowledge, including recent research articles

Table 6.1. Assessment Pathway for Developing Students' Capacity for Lifelong Learning

Assessment Pathway	Assessment Outline
Formative and summative aspects	The assessment pathway includes both formative nongraded assessment to help students motivate and learn, informally measure their learning progress and identify aspects for their further attention; and summative graded assessments to record students' achievement and also to further help them motivate and learn. Formative assessments are based on in-class activities, while summative ones take the form of two series of mini assessments, two written assignments, and a final exam as outlined below. Both formative and summative assessments are complemented by self-assessment.
Formative nongraded assessments:	The formative assessments are designed to help students make connections between business management theories with the "real" business world. Activities based on students' career aspirations and background knowledge, mini video case studies and articles from local media are for students to practice their thinking in group-based and whole-class discussions and receive an immediate formative feedback from their lecturer and peers.
Learning Contract (1)*	The Learning Contract is the main formative vehicle for developing students' thinking and process skills for lifelong learning by fostering a learner-centered learning culture. It sets the scene for creating a productive learning to learn environment of mutual trust and openness by engaging students with their expectations about key learning aspects of the course.
Mini summative assessments: InfoLit and weekly quizzes (1)*	Summative assessment is partly by a weekly series of mini assessments: InfoLit (Information Literacy) modules during the first half of the course, and weekly quizzes throughout the course. The knowledge required for these assessments also provides the building blocks for class discussions and subsequent assignments. Both these assessment series are available online 24-hours a day during the assessment period so that students can do them in their own time, place, and space.
Major summative assignments: 1. Towards Lifelong Learning, and (1) and (2)*	1. The Towards Lifelong Learning assignment helps students be proactive in learning and practicing higher level thinking skills, that is, analysis, synthesis, and evaluation. They draw upon their prior and current learning experiences to carry out analyses of their personal strengths and weaknesses for productive thinking and learning, as well as the opportunities and threats they faced in past and current learning environments respectively. Students then develop a strategy for maximizing their strengths and opportunities and present all this as a short report. Students' strategies are posted on an online discussion forum to facilitate their learning by sharing their perspective with others.

Table continues on next page.

Table 6.1. Continued

Assessment Pathway	Assessment Outline
2. Management Consulting Report (1), (2), and (3)*	2. The Management Consulting Report assignment helps students to develop their analytical skills for business management. They take the role of a management consultant and integrate a range of business models/frameworks to analyze a business case scenario in regional context. To produce their management report for their client, students use the strategic written communication skills that they have began to develop in the first assignment. They also draw together the research skills that they have learned in the InfoLit modules.
Self-assessment (1)*	With each assignment there is a detailed marking guide (rubric) that students are encouraged to use to self-assess the quality of their assignment while they work on it. This is to assist them to develop skills in self-critical reflection and appraisal. These skills are further developed in subsequent business management courses.
Final exam (1), (2), and (3)*	The final exam requires students to individually demonstrate their ability to synthesize and apply their knowledge in the context of broad business strategy, including strategic choices about structure, technology and culture. The 3 hour exam has three interrelated essay-based questions that cover the whole course but emphasize the topic areas not explicitly assessed in the coursework.

Note: * Indicates learning outcomes assessed.

and textbook theory, to help them challenge or endorse the roles and responsibilities they have originally agreed to.

> **Mini Summative Assignments:** The two weekly online multichoice assessments have been refined to encourage the development of students' capacity for lifelong learning by fostering sound study and work ethics. Information Literacy Modules branded as InfoLit (Avdjieva, Mitchell, & Callagher, 2004) and weekly quizzes enable students to master information literacy and test their understanding of the weekly readings in their own time, place, and pace.
>
> **Towards Lifelong Learning Assignment:** The introduction of this assignment as an implementation-oriented project (Lundeberg & Martensson, 2005) has been central to the newly developed assessment pathway for embracing and internalizing lifelong learning. To raise students' appreciation of what it takes to succeed in their degree and future careers, this assignment is designed to first activate students' prior knowledge and learning experiences and then provide opportunities to develop new knowledge and skills. The key learning objectives for this assignment are to develop students' ability to:

- Evaluate the role of the learning environment in developing their skills in lifelong and collaborative learning.
- Self-evaluate their desired approach to learning;
- Formulate strategies for developing lifelong learning and collaborative learning skills; and,
- Present their research findings, assessment and strategies as a coherent report with an executive summary.

To achieve these objectives, students draw upon prior experiences in teacher- and student-centered learning environments to conduct a SWOT (strengths, weaknesses, opportunities, and threats) analysis (Samson & Daft, 2003) to identify the intellectual skills and personal qualities that helped them succeed in each of these two environments. Then, they evaluate both environments in terms of providing opportunities for developing their skills in lifelong and collaborative learning by practicing the learning organization disciplines. Next, drawing upon the principles of motivation, students use their findings from the first two tasks to identify their desired approach to learning, or personal mastery, in their current context. Having recognized the impact of their strengths and weaknesses on their learning in a challenging learner-centered learning environment, students make a realistic self-assessment of their current and future learning needs. To formulate creative and practical strategies to assist them in becoming strategic lifelong learners, students set short and long-term goals for their current studies and future careers. In the process of goal setting, strategy formation, and implementation, students are encouraged to ask themselves, "What beliefs do we hold that cause us to value this intended outcome?" and "What makes us think that the strategies we selected will actually result in the outcomes we desire?" (Hinken, 2001).

This assignment acts as a powerful vehicle for helping students take responsibility for their learning, including developing their information literacy, doing their weekly readings, and testing their knowledge and understanding in advance of class discussions, and acting as management consultants to themselves and then to a hypothetical client.

> **Business Management Consulting Report:** In preparing this report students are able to capitalize on the knowledge, thinking, and process skills developed in doing their Towards Lifelong Learning assignment. To meet their learning objectives, however, they are to develop new skills, for example, revisit some of the business models that they had applied to advising themselves, and integrate them into more complex business frameworks to advise their client on the viability of a real business situation in regional context.
>
> **Self-assessment:** To encourage the development of students' self- and peer- assessment skills, the use of Criterion Referenced Evaluation Rubrics as summative feedback tools has been extended to include some formative feedback functions. The descriptors for the key criteria—content specific, generic scholarship, and generic communication—are used in class to create a shared understanding of the levels of achievement across a continuum. By engaging with the respective rubric, students can better manage their learning needs while preparing their assignments. To hone their self-assessment ability, they are encouraged to compare their self-assessment results with the marker's feedback and discuss any gaps.
>
> **Final exam:** Similarly to the Business Management Consulting Report, students take the role of a management consultant and are challenged to advise their client at strategic and operational levels by integrating theoretical frameworks across topic areas. As shown in Table 6.1, the final exam assesses all the three learning outcomes of the course.

This comprehensive learning strategy engages and assists students in achieving the challenging learning outcomes of the course. It is also coherent with the pedagogical and organizational learning principles as set out by Candy (2000) and Senge (2000) respectively. Further to the detailed presentation of the assessment strategies for developing students' capacity for lifelong learning given above, Table 6.2 demonstrates how clusters of these strategies help students acquire the six attributes and qualities of lifelong learners (Candy, 2000, p. 110) by practicing the learning organization disciplines.

ENACTING THE NEW ASSESSMENT PATHWAY

Insider action research (Coghlan, 2003) has been identified as the most appropriate method for working with living cases to formulate, test and refine new strategies for developing students' capacity for lifelong learning. Over the past eight semesters, *all* learners have been leveraging the opportunities created by the enquiry process for fostering a learner-centered culture. Through reflection-in-action and reflection-on-action (Schön, 1987), learners are able to collaboratively engage in the scholarly refinement of the Learning Contract and some aspects of the curriculum and thus take ownership of the new learning frameworks. Data collection includes students' formative and summative assessments, periodic focus groups and debriefs to reflect on the effect of the latest improvements made, and traditional end-of-semester student survey, respectively. Quotations from these sources appear in italics.

This critical reflection and interaction continues to shape the assessment pathway to lifelong learning as each new cohort of students brings in fresh ideas and unique perspectives. The learning experiences presented next, therefore, represent one interwoven story with multiple perspectives expressed over the past 4 years. To leverage the interpretive perspective of the insider action research methodology, the results of the assessment pathway to lifelong learning are presented and discussed concurrently.

Formative Nongraded Assessments: Learning Contract and Discussion Forums

The Learning Contract shown in Table 6.3 captures typical aspirations and expectations that new undergraduate students bring to the classroom. This initial document is refined throughout the semester. Column two reflects learners' consolidated personal masteries or shared vision to bind together around a common identity of *dedicated, approachable, polite, respectful, friendly, reliable; productive (not disruptive!); independent and collaborative* students whose sense of purpose is centered on obtaining *a high quality/well-recognized degree.* Having committed to

Table 6.2. Assessment Strategies for Developing Students' Capacity for Lifelong Learning by Practicing the Learning Organization Disciplines

Key Assessment Strategies (Formative and Summative) for Developing Students' Capacity for Lifelong Learning	Learning Organization Disciplines Practiced (Senge, 2000, pp. 7-8)	Attributes and Qualities of the Lifelong Learner (Candy, 2000, p. 110)
– Fostering and practicing a culture of intellectual inquiry and learning; – Online discussion forums as vehicles for generative conversations and knowledge sharing (e.g., virtual assignment and exam clinics, etc.).	**Mental Models** – Developing dialogue skills; – Enjoying generative face-to-face and virtual conversations; – Asking fundamental "Why" questions.	**An inquiring mind**
– Putting past and present learning experiences in perspective; – Conducting a contextual industry analysis and evaluation to see the "big picture."	**Systems Thinking** – Taking a holistic approach; – Understanding interdependency in order to manage change and its consequences.	**"Helicopter vision"**
– InfoLit Modules as a self-managed vehicle for lifelong learning; – Towards Lifelong Learning and Management Consulting assignments as drivers for practicing and advancing information literacy skills.	Driven by **Personal Mastery** – Developing Self Awareness; – Articulating your personal vision about lifelong learning alongside a realistic assessment of your current information literacy skills	**Information literacy**
– Sharing expectations about the course and the attributes and roles of a good teacher and student; – The Towards Lifelong Learning assignment as a vehicle for embracing change to build capacity for learning throughout life;	**Personal Mastery** – Developing self awareness; – Articulating personal vision alongside a realistic assessment of current reality ("Your future view, is the future YOU!")	**A sense of personal agency**

Table 6.2. Continued

Key Assessment Strategies (Formative and Summative) for Developing Students' Capacity for Lifelong Learning	Learning Organization Disciplines Practiced (Senge, 2000, pp. 7-8)	Attributes and Qualities of the Lifelong Learner (Candy, 2000, p. 110)
– The Towards Lifelong Learning assignment as a vehicle for developing the ability to self-assess learning needs, set goals and formulate strategies for developing the capacity for lifelong learning; – Assignment rubrics (criterion-referenced assessment tools) as feedback vehicles for refining existing learning skills and developing new ones.	Driven by **Personal Mastery** – Developing self awareness; – Articulating personal career vision alongside a realistic assessment of current learning skills ("Your future view, is the future YOU!" motto)	**A repertoire of learning skills**
– The Learning Contract as a vehicle for sharing and negotiating expectations to create a sense of purpose as a class. Collaboratively conducting a scholarly refinement of the Contract throughout the semester – Regular individual and interactive class & study group activities and debriefs as vehicles for formulating and reflecting on the effectiveness of learning strategies for developing independent & collaborative lifelong learning skills.	**Shared Vision** – Collectively created for a common purpose to encourage commitment towards achieving the vision; **Systems Thinking** – Understanding interdependency in order to manage change and its consequences. **Team Learning** – Developing awareness of attitudes and perceptions through inquiry and reflection; – Celebrating Diversity.	**Interpersonal skills and group membership**

abide by their Learning Contract, students and teachers engage in a dialogue to concert and refine their efforts towards building a productive learning environment where everyone learns, supports, and takes responsibility. By mutually encouraging each other to make suggestions to continuously strengthen the match between their behaviors and expectations, teachers and students share, in responsible ways, certain aspects of teachers' power, roles, responsibilities, and decisions on content and assessment. Students' posting on the discussion forums suggest that they welcome the opportunity to become involved in shaping their learning process: *I believe our contract will be effective so long as we revisit it and make changes to it if there's [sic] a need.* In becoming intrinsically motivated to succeed, students also show a deep appreciation of what it takes to realize their personal mastery: *I think that the ideas and responsibilities discussed in class are realistic to some extent … for example, having fun in class is great!!!! BUT that doesn't mean that everything we do in class is going to be fun [as a] good teacher should make us think about problems, make us challenge things.* Students also emphasize that to enrich their learning process **all** of them need to be encouraging each other to be open and willing to share their background knowledge and life experiences and thus help each other create new knowledge.

The refining of the Learning Contract is intertwined with the process of preparing the Towards Lifelong Learning assignment. At the beginning, some students tend to use the virtual clinic discussion forum as a place to fish for easy answers: *Please wot [sic] is Life Long Learning? Short Definition?"* Although such postings could be a threat to moving towards a deep approach to addressing learning needs, with patience and tact teachers can turn them into opportunities for embracing lifelong learning and personal responsibility, for example:

> Senge (2000) views lifelong learning as the fundamental means by which people engage with life and create their desired futures by practicing personal mastery. Lifelong learners take responsibility for what they are doing by self-managing their learning needs and processes. They learn how to identify their learning needs, be more critical of their work, as well as modify on the basis of feedback. The latter is essential to practicing the systems thinking discipline—your ability to leverage interdependencies. Thus they develop autonomy of learning—the ability to make strategic learning choices and to care about the quality of their efforts.

In this case, teacher's response initiated a healthy discussion about the essence of lifelong learning, which resulted in multiple refinements of the Learning Contract. Students saw their teacher as *a visionary leader building a learning organization*, while *what makes a good student* was seen as a commitment *to align underlying assumptions with espoused values* (Schein,

**Table 6.3.   Learning Contract
(Adapted From the Second Semester of 2005)—
Iteratively Refined Over the Course of
the Semester Through Drawing Upon Newly Acquired Knowledge**

Themes	*Negotiated Class Opinion* *(First Draft)*

Personal and professional expectations for this course	• Obtain a high quality/well-recognized degree
	• Benefit from a course related to real life/world /Gain knowledge and skills for practice in business/future career:
	   o Develop interpersonal communication and teamwork skills;
	   o Learn valuable management processes;
	   o Become open-minded and independent
	• Enjoy student–teacher interaction; have fun☺.

What makes a "good teacher"	• Enthusiastic, knowledgeable, well-organized, approachable, helpful, patient, and available • Keeps students engaged; does not let them "fly" (provides appropriate guidance)☺

What makes a "good student"	• Have a positive attitude; Take an active role! Doesn't act like a sponge!
	• Be dedicated, approachable, polite, respectful, friendly, reliable; productive (not disruptive!); independent and collaborative:
	   o Work hard; demonstrate good time management/complete work on time
	   o Help each other to learn: contribute; feel free to ask questions
	• "NO DOUBLE STANDARDS"☺

I, the undersigned, hereby state that I have read and understood the contents of our Learning Contract. I agree to the terms laid down in this contract and will work productively and to the best of my ability to ensure the success of my team and class respectively. If I fail to meet my team and/or class expectations, I will fully accept responsibility for any consequences of my behavior. I accept that the team and/or class may deal with any breaches of this contract as they see fit within reasonable measures.

1999). The introduction of the graduate profile (UABS, 2004, p. 17), SMART (specific, measurable, achievable, relevant, time-framed) goals and SWOT (Samson & Daft, 2003) analysis framework were instrumental to both refining the Learning Contract and engaging students in online discussions for evaluating the appropriateness of their desired approaches to learning for *getting where [they] want to be in the future*. Thus, students' past learning experiences helped them put their new learning into perspective.

Major Summative Assessments: Towards Lifelong Learning

Over the past six semesters, the Towards Lifelong Learning assignment enabled students to create a large pool of goals and strategies for becoming lifelong learners. When placed on a continuum, these range from short-term to forward-thinking goals that are well supported by relevant short-term ones. The former examples suggest that students have grasped the basics of goal setting and strategy formulation, but need to develop their ability to put their learning needs into perspective. The latter examples demonstrate students' ability to strategically articulate their personal mastery and creatively use it as a driver for identifying and addressing their on-going learning needs. This latter capability suggests that these students are well on their way of becoming lifelong learners. Furthermore, those aspiring to enhance the quality of their learning were very clear and open about the short-term implications of shifting from surface to deep learning on the efficiency of their learning. They were confident that in the longer-term they will be able to enjoy both high quality and efficiency of learning (Stroh, 2000).

In 2005, high achievement awards were introduced in response to students' creative suggestions to recognize the multiple aspects of excellence in becoming a lifelong learner. The awards encompass a wide range of categories such as Most Insightful Analysis of Past Experiences; Strongest Focus on MOTIVATION☺; Best Analysis of the Class as a Learning Organization; Strongest Career Focus; Best Set of Learning Strategies; and so forth. These awards boosted students' engagement with the discussion forum for sharing, discussing, and refining their strategies for developing their capacity for lifelong learning. The career focus winners, for example, demonstrated strong linkages between their short-term goals for study skills and long-term careers benefits: *ability to make self assessment of my learning needs at university means that I will be able to maintain my expertise in the workplace; learning to manage myself will help me manage others, and eventually, my own company.* Strategies for developing such skills—*communicating more with peers and teachers to build my self-assessment skills and confidence to exchange opinions with others*—show students' ability to leverage the opportunities offered by a learner-centered learning culture to improve *the learning process and make their learning environment more enjoyable.*

EFFECTIVENESS OF THE ASSESSMENT APPROACH

The potential of the formative and summative assessment pathway in fostering lifelong learning has already manifested itself in multiple ways. Its effectiveness for developing students' capacity for lifelong learning is reflected in the thinking and behavior that students demonstrate upon completing the course and the skills that are displayed. The impact of the assessment approach on students' personal growth also suggests that an embedded assessment pathway makes an effective vehicle for sustainable lifelong learning. This approach may also partially explain why graduates of the new degree had significantly better placement outcomes than comparison cohorts in traditional degree structures.

Immediate Impact on Thinking and Behavior

Students' insightful assignments and on-going feedback endorse the value of learner-centered culture and deep learning. In 2002, some students wondered *What do thinking, learning, and communication have to do with a business curriculum?* Four years on, at a debrief session, students endorsed the new assessment pathway by emphasizing that *an in-depth understanding of thinking and communicating for deep learning was most beneficial to [their] acculturation to university studies.* Even though students had experienced this assessment pathway for just one semester, the last time a student survey had a suggestion for "improvement" such as *Less focus on "deep learning,"* was in the first semester of 2004. The positive trend in student survey ratings also supports the effectiveness of the innovative curriculum and the resulting shift in students' perception of effective teaching. In 2005, students unanimously endorsed the usefulness of the authentic assessment pathway for taking a deep approach to managing their learning needs. The 100% student agreement with survey items such as: "The assessment methods required an in-depth understanding of the course content" and "The course helped develop deep understanding of the subject material," makes teachers confident that their students' deep understanding of lifelong learning skills and attitudes has positioned them for success in the twenty-first century.

Longer-Term Impact on Sustainable Personal Growth

The majority of students acknowledge the need for *perspiration* and *transformation*, but most importantly, more and more of them also see their journey towards lifelong learning as a process of *liberation*. At the Career Day 2005, the enthusiasm of the student ambassadors for the new business degree was contagious. A member of the student panel shared the consolidated insights from her cohort's first year experiences. She emphasized that *the BBIM degree teaches you how to learn on different levels.* After the very first semester of studies, students were convinced that in today's rapidly changing environment *you need to keep learning after you graduate in order to keep up with* [both] *technology and employers' expectation.*

What students learned and experienced in their first year business courses had already had a *huge positive impact on* [their] *personal life*—they have gained *an insightful viewpoint of the world* and feel like they are well on their way of becoming *a better person*. She emphasized that the learner-centered learning culture, particularly the opportunity to *find our lecturers most of the time, and communicate with them freely, know them at a personal level* was instrumental to students' personal growth within such a short period. Furthermore, *in the BBIM degree, students' opinions and needs are valued. You can grow with the degree! Individual feedback obtained from learning experience in the degree will become a good source for the further improvement of the degree and thus better meet students' learning needs for the uncertain future. If you are a person who likes challenges, this is the degree for you!* Another student captured the strong impact of the assessment pathway to lifelong learning as *Thank you for helping me plant a tree, so that I can sit in the shade in [the] future*.

GUIDING DESIGN PRINCIPLES AND STEPS FOR LIFELONG LEARNING

The following guiding design principles and steps for embedding structured opportunities to embark on a journey of management learning into the curriculum have been distilled from 4 years of intensive action research. They are centered on empowering students to take responsibility for their learning through a transformational learning experience. In embedding lifelong learning into the curriculum, the application of these principles is to be seen as a concurrent rather than a linear step by step process for creating a coherent curriculum as "assessment is most likely to lead to improvement when it is part of a larger set of conditions that promote change" (Astin et al., 1992). The principles of authenticity, relationship building and reflection filter through the seven design steps: (1) Create Curriculum for Lifelong Learning; (2) Create a Sense of Purpose and Identity: (3) Condition Students' Minds for Lifelong Learning; (4) Foster a Culture of Lifelong Learning; (5) Assess and Reward Lifelong Learning; (6) Encourage Individual and Collective Reflection; and (7) Sustain and Grow the Momentum.

Create Curriculum for Lifelong Learning

Creating a coherent curriculum with an embedded assessment pathway to lifelong learning is essential for developing students' capacity for lifetime of management learning. Such assessments not only measure students' learning, but also contribute to it. Hands-on experience clearly showed that the initial constructive alignment approach (Biggs & Moore, 1993) of setting challenging assignments based on teachers assumptions about student learning characteristics, and expecting students to live up to them, was not enough to force students with an ingrained surface approach to move into deep learning. The findings of this study concur with Weinstein and Meyer's (1994) and Candy's (2000) argument that lifelong learning skills should be developed by taking metacurricular rather than adjunct approach. "Learning how to learn" requires teaching both cognitive and metacognitive skills and needs to be placed at the heart of the undergraduate learning experience as in the case of the BBIM program. An add-on or separate subject approach does not provide opportunities for contextualization of knowledge and hence effective learning to occur. Furthermore, skills that had been effectively learned and applied in a learner-centered learning context, can be readily transferred into other educational and workplace contexts.

By the end of their first semester of studies, students have had the experience of setting SMART goals, researching topics and learning on their own and in study groups. The scaffolding or "staged withdrawal" of teachers' support is explicit and agreed at the beginning of the course as students have recognized this legitimate part of the educational experience is essential to enabling them to gradually take responsibility to manage their learning over their lifespan (Candy, 2000).

Create a Sense of Purpose and Identity

Leverage cultural diversity to advance everyone's learning. If culturally diverse student cohorts are to learn effectively, strategies need to be adopted that acknowledge their different backgrounds and learning experiences. An inclusive approach such as the development of a Learning Contract as a class, for example, helps us develop a shared understanding of what is considered to be important expectations for learning, goals and learning objectives, competencies, attitudes and behaviors. This mutual adaptation approach also allows us to acknowledge our differences and move forward by discussing multiple perspectives. It also helps *all* learners appreciate that joint sensemaking, where teachers and students work together to understand issues of relevance to learning, is extremely difficult and constrained by learners' assumptions. Nevertheless, in this way, *all* learners act as a resource to enable them to operate in a multicultural world (Dalglish, 2006).

The Learning Contract and particularly the Towards Lifelong Learning assignment also form an effective strategy for stimulating identity awareness and setting the scene for deep learning to occur by challenging the "comfort zone" of first year students. To create a meaningful sense of purpose and identity, however, students need to appreciate the importance of self-directed lifelong learning and commit themselves to developing their capacity for learning throughout their careers. This capacity has become essential in an environment where individuals are increasingly responsible for their own careers and employment (Edwards, 2003, in Billett & Pavlova, 2005).

Condition Students' Minds for Lifelong Learning

The majority of students still appear to bring to their undergraduate studies the mind-set acquired in a teacher-centered learning environment, where students "place instructional agents at the core of the instructional process" (Elen & Lowyck, 2000 p.421). Change management strategies for encouraging deep learning (Ramsden, 1992) are essential for motivating and enabling students to appreciate and internalize the need for lifelong learning. Relating new concepts to previous knowledge in the context of their current learning experiences (Entwistle, 1991) and career aspirations helps students appreciate that "learning how to learn" and self-directed learning are achievable skills in a learner-centered learning environment.

The strategies for moving towards a culture of initiative, collaboration and accountability (Kanter, 2004), where self-directed learning is both encouraged and rewarded, are firmly grounded in a constructivist approach to learning, underpinned by problem- and scenario-based learning. A range of management theories are at the heart of articulating and negotiating learning expectations, assessing students' learning readiness, and facilitating strategy formation and implementation.

Foster a Culture of Lifelong Learning

Fostering a productive learner centered learning culture where *both* students *and* teachers are open to learning is an important organizing principle for lifelong learning (Candy, 2000). As *context* is to a great extent what students *learn*, such an environment is crucial for achieving the challenging learning outcomes for the knowledge era that shape the graduate attributes of today's students. These attributes are another important aspect of a coherent teaching for learning framework as they give *all* learners a sense of purpose. In leveraging the opportunities presented by technology, flexible/e-learning serves as an enabler for preparing students to learn and operate successfully in the knowledge era. In engaging with technology in contexts that are meaningful to them, students do not just read about business management; they also take responsibility for learning in their own time, place and pace.

Assess and Reward Lifelong Learning

Assessment encourages transformational learning when it raises and illuminates issues that students really care about (Astin et al., 1992). Assessment methods that tend to focus on promoting and evaluating students' lifelong learning *attributes* and *skills* rather than the development of their *capacity* for lifelong learning are less likely to engage students with learning how to learn. Assignments such as Towards Lifelong Learning initiate the development of students' capacity for lifelong learning by encouraging transformational rather than reproductive learning. Transformational learning is authentic and involves experiential learning, which develops students' information literacy and problem-solving skills along with advancing reflective practice and critical self-awareness (Candy, 2000). It also engages students in self-directed and peer-assisted learning supported by flexible learning opportunities such as discussion forums, sharing strategies for lifelong learning and assignment clinics, as well as study groups. The high achievement awards are instrumental to boosting students' confidence and sustaining their learning process.

More and more students see the Towards Lifelong Learning assignment as a vehicle for becoming better learners as it encourages them to pay attention not just to the outcomes of their learning, but also to the strategies and experiences that have lead to those outcomes. They become excited and involved when they are given the opportunity to be their own consultants for lifelong learning. The rewarding aspects of this experience were insightfully captured by one student as: "*The true value of learning lies in self-knowledge, the first step to wisdom.*"

Encourage Individual and Collective Reflection

"Possession of effective learning-to-learn skills is an important prerequisite for effective lifelong learning to occur" (Cornford, 2002, p. 367). Through critical content and process reflection students uncover the tacit assumptions that have shaped their prior learning (Mezirow, 2000). Enabling them to take a metacognitive perspective to their own learning raises their self-awareness and interest in learning to learn (Pellegrino, Chudowsky, & Glaser, 2001). Sharing and assessing beliefs about why they value their approaches to learning and the intended outcome, as well as why they have assumed their previous strategies would work (Hinken, 2001), engages students in a double-loop learning cycle (Argyris & Schön, 1978). Linking critical reflection to action empowers students to act autonomously and enables them to challenge and change the status quo. Collaborative initiatives such as the Learning Contract provide excellent opportunities for continuous reflection and refinement by *all* learners. In the process students are also able to experience, understand and reflect on the larger system within which they act, as well as become aware of their interdependency with the larger context (Senge, 2000).

Sustain and Grow the Momentum

Changing learners' perceptions about different ways of teaching and learning (Kane, 2004) is just the first step of the important and challenging process of developing students' capacity for lifelong learning. The next step—sustaining and growing the momentum of a learner-centered learning culture—is critical to enhancing students' capacity for lifelong learning. Building upon the Towards Lifelong Learning assignment across subsequent courses is essential for promoting learning by a process of further action and reflection (Frank, 1996). Even though the importance of the principle of sustaining and growing the momentum is well recognized, reflections of year two students doing the Communication Processes course strongly suggest that there is significant room for improvement in this respect. While students' postings on the online discussion forum sound very encouraging, their critical reflections on other courses clearly demonstrate a desire for the opportunities for developing their capacity for lifelong management learning to continue:

> *I am very much looking forward to this paper. Teaching outside a normal lecturing format really intrigues me. Moving onto getting the students doing the teaching and the "lecturer" helping to guide the students through the learning process really provides an opportunity for students to take the iniative [sic] and get involved in their learning. This "buy in" is a hell of a lot more rewarding as the learning that is being done has a lot more weight compared to when it is jst [sic] regurgitated by lecturers to students year after year.*

> *The progression towards this style of teaching reminds me of the first essay we had to do last year about TCL [Teacher Centered learning] vs SCL [Student Centered Learning]. After that we were all aware of the differences but stil [sic] felt a lot of our papers were stil [sic] very much TCL to a degree.*

Bus 291 smashes that philosophy and we the students get the power of teaching in the class room, I like that idea. Its [sic] not like the teacher knows everything.

I say proceed with chaos and I'm sure the resulting LO [Learning Objectives] will reflect everything we put into it.

I enjoyed the radical approach to learning that went on today. This must be a giant leap forward towards the SCL that we learned about in the first year business course. The amount of value that we get out of this course corresponds to how much effort we put in, and one thing I felt throughout the meeting was that a lot of people felt comfortable to take on the new approach.

It is all very encouraging and here's [sic] hoping it all goes well—or rather, goes completely wrong!

Students' refreshingly thoughtful approach to what they are doing and most rewardingly perhaps, their sense of responsibility and desire to have more courses that provide them with exciting learning opportunities, seem to confirm that the progression through the core business courses is gaining more and more traction. Regarding the BBIM program as a whole, the way forward lies in advancing the climate of intellectual inquiry —a key factor for producing lifelong learners:

The most vital determinant of whether or not graduates choose to become lifelong learners is the climate of intellectual inquiry in the institution, and the single most important factor influencing this climate is whether or not the academic faculty members themselves manifest a lively curiosity, a passion for their subject and a predisposition towards being continuing lifelong learners themselves. (Candy, Crebert, & O'Leary, 1994, p. xiii, in Candy, 2000)

Given that the impact and advancement of my initiative to embed lifelong learning into the curriculum is constrained by its contextualty and continuity, mechanisms for staff succession and broadening further the application of the guiding principles is crucial for sustaining and growing the momentum.

CONCLUDING REMARKS

The embedded assessment pathway for a lifetime of management learning evolved over 4 years of my action research. It increased effectiveness of learning in the first-year undergraduate business course, and initiated transformation throughout the degree program. It also informed the field of organizational learning and innovation management in management education. The challenges of the twenty-first century require innovative assessment pathways for developing students' capacity for lifelong learning in an authentic way. Interdisciplinary theoretical frameworks that take into consideration the needs of students in the knowledge era are particularly helpful for creatively embedding such pathways into business curricula. The implementation of pedagogical principles is significantly facilitated through the application of career and organizational learning theories that engage students with their current needs and career ambitions. The Learning Contract and Towards Lifelong Learning assignment are focal points in an effective assessment pathway for developing students' ability to identify and address their evolving learning needs in the context of their changing environment. Through a process of reflection in and on action, students start developing their "learning to learn" skills while dealing with real life challenges.

Working with real life challenges and collaborating with their peers provides students with a qualitatively different learning experience, which has a number of positive effects. Inclusive approaches such as negotiating a Learning Contract as a class go beyond just engaging and inspiring students to achieve their aspirations. They also help students develop a shared understanding of what *all* learners consider as important competencies, attitudes, and behaviors. This mutual adaptation approach is perceived as valuable, useful, and fun as it allows students to acknowledge differences and move forward by discussing multiple perspectives. In this way, *all* students act as a learning resource that will enable them to learn how to operate in a multicultural world.

Developing students' overall ability to manage their learning is critical for enabling them to shape their own destinies (Candy, 2000). To help students develop this ability, key thinking and learning concepts and principles are to be explicitly embedded into course content, delivery, and assessment. By developing a deep understanding of these concepts and principles and their interrelatedness, students acquire metacognitive skills that raise their awareness of the central role of lifelong learning for realizing their career aspirations.

This strategic pathway successfully puts year one undergraduate business students on the first steps of a lifetime journey of continuous learning. By starting with learning in the context of content, future managers are empowered to begin developing their capacity for lifelong learning while learning to become managers. In this way, they have the unique opportunity to leverage their newly acquired management knowledge by applying a range of management theories to their own professional and personal development as lifelong learners. Even though the innovative BBIM degree program is still in its early days and the need for sustaining and growing the momentum poses serious challenges, the assessment pathway to lifelong learning prepares students well for the realities of today's business world. It has been very gratifying to see an increasing percentage of our graduates move on from university into challenging roles with global companies where they thrive on changes brought about by technology, market place demands and global competition (Avdjieva, 2005). Students' appreciation for having developed their capacity to take a strategic approach to their learning and career aspirations is encapsulated in a recent e-mail from one of my alumni:

> *I do have some good news to brighten your day up—KPMG have offered me a graduate role in the Audit and Risk Advisory department starting in July 2007. :-)*
> *Thank you very much for helping me achieve this position and goal. All the hard work has finally paid off!*
> *Many thank you's [sic] for your help and care."*

Regarding sustainability, a dialogue about teaching and learning needs to occur at both program and faculty/school level. Over time this dialogue could grow and shape as a core institutional process of inquiry (Maki, 2004), which among other things will support the design and delivery of coherent assessment pathways to lifelong learning. In an environment where the quality of teaching and learning is genuinely valued and practiced (Astin et al., 1992), assessment becomes a powerful engine for promoting and sustaining lifelong learning.

In closing, I should caution that the learning strategies presented in this chapter are simply a starting point for creating an experience that provides a social dynamic conducive to developing students' capacity for engaging with a lifetime of management education. The success of these strategies depends not on methodology alone but, ultimately, on the constantly-evolving, dialectical relationship between methodology and *all* learners (Kane, 2004). Hence, I encourage readers to use the guiding principles and steps presented in this chapter as vehicles for crafting their own unique pathways to a lifetime of management learning. I also note, that these principles and steps lend themselves to a wide range of subject areas, with the particulars adjusted to suit disciplinary body of knowledge, norms and aspirations.

NOTE

1.   "What the ancient Greeks viewed as *paideia* was the cultivation of each individual's natural, in-born potential in every domain of social activity, which cannot be achieved through fixed programmes" (Antonacopoulou, 2002, p. 198).

REFERENCES

Antonacopoulou, E. (2002). Corporate universities: The domestication of management education. In C. Wankel & R. DeFillippi (Eds.), *Rethinking Management Education for the 21st Century* (pp. 185-207). Greenwich, CT: Information Age.

Argyris, C., & Schön, D. A. (1978). *Organizational learning.* Reading, MA: Addison-Wesley.

Arthur, M. B., Inkson, K., & Pringle, J. (1999). *The new careers: Individual action and economic change.* Thousand Oaks, CA: SAGE.

Astin, A. W., Banta, T. W., Cross, K. P., El-Khawas, E., Ewell, P. T., Hutchings, P., et al. (1992). *AAHE assessment forum: 9 principles of good practice for assessing student learning.* Retrieved January 15, 2008, from, http://www.assessment.tcu.edu/assessment/aahe.pdf

Avdjieva, M. (2005). Learning to Foster builders of knowledge economy. *International Journal of Learning, 12*(8), 223-234.

Avdjieva, M., Mitchell, L., & Callagher, L. (2004, June 13-16). Let me learn—time, place, and pace: Information literacy in a flexible learning environment. In P. Danaher (Ed.), Whose responsibility and what is your contribution? *Proceedings of the 3rd International Lifelong Learning Conference, CQU,* Yeppoon, Australia, 32-38.

Bar-Lavie, B.-Z. (1987). *Enhancing meaningful learning in an environmental education program: A case study of a class empowered through the use of novak's and gowin's principles of learning how to learn, concept mapping, interviewing and educating.* Unpublished doctoral dissertation., Cornell University, United States—New York.

Biggs, J., & Moore, P. (1993). *The process of learning.* New York: Prentice Hall.

Billett, S., & Pavlova, M. (2005). Learning through working life: Self and individuals' agentic action. *International Journal of Lifelong Education, 24*(3), 195 -211.

Boyatzis, R. E. (2000). Management education: Coming of age. *Selections, 16*(2), 14.

Boyatzis, R. E. (2004). Self-directed learning. *Executive Excellence, 21*(2), 11.

Boyatzis, R. E., Cowen, S. S., & Kolb, D. A. (1995). A learning perspective on executive education. *Selections, 11*(3), 47.

Boyatzis, R. E., & Kram, K. E. (1999). Reconstructing management education as lifelong learning. *Selections, 16*(1), 17.

Boyatzis, R. E., & McLeod, P. L. (2001). The guest editors' corner: Our educational bottom line: Developing the whole person. *Journal of Management Education, 25*(2), 118.

Candy, P. C. (2000). Reaffirming a proud tradition: Universities and lifelong learning. *Active Learning In Higher Education, 1*(2), 101-125.

Catts, R. (2004). *Lifelong learning and higher education—reflections and prospects.* Paper presented at the 3rd International Lifelong Learning Conference "Whose Responsibility and What is Your Contribution?" CQU, Yeppoon, Australia. Retrieved January 15, 2008, from http://elvis.cqu.edu.au/conference/2004/papers.htm

Coghlan, D. (2003). Practitioner research for organizational knowledge: Mechanistic- and organistic-oriented approaches to insider action research. *Management Learning, 34*(4), 451-463.

Cornford, I. R. (2002). Learning-to-learn strategies as a basis for effective lifelong learning. *International Journal of Lifelong Education, 21*(4), 357-368.

Dalglish, C. (2006). The international classroom, challenges and strategies in a large business faculty. *The International Journal of Learning, 12*(5), 85-93.

Devlin, M. (2002). Taking responsibility for learning isn't everything: A case for developing tertiary students' conceptions of learning. *Teaching in Higher Education, 7*(2), 125-138.

Drucker, P. F. (1993). *Post capitalist society* (1st ed.). New York: HarperBusiness.

Elen, J., & Lowyck, J. (2000). Instructional metacognitive knowledge: A qualitative study on conceptions of freshmen about instruction. *Journal of Curriculum Studies, 32*(3), 421-444.

Elliott, C. J., Goodwin, J. S., & Goodwin, J. C. (1994). MBA programs and business needs: is there a mismatch? *Business Horizons, 37*(4), 55-61.

Entwistle, N. (1991). Approaches to learning and perceptions of the learning environment: Introduction to the special issue. *Higher Education, 22*(Special Issue), 201-204.

Frank, H. D. (1996). Learning to learn at the university. *Education + Training, 38*(8), 4-6.

Frielick, S. (2004). *The zone of academic development: An ecological approach to learning and teaching in higher education.* Unpublished manuscript, University of the Witwatersrand, Johannesburg.

Garratt, B. (1999). The Learning Organisation 15 years on: Some personal reflections. *The Learning Organization, 6*(5), 202.

Glenn, C. A. (2000). Learning how to learn. *New York Times*, pp. 4A, 12.

Gookin, J. (Ed.). (2003). *NOLS wilderness wisdom: Quotes for inspirational exploration.* Mechanicsburg, PA: Stackpole Books.

Hanna, D. (2003, July/August). Building a leadership vision: Eleven strategic challenges for higher education. *EDUCAUSE Review.*

Hinken, B. (2001). Working In high-leverage zones with the double-loop learning matrix. *The Systems Thinker® Newsletter, 12*(8). Retrieved on January 15, 2008, from http://www.pegasuscom.com/levpoints/doubleloopmatrix.html

Kane, L. (2004). Educators, learners and active learning methodologies. *International Journal of Lifelong Education, 23*(3), 275-286.

Kanter, R. M. (2004). *Confidence: How winning streaks and losing streaks begin and end.* New York: Crown Business.

Kolb, D. A. (1984). *Experiential learning: experience as the source of learning and development.* Englewood Cliffs, NJ: Prentice-Hall.

Lundeberg, M., & Martensson, P. (2005). Real real world projects. In C. Wankel & R. DeFillippi (Eds.), *Educating managers through real world projects* (pp. 47-64). Greenwich, CT: Information Age.

Maki, P. L. (2004). *Assessing for learning: Building a sustainable commitment across the institution*: Stylus.

Marsick, V. J., & Watkins, K. E. (1999). Looking again at learning in the learning organization: a tool that can turn into a weapon! *The Learning Organization,* 6(5), 207.

Mezirow, J. (2000). *Learning as transformation: Critical perspectives on a theory in progress* (1st ed.). San Francisco: Jossey-Bass.

Pellegrino, J. W., Chudowsky, N., & Glaser, R. (Eds.). (2001). *Knowing what students know: The science and design of educational assessment—Committee on the Foundations of Assessment, Board on Testing and Assessment, Center for Education, Division on Behavioral and Social Sciences and Education, National Research Council (U.S.).* Washington, DC: National Academy Press.

Pelsma, D., & Arnett, R. (2002). Helping Clients cope with change in the 21st century: A balancing act. *Journal of Career Development, 28*(3), 169.

Ramsden, P. (1992). *Learning to teach in higher education.* New York: Routledge.

Rothwell, A., & Ghelipter, S. (2003). The developing manager: Reflective learning in undergraduate management education. *Reflective Practice, 4*(2), 241-254.

Salmi, J. (2002). *Constructing knowledge societies: New challenges for tertiary education.* January 15, 2008, from http://www-wds.worldbank.org/servlet/WDSContentServer/WDSP/IB/2002/11/01/000094946_02102204203142/Rendered/PDF/multi0page.pdf

Samson, D., & Daft, R. L. (2003). *Management* (Pacific Rim ed.). South Melbourne, Victoria, Australia: Thomson.

Schein, E. H. (1988). Management education: Some troublesome realities and possible remedies. *The Journal of Management Development, 7*(2), 5-15.

Schein, E. H. (1999). *The corporate culture survival guide: sense and nonsense about culture change* (1st ed.). San Francisco, CA: Jossey-Bass.

Schön, D. A. (1987). *Educating the reflective practitioner: Toward a new design for teaching and learning in the professions* (1st ed.). San Francisco: Jossey-Bass.

Senge, P. M. (2000). *Schools that learn: A fifth discipline fieldbook for educators, parents, and everyone who cares about education* (1st ed.). New York: Doubleday.

Stroh, D. P. (2000). Conflicting goals: Structural tension at its worst. *The Systems Thinker® Newsletter, 11*(7), 6-7.

UABS. (2004). *Teaching and Learning Manual: BBIM Graduate Profile.* Auckland, New Zealand: University of Auckland Business School.

Weimer, M. (2003). Focus on learning, transform teaching. *Change. New Rochelle,* 35(5), 48-55.

Weinstein, C. E., & Meyer, D. K. (1994). Learning strategies, teaching, and testing. In T. Husen & T. N. Postlethwaite (Eds.), *The International Encyclopedia of Education* (2nd ed., pp. 3335–3340). Oxford, England: Pergamon Press.

Zohar, D. (2004). *A new capitalism we can live by.* Retrieved January 15, 2008, from http://www.pegasuscom.com/levpoints/zoharint.html

CHAPTER 7

WHAT HAVE WE LEARNED ABOUT STRATEGIC LEADERSHIP DEVELOPMENT?

Robert M. Fulmer and Jared Bleak

Great leaders deliver great results. This statement has been shown to be true across many studies and especially in companies that are effective in developing leadership talent. How do these companies do it? How are great leaders—who in turn build great organizations—created? This chapter details guiding principles for leadership development that emerge from the recent research literature. In addition, it articulates other broad themes and best practices in leadership development gleaned from a study of best-practice companies. These companies have shown that by following the principles outlined, they can effectively improve leadership development in their organizations as well as increase the focus on learning and development among employees.

INTRODUCTION

Great leaders deliver great results. This is perhaps the most profound finding from research on leadership development over the past decade. It has been clearly articulated by astute gurus and seen by forward thinking

University and Corporate Innovations in Lifelong Learning, pp. 167–185
Copyright © 2008 by Information Age Publishing

chief executive officers (CEOs) as a key to developing true competitive advantage. Truly, organizations with strong leaders and superior leadership development strategies deliver better results. In short, developing great leaders delivers great results and is a key leading indicator of business success.

Of course, leadership has never been an easy proposition. Observers have, throughout history, wondered if there were enough capable leaders to manage the challenges facing all types of organizations. Today, business and governmental organizations face something of a "perfect storm" of problems that have profound implications for current and future leaders.

- Competition is now coming from unexpected quarters. Because of the rules of the business game are changing with this competition, current leaders represent what the business needed in the past not the present or the future.
- The talent pipeline often lacks sufficient numbers to replace leaders that are or soon will be leaving—often due to the increasing "war for talent" that increased competition has sown.
- The organization's expansion goals outstrip the amount of talent needed to support them.
- Globalization and increasing technological demands make the leader's job more difficult than ever.
- Problems with strategic direction, organizational alignment, and employee commitment (e.g., unclear direction, poor alignment, and little commitment) continue to exist and are exacerbated in the current competitive environment.
- Human resources and those responsible for leadership development feel increased pressure to demonstrate value, particularly in terms of return on investment for leader development and other education and training initiatives.
- Leadership development initiatives are not integrated with business needs, and consequently, are of questionable value to internal customers.

The "perfect storm" of organizational challenges and leadership pressures has prompted study after study hoping to determine a key to survival. And in study after study—superior financial and organizational performance (or otherwise) has been linked to leadership. This comes as no surprise to those who have worked with or for a great leader. Good results follow good leadership. We are motivated by good leadership, guided by good leadership, and even held accountable by good leadership. In fact, employees who are led by strong leaders are more satisfied, engaged, and loyal than employees with weak leaders (Bernthal & Wellins, 2004). Most of all, we are often developed into good leaders ourselves as a result of being taught by and following the example of leaders who were role models, mentors and teachers.

These findings have been confirmed across different dimensions of leadership development. For instance, the Corporate Leadership Council (2004) found that organizations with strong leadership bench strength have approximately 10% higher total shareholder return than their weaker peers. Similarly, companies with above average financial returns have more comprehensive succession planning processes and are more committed to developing future leaders (Salob & Greenslade, 2005).

What brings these results? Previous research in leadership development has yielded five guiding principles for leadership development in general. Companies have shown that by following these principles they can effectively improve their leadership development results and streamline their organization's focus on leadership development.

These principles are:

1. Start with the top
2. Link leadership development directly to the business—and deliver results
3. Build an integrated leadership strategy
4. Drive consistency in the execution of leadership programs and practices
5. Hold leaders and the organization accountable for results—both developmental and business results

The research has shown that individually each of these principles will yield positive results; however, practiced together, they can propel an organization to new heights in leadership development.

1. Start at the Top

The engagement of CEO support for leadership development is often what separates the top performing companies from the rest. In a study of the top 20 companies for leaders, Hewitt (Salob & Greenslade 2005) found that 100% of these top companies involved the CEO in leadership development and many initiatives were sponsored directly by the chief executive, compared with 65% of other companies studied. Similarly, board level involvement also makes a difference in leadership development. A majority of top companies (65%) involved the board in leadership development activities and processes, compared to only 31% of other companies.

However, involvement of senior leaders does not just stop with endorsing and sponsoring programs. A current trend is to use top leaders as teachers in developmental programs as well as coaches and mentors to high potentials. In fact, 75% of leading learning and development organizations identified the use of senior executives as faculty in programs as the leading trend in the near term. In addition, just over half of the respondents from this same group noted that the use of executives as coaches would also be a significant trend (Bolt, 2004).

GE's Crotonville became a household name because of the importance placed on it by Jack Welch. And not only did he espouse the strategic importance of learning and development, but he modeled it by staying deeply involved in the company's efforts (Bartlett & McLean, 2003). Other examples of executive involvement at the very highest levels include PepsiCo's Roger Enrico and Caterpillar's Jim Owens. Both these leaders have been intimately involved in their organization's leadership development strategies and have seen great results from their efforts.

Using senior executives as teachers and coaches can also be a risky proposition. If training time is not given to improve their teaching and coaching skills, often senior executives become frustrated with their lack of success and the inherent difficulty of teaching, while developing leaders are disillusioned through the process. Giving presentations, which executives do very well, is different from teaching, and executives often need to be taught how to teach if this strategy is followed.

2. Link Directly to the Business and Deliver Results

Leadership development should begin and end with the business objectives and well as personal development needs in mind. Hewitt (2005) found that the top 20 companies in the United States in leader development closely linked development strategies with business strategies. This was done even over the temptation to build development practices that were composed of "best practices" from other companies or heralded in benchmark studies or training magazines. Indeed, alignment with business strategy and priorities was seen to win out over a hodgepodge of benchmark programs.

As companies become more and more attuned to and concerned with measuring the impact of leader development activities on business success, they are developing better methods of assessing this. For instance, 70% of corporate universities measure improved product/service quality as well as improved customer service. And 59% measured reduced operating costs as a result of leader development. Other measures include increased revenues (51%), improved sales efficiency (49%), and increased profits (48%) (*Sixth Annual Benchmarking Report*, 2004).

Yet with solid measures available, less than one company in five currently tracks business results from leader development activities (Bolt, 2004) as compared to over three of four companies that measure participant satisfaction and learning (*Sixth Annual Benchmarking Report*, 2004).

Challenges that are associated with measuring business impact explain much of the difficulty of the task. These include creating a common language that defines value, gaining access to appropriate business data, and finding matched samples to contrast against leader development participants.

3. Build an Integrated Leadership Strategy

Perhaps the most significant, overarching trend in leader development is the pressure and need to organize development activities and initiatives into an integrated strategy. In a 2004 study, 69% of respondents noted that the "creation of an integrated strategy and system for all executive development" was the leading priority of their learning and development organizations (Bolt, 2004, p. 13). This result replicated a 2000 study as well (Bolt, 2000). Of course, these results show that this is a key priority of learning and development organizations, and that it is difficult to measure and to show causality to the recurring results.

Many company learning and development organizations see leadership development as a bunch of puzzle pieces representing initiatives and programs that somehow fit together but do not seem to ever come together in the right way. These pieces include competency models, 360°s and other assessments, developmental job rotations, experiential and action learning, talent management, succession planning, rewards and recognition, and coaching and mentoring. A leadership development architecture can bring these often disjointed elements together into a consummate whole that has a greater chance of delivering real results (Duke Corporate Education, 2005). This architecture must be integrated and linked to the strategy and needs of the business in order to increase the potential for real impact and then communicated widely to engender support (Bolt, 2004).

4. Drive Consistency in the Execution of Leadership Programs and Practices

The best companies for leaders consistently execute on the strategies that make for good leadership development. They create enterprise wide standards, practices, and metrics for leadership; cascade programs and processes down through the organization to improve impact and drive cultural change; include flexibility in centralized leader development programs in order to address specific business needs; and customize developmental solutions for business units in order to better ensure senior management support and engagement (Corporate Executive Board, 2004; Fulmer, 2005; Salob & Greenslade, 2005; Saslow, 2004).

An important leverage point in leadership development efforts is the high-potential leader population within companies. Accelerating the development of high potentials was listed as a key objective by 62% of learning and development professionals (Bolt, 2004). However, even with this objective in mind, 46% of companies have no systemic process for identifying and developing candidates for key leadership positions, including high potentials (Bernthal & Wellins, 2004). And 37% of companies see their ability to identify leadership potential as a serious weakness (Bernthal & Wellins, 2004). Among the top companies in leader development, 95% identify high potentials as compared to 77% of other companies. Additionally, 68% then inform those high potentials of their status and 72% track their progress and turnover systematically (Salob & Greenslade, 2005). Even greater differentiation in the development of high potentials can be seen in the techniques and methods used. Ninety-five percent of top companies provided increased access to senior leaders for their high potentials as compared to 45% of other companies. Similarly, top companies provided internal training (90% vs. 51%), developmental assignments (89% vs. 43%) and mentoring and coaching (58% vs. 24%) at a much higher rate than did companies not considered benchmarks for leadership development (Salob & Greenslade, 2005).

Even when a good high potential development program is in place, without an equally effective succession management strategy and process, these efforts can end in frustration. Overall, half of internal candidates selected for leadership positions fail when there is no succession management system in place (Bernthal & Wellins, 2004, p. 3). And if they had the opportunity, organizations would rehire only 62% of their executives (Rioux & Bernthal, 2006, p. 1). To increase the odds of success, an effective succession management process should include visible support by senior management and line leaders who are involved in identifying and developing succession candidates, a time frame for achieving planned development actions, flexibility to change in response to strategic needs or competitive pressures, and the sharing of information with candidates (Fulmer & Conger, 2004).

5. Hold Leaders and the Organization Accountable for Results—Both Developmental and Business

Holding people and the organization accountable for developmental efforts is a trend that continues to gain momentum, especially in an increasingly competitive environment where any investment or outlay is carefully considered and monitored for a return. In fact, 52% of learning and development professionals planned to use systematic measurement/ evaluation to measure the impact of their development efforts (Bolt, 2004).

Best practice firms anchor their leadership development efforts with lean competency models that are tied to performance and reward systems (Salob & Greenslade, 2005). A clear, lean set of competencies was heralded as top companies in leadership development integrate their competencies into succession planning (100% of top companies vs. 78% of others) and make the competencies a baseline for identifying and then developing high potentials as part of succession planning. In the top quartile of leadership development companies identified by Hewitt (2005), metrics were integrated with succession planning 71% of the time, versus only 45% of the time in companies in the bottom quartile. These companies also more fully integrated competency measures into formulas for base pay (60% vs. 30%), annual incentives (60% vs. 31%), and long-term incentives (65% vs. 23%) (Salob & Greenslade, 2005).

Top leadership development companies also use competencies as metrics in the performance management processes. They are set as behavior standards for leaders and managers and pay is influenced by performance against them. Of course, a key in this is a set of clear, easily understandable and readily observable competencies.

Even with these results, many companies do not measure results in learning & development as they should. In a study that looked specifically at European based multinationals, 63% reported never measuring return on investment in learning & development (Execsight, 2004), even though these same firms reported that the importance of learning and development was higher than ever before (p. 44). There is clearly more work to be done in holding people and organizations accountable for learning and development results.

RESEARCH BACKGROUND: MEETING CURRENT CHALLENGES

Given the challenges to develop themselves and their people for the future faced by today's organizations, APQC, the Center for Creative Leadership, and Duke Corporate Education joined together to conduct a 2006 benchmarking study to achieve the following objectives:

- knowledge of how to elevate the importance of the leadership development function as a must-have for executing strategy (not a nice-to-have for developing individuals);
- a clear understanding of why an integrated leadership development architecture is vital to business success;
- awareness of current development and implementation strategies; and
- insights into how to evaluate leadership development programs for success at the individual and organizational levels.

This chapter introduces the highlights of our recent research on strategic leadership development along these five dimensions, including what we found as "best practices." These findings will be treated in more detail in subsequent chapters.

The benchmark organizations that were selected were subjected to deep, detailed study through structured data collection and site visits. The goal of the project was to examine these organizations and determine best practices in the following areas:

- Tying leadership culture, values, practices, and development to business strategy;
- Creating strategically relevant collective learning opportunities;
- Integrating various development initiatives for maximum impact into an overall leadership development architecture; and
- Using leadership development to support the execution of business strategy and meeting long-term needs for developing individual competencies while also building immediately needed organizational capability to address business challenges.

BUILDING 2020 LEADERSHIP VISION

High potentials in many leadership development programs will be at the very top of their organizations in 10-15 years. The challenge of developing leaders with 2020 vision thus becomes more than a double entendre. The results of our research confirm in many important ways much of the work on leadership development to date, while also making important additions and clarifications. Our results fall into four broad themes:

1. Developing leadership strategy
2. Building an integrated architecture for strategic leadership development
3. Implementing successful, strategic leadership development
4. Evaluating success

Within these broad themes, we have broken out the key findings from the research into several more specific messages. Each of these key messages is previewed below as a prelude to a more thorough discussion in later chapters.

I. Developing Leadership Strategy

Organizations Have Teachable Moments too

Much has been written about the importance of providing developmental opportunities for individuals at the appropriate "teachable moment." There is ample evidence that managers benefit more from educational experiences that are "just in time" for them to use them rather than "just in case" they eventually need a new set of skills. These moments often occur when individuals have just been asked to change their identities—that is, become managers rather than individual contributors, managers of managers or general managers with overall operational responsibility for a business unit.

Similarly, organizations seem to have moments when the development and articulation of a leadership strategy are especially appropriate. In our research, it appears that these opportunities generally occur when there is a new CEO who wishes to align the organization around a new strategy, when two organizations have merged or when there is a significant organizational crisis.

For example, when Jim Owens became CEO of Caterpillar in 2004, one of his early decisions was to empower the Leadership College of Caterpillar University to create a "leadership Quest" program for the firm's high potentials. This program built on an earlier initiative that created the firm's "leadership framework" or competency model and was intended, according to Owens, to "give our next generation of leaders an infusion of 'yellow blood.' "

In 2002, Washington Group International emerged from chapter 11 with a four person "Office of the Chairman" headed by Stephen Hanks as CEO and a new three-fold mission statement that identified "People" and their development as first priority. According to Hanks, "The company that develops talent the fastest will take the hill."

Each benchmark company used a key organizational transition to develop, articulate, and align a new leadership strategy with the strategic direction of the firm. These transitions became teachable moments for the organization and formed crucial starting points for achieving excellence in leader development.

Linking Corporate Strategy and Leadership Development Strategy Creates Winners

The direct link between a leadership development strategy and corporate strategy provides great benefit to an organization and its employees. Alignment with the corporate strategy is clearly a key concept for successful leadership development. Organizations that realize this establish a leader development philosophy that permeates all levels of the organization and is meaningful to all employees.

This was clearly evident in the benchmark companies we studied. All of these organizations tied leadership development to corporate planning as well as the business strategy.

At Caterpillar, alignment is achieved by receiving input from the executive office, business units, and process owners of the critical success factors. To further embed leadership development into the business strategy, metrics were established to connect leadership to the business. PwC links development activities to its strategy to become the "distinctive firm." Programs that are successful are designed to reinforce corporate strategy, thus ensuring linkage and success. PepsiCo's leadership development strategy is grounded in the belief that strong leaders are needed for success in the marketplace.

As these short examples show, each benchmark company worked hard to ensure that emerging leaders are prepared for the future and its realities and not bogged down with the past.

Executives use Leadership Development as a Powerful Tool to Formulate, Translate, and Communicate Strategy

While education is a relatively small portion of the entire developmental process for leaders, carefully crafted learning initiatives can be important in providing input from throughout the organization, effectively communicating the reasons for and implications of corporate strategy to managers who will need to translate the strategy for employees throughout the organization so they understand their role in making it happen.

Various studies have concluded that 60-70% of all strategies fail to be successfully implemented. Our benchmark companies seem to have discovered that one way to beat these odds is to ensure that everyone in the organization understands the strategy, the reasons for it, and their role in making the strategy happen. These companies also understand that effective developmental activities can be an effective means of sharing the information and providing some of the tools for successful implementation.

Lean Competency Models and Values are the Foundations of Strategic Leadership Development

A simple leadership model with a concise statement of values serves as an important point of focus in leadership development. None of the best practice partners had a "scientifically valid" competency model; most had created their own or adapted it from a set of competencies developed by an outside firm.

The benchmark companies in our research kept their values and competencies simple and straightforward, understanding that competencies should apply at all levels within an organization and directly lead to better performance.

II. Building an Integrated Architecture for Strategic Leadership Development

Strategic Leadership Development is a Partnership Between Senior Executives and Multiple Human Resource Systems

Senior executive support, usually starting with the CEO, is vital for success in strategic leadership development. Yet, even the most effective CEO cannot assure success without the involvement of the entire human resource system. Conversely, training and education professionals will not be successful unless they reach out and collaborate with their colleagues in line positions and in other human resource specialties.

For example, within Cisco's human resource (HR) function, the organization's Worldwide Leadership Education group works with leaders to identify candidates for its leadership development programs. Executives then help to design the programs, ensuring that the program meets business needs and aligns with strategy.

At Washington Group International, corporate leadership and the business units share responsibility for leadership development. The development and strategy office is responsible for the design, development, implementation, and maintenance of the programs while the office of the chairman reviews, approves, and provides feedback on moving forward with development. The 14-member senior executive leadership team meets regularly to discuss leadership development.

As leadership development increases in importance in corporations, partnerships with executives and HR will have to continue to be strengthened in order for these efforts to succeed.

Strategic Human Resource Development (HRD) is a key Part of the Corporate Planning Cycle

Another test for determining if developing leaders is a strategic priority for a company is to see if there is a HRD component to the planning cycle. The benchmark companies in this study make people planning something that every key executive is expected to address in concert with their human resource partners (usually including succession planning) and their immediate superior. In other words, it makes sense to consider what key players are expected to implement the strategy and what assistance they need to enhance the probability of success.

Washington Group International leverages its annual strategic and business planning sessions to discuss employee development and leadership development needs for the organization. Similarly PepsiCo's career growth model aligns with the organization's annual operating calendar.

These last two findings lead to a strong conclusion that the successful development of leaders requires a strategic alignment of planning and all human resource systems.

HRD can win the Support of top Management by Involving Them in Strategic Learning Initiatives and by Knowing the Business

Most of the exemplars in this study have a high degree of executive involvement in the delivery of key corporate programs. Similarly, executive involvement in programmatic design can ensure that program content addresses topics of genuine concern to this key constituency and contribute to higher levels of support for the ongoing initiative.

At Cisco Systems, each program has an established cross-functional steering committee that ensures linkage between the program and the business. The business leaders on the steering committees help drive the design of the programs and recruit appropriate executives into the classrooms. During the design phase of the program, the steering committees meet often, approximately once a month. In addition, the programs employ the role of "executive faculty," people who bring participants a strategic perspective.

A board of governors for Caterpillar University includes the CEO and senior executives who approve learning budgets and priorities as well as determine policy. An advisory board for each college includes senior leaders from business or "user" groups. This group has geographic and subject matter mix and membership from most of Caterpillar's business units.

While it is important to involve line executives who have a deep understanding of the business challenges facing an organization, this is not enough to ensure programmatic success. Successful HRD partners must also understand the business as well as leading edge leadership concepts.

Leaders who Teach are More Effective Than Those who tell

One of the surprising findings of this project was the degree to which senior executives practice the concept of "leading by teaching." At PepsiCo, Senior Vice-President of Corporate Training and Development Paul Russell, speaks of "the magic of leaders developing leaders." According to Russell, the missing adult learning principle is that

> people learn best when they get to learn from someone they really want to learn from! At PepsiCo, the 'teachers' our executives want to learn from are our own senior leaders. They are world class, widely respected and have proven that they can do it HERE!

Senior executives are asked to share their personal perspectives, build participant confidence, and skills while demonstrating support for their growth. Of equal importance, senior leaders get greater teamwork from participants and get to know key young leaders, while developing more loyalty, motivation, productivity, and better alignment around vision and key strategic initiatives. PepsiCo leaders are encouraged to think of learning as an important "arrow in their quiver" for helping to drive change. At PepsiCo, learning becomes something to live, not just another thing to "endorse."

Corporate Learning Initiatives Tend to Focus on High Potentials

Substantial organizational impact can be gained by involving small numbers of people with high potential who will return to their regular jobs and translate their learning for others in various operations.

Similarly, many key corporate programs can be adapted by business groups who wish to provide a similar experience for their key people that aligns with the corporate emphasis.

While PricewaterhouseCoopers designed its PwC University experience for 2000 U.S. partners, and Caterpillar involved all managers in their 2005 strategy rollout, most key corporate initiatives in our study were focused on high potentials. Caterpillar's Leadership Quest involves approximately 50 key midlevel leaders per year. PepsiCo's CEO program involves approximately 40 high potentials each year. Washington Group International's Leadership Excellence and Performance project began in 2002 and had graduated 48 participants by mid-2006. Cisco's Executive Leader Program focuses on the company's strategic intent and serves approximately 40 top leaders annually. This program was designed for employees who are newly promoted to the vice-presidential level, or who are filling a vice-presidential role.

III. Implementing Successful, Strategic Leadership Development

Leaders in HRD do it Themselves—Often With Expert Assistance

A somewhat surprising finding was the degree to which the exemplar firms maintained control of the design and delivery of their leadership development programs while leveraging input from trusted outside partners or advisors. All had relatively small staffs for the HRD function, yet had delegated relatively little to outsiders.

Since PwC is a professional services firm, it has a greater involvement with outside professionals—thinking that their partners' time can be better spent on helping their own clients than trying to become experts in HRD. PwC's Learning and Education Group has 250 employees; however, most of them are involved in technical and professional learning. A very small group involved in leadership and partner development is totally involved in every aspect of their programs but rely on external vendors for some design and most delivery.

Washington Group International's leadership development is coordinated by the three senior level HR executives. They uses outside consultants to a limited degree and rely on their officers to do much of the actual instruction along with some former executives who have taken early retirement but still know the firm, its culture and industry.

Caterpillar worked closely with the Hay Group to set up its "Building Great Leaders" program and leadership framework and asks Duke

Corporate Education to facilitate the "Leadership Quest" program and to coach officers in planning their sessions in the course.

Human Resources Departments Leverage Their Talents With the Judicious us of Consultants

While leadership development remains firmly under the control of the company, the lean corporate staffs in the benchmark companies leverage their time and talents with the judicious use of outside expertise. Because of the emphasis on knowing the business and on lead staffing, most of the benchmark companies involved outside firms or specialists in both the design and delivery of their learning initiatives. Yet, no matter how busy they are, they never completely turn over either challenge to others.

In none of the benchmark companies is leadership development an island. There is a growing trend toward a partnership and alignment with succession planning and performance management as well as other HR activities. Happily, the leadership development silo seems to have been punctured and is hardly recognizable among the benchmark companies in this study.

Integration of Leadership Development With Other Talent Management Systems Creates Synergies

Organization's committed to leadership development understand its relationship with other talent management systems and practices. The best-practice partners incorporate their leadership development programs with others such as performance reviews, management development, and succession planning.

The benchmark companies have invested heavily in their people. In doing so, it is inevitable that they integrate leadership development with other talent management systems in order to receive the maximum benefit.

Washington Group International is such a strong proponent of this mindset that they integrate every aspect of talent management. This process begins with establishing a vision of what positions will need to be filled and then forecasting, identifying, and preparing candidates for these positions. Subsequently, employee development plans are carefully crafted for each employee. An overall employee development strategic plan then feeds the succession planning process, which in turn is used in the leadership development program.

Cisco uses executive coaches to accelerate development as part of its high-potential program. In this program, high potentials are paired with an external executive coach for a year and even though the coach is an external resource, he or she is fully trained and knowledgeable in "the Cisco way" prior to the assignment.

IV. Evaluating Success

Developing People is a Growing Measure of Executive Success

Best practice partners take the development of people very seriously. They seem to believe that financial results are a "lagging indicator" of organizational success, while people development is a "leading indicator." Consequently, people development is becoming an important part of the assessment of executive performance.

PepsiCo has historically allocated one-third of incentive compensation for developing people with the remainder for results. In 2007, the company is moving to an equal allocation of incentive compensation for people development and results. Pepsi also utilizes the results from its semi-annual climate survey and 360 degree feedback as part of the performance review process.

Caterpillar found that their managers were superb at the "execution" portion of their leadership framework, satisfactorily in the "vision" category but needed more attention to the "legacy" (developmental) set of behaviors. Consequently, they have begun to focus on this theme in learning programs and in performance assessment.

Return on Learning is Increasingly Measured by Corporate Success Rather Than Individual Performance

All of the benchmark companies were familiar with the Kirkpatrick (2005) and Phillips (2003) models of evaluation. However, Caterpillar was, perhaps, the most rigorous in attempting to measure the return on its learning investment.

Since Caterpillar University was established during a recession, this may have forced them to establish the value proposition for learning early in their history. As part of this, Caterpillar University created a document called the "Business of Learning" where each college developed a value proposition for key initiatives based on net benefits, ROI (return on investment), and other standards. This later evolved into the enterprise learning plan, a 161-page document that discussed the state of learning at Caterpillar, articulated the value proposition for learning, and estimated the ROI for Caterpillar University at 50% for 2003. This was then followed by seven detailed ROI studies. These leveraged focus groups, surveys, and in-depth discussion with participants. It identified the benefits, dollar benefits, costs, net benefits, and ROI. Having established the value proposition, Caterpillar doesn't repeat this process for all subsequent iterations of a program and are beginning to speak about "Return on Learning" rather than the more formalized process for ROI.

PepsiCo does not attempt to measure the value created by a program, but the CEO attends each of the major high potential programs and is the primary facilitator. Since she is intensely involved with program design and delivery, ratings are less of an issue. At the end of each program, each participant is asked to send the CEO an e-mail indicating what he or she will be doing differently as a result of attending the session. Six months afterwards, they are also asked to send the CEO another e-mail reporting on how well they have done in meeting their commitment.

Cisco collects both quantitative and qualitative measures. Worldwide Leadership Education has a formal system for measuring the outcomes of leadership development strategy. Examples of metrics include "price range for a one week course," "customer satisfaction scores," "percentage of class graduates who have used learnings in their jobs and had a positive impact," and "percentage of learners who stay with the company." The team concentrates on metrics showing the application of learning to jobs and changes in business results. An example is the retention percentage for employees going through the programs compared to the general employee population, which has turned out to be quite favorable for Cisco—approximately 93% across the organization.

Successful Programs are a Process Rather Than an Event

At one time, corporate educational programs were a disconnected series of independent events. Today, they are typically part of an integrated career development plan that is tied to strategic objectives with specific, actionable objectives. They are seldom 1 week discrete events and often include team or individual applications.

The Cisco Leadership Series operates in a 3-phase structure that facilitates the employee's ability to put learning into action. It is an "events to process" model. Employees involved in the various programs progress through each phase: preparation, program, and application on the job. While the face-to-face portion of Cisco's programs may only be 5 days, the participant is involved in the process for 8-10 months.

Caterpillar's core leadership programs leverage key transition points in its leaders' careers and build on one another in a building-block fashion. Underlying all of its programs is its foundational Making Great Leaders program. These transitions take place as individuals move from supervisor (i.e., frontline leader), to manager (leader of leaders), to department head, and finally to executive. A person's movement through these programs and transitions is all part of her developmental journey at Caterpillar.

GETTING TO GREAT RESULTS—A SUMMARY

No business or strategy is good enough to succeed without strong leadership. And this strong leadership has been shown to be at the essence of exceptional organizational performance.

Leadership and learning should play a critical role in enabling organizational growth and transformation. Today's leaders must be flexible, collaborative, able to leverage subject matter expertise, and willing to continue their learning journey. The same characteristics should also be true for their organizations. Ideally, the leadership strategy should be aligned with the corporate strategy. Individual developmental plans should be aligned with the emerging needs of the firm, and all human resource systems should be aligned in support of business objectives. Staff professionals with responsibility for any aspect of talent management should forge productive, business-focused partnership with their line counterparts and with their outside providers and consultants.

The benchmark companies in our study understand these principles well and created best in class leadership development strategies, practices, and measures that in turn contribute to overall financial and strategic success. They know that great leaders deliver great results.

ACKNOWLEDGMENT

Unlike the rest of the book, this chapter reports on "applied research" (rather than traditional academic research) that reflects questions and concerns of sponsoring organizations. While referencing other applied studies, the major trust of the chapter is from the authors; 2006 "best practice study" sponsored by American Productivity & Quality Center, Center for Creative Leadership, Duke Corporate Education and 14 contributing corporate sponsors from four continents.

REFERENCES

Bartlett, C. A., & McLean, A. N. (2003). *GE's talent machine: The making of a CEO.* Boston: Harvard Business School.

Bernthal, P., & Wellins, R. S. (2004). *Leadership forecast: 2003-2004*. Bridgeville, PA: Development Dimensions International.

Bolt, J. (2000). *Executive Development Trends 2000*. San Francisco: Executive Development Associates.

Bolt, J. (2004). *Executive Development Trends 2004: Filling the talent gap*: Executive Development Associates.

Corporate Executive Board. (2004). *Driving performance and retention through employee engagement*. Washington, DC: Author.

Duke Corporate Education. (2005). *Creating a leadership architecture* (internal document). Durham, NC: Author.

Execsight. (2004). *Leadership development in european organisations: Challenges and best practices*. Palo Alto, CA:The Danish Leadership Institute and Institute of Executive Development.

Fulmer, R. M. (2005). *Next generation HR practices*. Houston, TX: APQC.

Fulmer, R. M., & Conger, J. A. (2004). *Growing your company's leaders: How great organizations use succession management to sustain competitive advantage*. New York: AMACOM.

Kirkpatrick, D. L. (2005). *Evaluating training programs: The four levels* (3rd ed.). San Francisco: Berrett-Koehler.

Phillips, J. J. (2003). *Return on investment in training and performance improvement programs* (2nd ed.). Burlington, MA: Butterworth-Heinemann.

Rioux, S. M., & Bernthal, P. (2006). *Succession management practices*. Bridgeville, PA: Development Dimensions International.

Salob, M., & Greenslade, S. (2005). *How the top 20 companies grow great leaders*: Lincolnshire, IL: Hewitt Associates.

Saslow, S. (2004). *Current challenges in leadership development*. Palo Alto, CA: Institute of Executive Development.

Sixth Annual Benchmarking Report. (2004). New York: Corporate University Xchange.

CHAPTER 8

FRAMING ARTS-BASED LEARNING AS AN INTERSECTIONAL INNOVATION IN CONTINUING MANAGEMENT EDUCATION

The Intersection of Arts and Business and the Innovation of Arts-Based Learning

Nick Nissley

Similar to a fusion chefs' creative disillusionment with traditional cooking, there is a sense of disillusionment being expressed by those in continuing management education. The disillusionment is fueled by the increasing criticism of management education, for underemphasizing the creative skills that leaders and managers require for coping with a rapidly changing and complex global business environment. At the same time, there's a growing recognition by management educators that many of these required skills can be found in those creative arts that have typically existed outside the business school. However, coupled with the disillusionment is a growing

University and Corporate Innovations in Lifelong Learning, pp. 187–211
Copyright © 2008 by Information Age Publishing

sense of possibility—emerging at the intersection of arts and business. Similar to fusion chefs, these continuing management educators are beginning to work in this intersection of arts and business and have found arts-based learning as an expressive means to generate innovative and stimulating continuing management education experiences. This chapter explores the learning fusion or intersectional innovation occurring within continuing management education – the intersection of arts and business— and the emergence of the innovation of arts-based learning in continuing management education.

CREATIVE DISILLUSIONMENT IN CONTINUING MANAGEMENT EDUCATION

In *The Medici Effect* (Johansson, 2004), argues that innovations occur when people see beyond their expertise (e.g., continuing management education) and approach situations actively, with an eye toward putting available ideas together in new combinations. Johansson calls that space the "intersection," and his book describes "intersectional innovation." The main thesis of the book asserts that there is an exponential power when many people from single-disciplinary backgrounds come together to create something multidisciplinary.

To further elaborate this idea of intersectional innovation, and seek to more deeply engage the reader's senses, consider this idea of intersectional innovation as being similar to fusion cuisine. The nature of fusion cuisine might be described as a demonstration by chefs of their creative disillusionment with traditional cooking. Their expression is framed by a determination to make food more interesting, to generate excitement about diverse ingredients from different cooking traditions that contribute to the overall excellence of the dish while retaining the individual flavors or characters of the ingredients. The key to the culinary art of fusion cuisine is its ability to generate innovative food experiences.

Similar to the chefs' creative disillusionment with traditional cooking, there is a disillusionment, coupled with a sense of possibility, being expressed by those in continuing management education (e.g., Adler, 2006; Austin & Devin, 2003; Beckwith, 2003; Boyle & Ottensmeyer, 2005; Buswick, Creamer, & Pinard, 2004; Schein, 2001; Seifter & Buswick, 2005). The sense of possibility is emerging at the intersection of arts and business and the emerging innovation of arts-based learning within continuing management education. These educators are broadly exploring the intersection of arts and business. And, they are seeking to find connections between management education and specific arts disciplines, for example: *film* (e.g., Champoux, 1999, 2000), *theatre* (e.g., Clarke & Mangham, 2004; Corsun, Young, McManus, & Erdem, 2006;

Ferris, 2002; Gibb, 2004; Monks, Barker, & Mhanachain, 2001; Nissley, Taylor, & Houden, 2004), *literature* (e.g., Cohen, 1998) and *poetry* (e.g., Burrell, 2007), and *music* (e.g., Linstead, 2006), and *dance* (e.g., Denhardt & Denhardt, 2006). Similar to the fusion chefs, these educators are seeking more expressive ways of engaging in their management education practice—to generate innovative and stimulating continuing management education experiences.

This chapter explores the learning fusion or intersectional innovation occurring within continuing management education—the intersection of arts and business—and the emergence of the innovation of arts-based learning in continuing management education. Nissley (2002) initially chronicled the emerging innovation of arts-based management education in 2002. Since then, in a mere 5 years, a flourishing practice has emerged. This chapter picks up where Nissley's (2002) work left off, without repeating the in-depth chronicling of the innovation, prior to 2002.

THE INTERSECTION OF ARTS AND BUSINESS AND THE INNOVATION OF ARTS-BASED LEARNING

Presently, within continuing management education we're experiencing an intersectional innovation—the intersection of arts and business and the innovation of arts-based learning (e.g., Adler, 2006; Austin & Devin, 2003; Beckwith, 2003; Boyle & Ottensmeyer, 2005; Buswick, Creamer, & Pinard, 2004; Darso, 2004; Nissley, 2002; Seifter & Buswick, 2005; "The Arts in Business," 2001). This intersection is being fueled by the creative disillusionment of both educators and managers with traditional approaches to continuing management education, which has given rise to arts-based approaches to learning. In this innovative approach of arts-based learning, learners engage with artists and arts practices as a vehicle for learning. Almost 15 years ago, Barry (1994) described how "analogical-based methods" could be used in management education. Today, terms such as "artful creation" (Nissley, 2004) and "artful making (Austin & Devin, 2003) are commonly used when one seeks to explain, "how the arts can improve business" (Buswick, Creamer, & Pinard, 2004) or how one may use "an arts technique to facilitate leadership development" (Di Ciantis, 1995). In arts-based learning, learners use the artists' spaces and engage in artistic processes, in addition to the traditional management education classroom, as invitations to new ways of approaching continuing management education.

Dr. Nancy Adler (2006), one of the world's most prominent scholars of organizational leadership, from Montreal's McGill University's Faculty of Management, makes the following assertions in the *Academy of*

Management Learning & Education journal. Dr. Adler asserts that organizations, communities, and nation-states are calling on their people for more creativity and innovation. As we enter the twenty-first century, Adler observes, we are seeing increasing numbers of leaders bringing artists and artistic processes into their organizations—as we are beginning to think more creatively about continuing management education. She asks the reader to consider the following examples of the intersections of arts and business being pursued through arts-based learning in continuing management education.

- The invitation of a poet, David Whyte, to address senior executives at companies such as McDonald Douglas, a global aerospace company and aircraft manufacturer.
- The collaboration of a Harvard Business School professor with a theater director in 2003 to author the book *Artful Making: What Managers Need to Know About How Artists Work*.
- Denmark's world renowned Copenhagen Business School's opening of the world's first business-school-based Center for Art and Leadership.
- Leading business schools worldwide adding arts-based courses to their curriculum, including: (1) Wharton's compulsory MBA workshop "Leadership through the Arts," facilitated by the noted dance company Pilobolus; (2) at MIT, three of the 2003/2004 Sloan Leadership courses had arts-based components, including "Unconventional Leadership: A Performing Advantage" and "Leadership as Acting: Performing Henry V"; and (3) the University of Chicago's required Leadership Exploration and Development course, where MBAs write, produce, and showcase a film.

These examples, and others (e.g., Buswick, Creamer, & Pinard, 2004; Mirvis, Ayas, & Roth, 2003; Seifter & Buswick, 2005) offer a glimpse of a future where managers/leaders and artists work collaboratively, seek inspiration from one another, and make use of artistic processes to inform new ways of approaching their personal and professional development in management education. Dr. Adler is not alone in her observations of this phenomenon. Dr. Lotte Darso (2004), author of *Artful Creation: Learning-Tales of Arts-in-Business*, has also said that the arts and artists have a role to play in helping leaders and organizations realize success in the creative economy. In fact, leadership experts such as Chuck Palus and David Horth (2002) from the Center for Creative Leadership (*The Leader's Edge: Six Creative Competencies for Navigating Complex Challenges*) and Mary Jo

Hatch and colleagues (2005), authors of *The Three Faces of Leadership: Manager, Artist, Priest*, have begun to describe the intersectional innovation of where the arts and artists are informing continuing management education and leadership learning. To lead in the creative economy they suggest leadership competencies more closely aligned with artists and found in artistic practice, than in the traditional technical sphere of the practices of managing in the workplace.

One may understand such creative disillusionment as a response to Peter Vaill's (1974, 1989) assertion, over 30 years ago, that management is not "paint by numbers." Vaill was a leading voice within management education, later joined by others such as Marsick (1990), Chalofsky (1996), and Gibb (2005) within the practice of human resource development, calling for us to look beyond the traditional positivistic paradigm (way of knowing). Intersecting with a broader disillusionment within the interdisciplinary field of organizational studies, organizational aesthetics has emerged as a subspecialty (e.g., Strati, 1992, 1999; Linstead & Höpfl, 2000; Taylor & Hanson, 2005). Generally speaking, organizational aesthetics provides us with an other way—an aesthetic way —of understanding organizational life. Ironically, Vaill's assertion that management is not "paint by numbers," inspired an intersectional innovation in continuing management education that has been inspired by the arts metaphor – simply not the prescriptive "paint by numbers" metaphor, but a richer and much more complex understanding of how arts-based learning can enrich the practice of continuing management education. In fact, models describing how arts-based learning relates with management education have been offered in the emerging literature (e.g., Austin & Devin, 2003, pp. 15-16; Darso, 2004, pp. 149-159; Hatch, Kostera, & Kozminski, 2005, pp. 132-141; Nissley, 2004, p. 292; Palus & Horth, 2002, p. 6; Taylor & Ladkin, 2007; Woodward & Funk, 2004). Appendix A offers an overview of the emerging models, describing how arts-based learning has been born from the intersection of arts and business and is relating with management education. Appendix B offers, more specifically, select emerging models describing the innovation of arts-based learning in management education.

While this chapter documents the intersection of the more theory-based aesthetic epistemology (aesthetic ways of knowing) literature with the more practice-inspired arts-based learning literature, it does not seek to suggest arts-based learning as a new paradigm in continuing management education, opposing the traditional paradigm of logical positivism. It does more modestly, however, mindful of multiple ways of knowing; seek to identify arts-based learning as an *other* means of viewing and understanding the evolution of continuing management education. The ideas presented in this chapter may be viewed as building upon Morgan's

(1986) *Images of Organization*, to include art as a metaphor for understanding continuing management education. Our understanding of arts-based learning within the field of management education has expanded significantly in the past 10 years, beyond the metaphorical conceptualizations of "the art of good teaching" in management education ("The Art of Good Teaching," 1997). As the examples noted in this chapter suggest, practitioners have moved beyond the "art of" metaphor. Today, "the art of" metaphor is only one way the arts and business have intersected to inform the practice of continuing management education. Darso (2004) documents four additional ways in which businesses use the arts: (1) decoration—the artwork in lobbies/corridors, and the pictures on office walls (e.g., corporate art); (2) entertainment—bringing the arts/performances into the office space (e.g., giving employee tickets to arts events); (3) instrument—when business uses the arts as an instrument for management/leadership development (e.g., teambuilding, communication skills development, etc.); and 4) strategic transformation —when the business integrates the arts in areas such as vision and values, creativity and innovation, branding, and marketing.

This chapter focuses on what Darso (2004) refers to as the "instrument" type of arts and business intersection. First, an examination of the literature that is documenting and defining this emerging innovation of arts-based learning is presented. Then, the reader is presented with a single case/portrait (e.g., Lawrence-Lightfoot & Davis, 2002) of arts-based learning in continuing management education, at Canada's Banff Centre for Continuing Education. The Banff Centre is an outstanding example of arts-based learning in continuing management education/leadership development, and affords the reader insights to the practice.

At the heart of the Canada's Banff Centre and their leadership development programming, is a recognition of the limitations of the technical proficiencies of leadership. The Banff Centre is self-described as Canada's premier institution of creativity—an intersectional space for the continuing education of artists and organizational leaders. It has over a half-century of experience understanding how artists and artistic processes can inform the practice of leadership. At The Banff Centre, they have built on the research identified in Appendices A and B, research that suggests aesthetic competencies of leaders and artful making as innovative means of management education. Such research informs The Banff Centre's practice of leadership development—which occurs outside the traditional confines of the four walls of a classroom. Literally, at the Banff Centre you learn to "think outside of the box." In their programs, leaders also visit the actor's stage, the potter's studio, the musician's performance space. Participants use these spaces, in addition to the classroom, as invitations to new ways of learning about leadership—these spaces are real examples of the intersection of arts and business and the innovation of arts-based learning in continuing management education.

REVIEWING THE LITERATURE AND PRACTICE OF ARTS-BASED LEARNING IN CONTINUING MANAGEMENT EDUCATION

In this section, the literature (research and practice-based) and vehicles (conferences, institutions, communities of practice, and formal management education programming) that enable arts-based learning in continuing management education are presented and examined.

Scholarship: Research-Based

Nissley (2002) was the first to comprehensively investigate and report on the emerging innovation of arts-based learning in management education, in *Rethinking Management Education*. However, the practice of arts-based learning was by no means, new. Rather, the management education literature was finally catching up with the practice. The creative disillusionment with management education's preoccupation with logical-positivist prescriptions had been fomenting for years (e.g., Vaill, 1974; 1989). And, a quarter-century later, Schein (2001, p. 81) provocatively asked, "Why is art relevant to other elements of society like business or government? Why should managers learn anything about art and the role of the artist?" As founding editor of the Society for Organizational Learning Journal, *Reflections*, he went about answering that question, by publishing a special edition, dedicated to "The Arts in Business and Society." Just 3 years later, Lotte Darso (2004), who was then working for the Creative Alliance, one of six research consortia at the Learning Lab Denmark—whose purpose was to accentuate the learning potential of the interplay between arts and business—authored, *Artful Creation: Learning-Tales of Arts-in-Business*. Darso's research provided a map of this emerging innovative learning practice—almost overnight offering a glimpse of how management education practitioners were engaging with arts-based learning, all over the globe. Then in just another 2 short years, Nancy Adler's (2006) article in the *Academy of Management Education and Learning Journal*, heralded the coming of age of arts-based learning as a management education innovation, when she asserted: "the time is right for the cross-fertilization of the arts and leadership." Adler's paper was also nominated for "best paper" recognition at the Academy of

Management—creating greater acceptance and credibility for arts-based learning in management education.

In addition, other scholarship has emerged in the last 5 years, further documenting the field's emergence. For example, Heemsbergen (2004), a faculty member at The Banff Centre's Leadership Development Program, has linked arts-based learning with neuroscience research, offering new insights to how arts-based learning contributes to the effective development of leaders. Similarly, Harvard Business School's Rob Austin collaborated with Swarthmore College's Professor Emeritus of Theatre, Lee Devin (2003, p. xxii), to describe "artful making" as an alternative to traditional approaches to management practice. Expressing their creative disillusionment, with such traditional approaches, they assert, "Managers should look to collaborative artists rather than to more traditional management models if they want to create economic value in this new century." And, another Harvard Business School colleague, Stan Davis, along with David McIntosh (2005) authored, *The Art of Business*, which similarly asserts an other way of looking at business and management practice, which moves beyond the traditional focus upon the economic flow of business, and suggests that business also has an artistic flow. Specifically, they identify elements of artistic flow: artistic *inputs* such as imagination, artistic *processes* such as creating, and artistic *outputs* such as beauty. This literature asserts an intersection of arts and business.

Scholarship: Practice-Based

The literature references mentioned above and framed in Appendix A (e.g., Adler, 2006; Austin & Devin, 2003; Darso, 2004; Davis & McIntosh, 2005) are central to understanding the emergence of the intersection of arts and business. However, while these authors reported on the structural emergence of the field growing from the arts and business intersection; practitioners were also beginning to contribute to the literature, reporting specifically on the emergent innovation: the practice of arts-based learning in management education. For example, while Darso's (2004) publication chronicled the structural emergence of arts-based learning, Seifter and Buswick's (2005) editing of a special edition of the *Journal of Business Strategy* (Arts-Based Learning for Business), offered an in-depth understanding of the practice of arts-based learning. Their special edition offered insights to nearly every art form's applicability to management education (from theatre to jazz), as well as insights to the type of organizations that are using these innovative approaches (e.g.,

Unilever and McGraw-Hill companies). Also, Seifter and Buswick offered an annotated bibliography, allowing a broad-based view of the field.

Other practitioner accounts of arts-based learning have emerged. For example, overviews of the emerging practice have been shared (e.g., Beckwith, 2003; Buswick, Creamer, & Pinard, 2004). And, literature regarding specific arts and business intersectional engagements, where arts-based learning is being practiced has emerged (e.g., Boyle & Ottensmeyer, 2005; Jones, 2006; Mirvis, Ayas, & Roth, 2003). And, literature describing arts-based learning methodologies have also begun appearing (e.g., Halpern & Lubar, 2004; Di Ciantis, 1995; Palus & Horth, 2002, 2001; VanGundy & Naiman, 2003; Woodward & Funk, 2004).

Conferences

In addition to the emerging scholarship, a number of conferences have sprouted, focusing on the intersection of arts and business. Most notably, for example, September 2002 saw the beginning of the Art of Management and Organization Conference (2007) in London. The conference aim was, and continues to be, the exploration and promotion of the arts (in the most inclusive sense) as a means of understanding management and organization(al) life. This conference has given rise to a vibrant global community of praxis—including scholars and practitioners. The conference has resided in London (2002), Paris (2004), and Krakow (2006); and in 2008—it will travel to Banff, Canada. This movement of the conference, from Europe to Canada, reflects the growing diversity of the community—which touches every continent.

Second, IDRIART, the Initiative for the Development of Intercultural Relations through the Arts (2007), was born out of recognition that the healing forces inherent in art must take on a more social role in answer to increasing isolation among people and cultures. For the past 20 years IDRIART has been trying to build a creative environment where people from different walks of life and from different countries, can use the arts as a vehicle for personal transformation and societal change. IDRIART operates as a nonprofit organization, and was founded in 1981, by Miha Pogacnik, violinist and cultural ambassador of Slovenia. The philosophy of the organization is: that artists and their audiences purposefully travel throughout the world and gather in places that really need them. In these places IDRIART can take the initiative to intervene in political, social, and cultural situations. Pogacnik has convened the festival of art and business which has taken place at the Borl Castle, in eastern Slovenia.

Formal Postsecondary Management Education Institutions

In the past 10 years a number of institutions, rooted in the intersection of arts and business and the innovation of arts-based learning in management education have emerged, spread across the globe, but mostly located in Europe (see Appendix C).

First on the scene was the Creative Alliance, one of six research consortia at the Learning Lab Denmark—whose purpose was to accentuate the learning potential of the interplay between arts and business. Second, and also in Denmark, Copenhagen Business School's Centre for Art and Leadership (2007), is a research center in the Department of Management, Politics, and Philosophy. The Centre concentrates its efforts in three areas:

- The creation of an international network of researchers, organizations, and artists that share the Centre's ambitions and its vision of the connection between art and leadership. This is also intended to prepare the ground for exemplary research in this area.
- The installation of art in a theoretical context and perspective in which leadership is imbued with new and effective insights. Here concepts are clarified and a common language is created—one that is rooted in a unique theoretical approach to the relation between art and leadership.
- The establishment of a collaborative relation to the business community, to organizations and to social institutions with the aim of stimulating learning and creative growth.

Third, the University of Trento's (Italy) Research Unit on Communication, Organizational Learning, and Aesthetics, RUCOLA, (2007) led by Antonio Strati, is a group of scholars and researchers collaborating since 1993 on the basis of common professional interest in specific aspects of organizational aesthetics and aesthetic ways of knowing organization(al) life. Fourth, Stockholm University's School of Business (2007) has a research program on arts and business (fields of flow) led by Pierre Guillet de Monthoux. They express the creative disillusionment, mentioned earlier, asserting, "For a long time, business administration has turned to science with respect to learning about life in organizations and enterprises. We wish, however, to investigate the role of art in enterprise and organizing."

Continuing Management Education With Arts-Based Learning Programming

In addition to the formal postsecondary management education institutions noted above and reported in Appendix C, there are a number of programs (versus entire institutions) that are focusing on continuing management education by integrating arts-based learning into their programming (see Appendix D). It should be noted that these two institutional delivery methods mentioned in Appendices C and D are only the proverbial *tip of the iceberg* in terms of how the practice of arts-based learning is occurring. In fact, much of the practice is being carried out by entrepreneurial individuals with consultancies (see Nissley, 2002). While these individuals constitute a majority of the market in terms of the provision of arts-based learning continuing management education, their coverage is beyond the scope of this chapter.

Leading business schools worldwide are adding arts-based learning programs to their curriculum. First, Wharton (at the University of Pennsylvania, United States) has a compulsory MBA workshop "Leadership Through the Arts," facilitated by the noted dance company Pilobolus. Similarly, McGill (Canada) University's MBA students participate in a course titled, "The Art of Leadership," taught by distinguished scholar, Dr. Nancy Adler. In the course, McGill MBA students spend 3 weekends exploring all forms of the arts and reflecting on their personal experiences to tap into their leadership potential. Second, at the Massachusetts Institute of Technology (MIT), three of the 2003/2004 Sloan leadership courses had arts-based components, including "Unconventional Leadership: A Performing Advantage" and "Leadership as Acting: Performing Henry V." In addition, The School of the Museum of Fine Arts (SMFA, 2007) in Boston, has begun offering a unique, studio-based visual arts workshop designed in partnership with MIT's Sloan School of Management and developed especially for business leaders. The intensive, hands-on workshop utilizes the SMFA's unique interdisciplinary approach to stimulate new and creative ways of thinking and problem solving while utilizing the primary communication and teamwork skills essential in business. Third, in the University of Chicago's required Leadership Exploration and Development course, MBAs write, produce, and showcase a film. Similarly, the University of Chicago's Executive Education programming offers a course titled, "Leadership as Performance Art," taught by distinguished professor, Harry Davis. Through the lens of theater, this program engages participants with perspectives and skills necessary to become more authentic *actors* in connecting to diverse audiences as well as more powerful *directors* in bringing forth the talents of others within their organizations.

In addition to both the formal post secondary management education institutions noted above and reported in Appendix C, and the programs that are focusing on continuing management education by integrating arts-based learning into their programming noted in Appendix D, a couple of unique hybrid programs have risen to the top in North America and Europe (also noted in Appendix D). First, the U.K.'s arts and business's creative development (2007) programming brings the unique experience of the arts into a business context, by focusing on stimulating imaginative and innovative thinking. They do this through learning activities (e.g., teambuilding, communication training, leadership development, problem solving, etc.), change programs, and the creation of imaginative events. Tim Stockil was the founder of arts and business's arts-based learning programming, and a pioneer of arts-based learning in continuing management education throughout the United Kingdom. Similarly, in North America, the Creativity Connection (2007), born from the Arts and Business Council of the Americans for the Arts, and led by Harvey Seifter, helps corporations to surface creativity through high-quality arts-based learning programs that are designed to foster creative thinking, enhance organizational learning, and strengthen employee skills in critical areas such as collaboration, conflict resolution, change management, intercultural communication, and public performance.

Communities of Practice

Networked communities of practice have sprung up over the past 5 years (see Appendix E), in response to the globalization of arts-based learning, and the availability of technology to enable active participation across great divides. Most notable, AACORN, the Arts, Aesthetics, Creativity, and Organization Research Network (2007), was founded to develop and promote the field of organizational aesthetics (broadly defined). It connects a global network of individuals. Similarly, but more geographically focused in the southern hemisphere (in Asia Pacific and Australia), The Creative Skills Training Council (2007) is an online community of creative practitioners made up of business executives, academics, designers, artists, behavioral, and cognitive scientists involved in advancing the practice of creative skills training in business, organizations and government through arts-based processes and creativity tools and systems.

In this section, the literature (research and practice-based) and vehicles (conferences, institutions, communities of practice, and formal management education programming) that enable arts-based learning in continuing management education were presented and examined. Next, the reader is presented with a single case/portrait (e.g., Lawrence-Lightfoot & Davis, 2002) of arts-based learning in continuing management education, at Canada's Banff Centre for Continuing Education. The Banff Centre is offered as an outstanding example of arts-based learning in continuing management education, and affords the reader insights to the practice of arts-based learning in continuing management education.

THE BANFF CENTRE

Founded in 1933 by the University of Alberta, Department of Extension, with a grant from the U.S.-based Carnegie Foundation, The Banff Center began with a single course in drama. Its success generated additional arts programs and the Centre became known as the Banff School of Fine Arts in 1935. While arts programming continued to grow and flourish, management programs were introduced in 1954. The Banff Centre is all about *inspiring creativity*. Today, The Banff Centre is recognized as one of the world's premier centres for creativity.

ART-INSPIRED LEADERSHIP DEVELOPMENT

For over a half-century, the Banff Centre has conducted management and leadership development programming, making it one of Canada's first centres for leadership development. No where else in the world does an arts education and leadership development organization coexist, as does The Banff Centre. For over a half-century, The Banff Centre's Leadership Development Programs have capitalized on this relationship—learning from what artists have to offer leaders and their development. Not only is The Banff Centre one of Canada's oldest and most venerable institutions for leadership development, it is also the world's pioneer in arts-inspired creative leadership development, where arts-based learning informs the design and delivery of all of their leadership development programming. Here arts and leadership intersect in the multidisciplinary environment of The Banff Centre. As Canada's premier center for creativity, the The Banff Centre has come to understand how artists and artistic process can inform, and benefit, the development of leaders and the practice of leadership. This arts-based learning approach to continuing management education/leadership development at The Banff Centre makes the center unique, unlike any other leadership development institution in North America, and possibly the world.

A LAB SPACE DESIGNED TO ENABLE THE INTERSECTION OF ARTS AND BUSINESS

Laboratories, by definition, are spaces and resources dedicated to creativity and innovation. The Leadership Learning Lab at The Banff Centre has a mandate similar to a traditional laboratory: generating creative ideas and innovative solutions—to continuously improve the Centre's Leadership Development programming. The lab's discoveries— about how to creatively support the process of leadership development— are now a regular feature in the leadership programs offered by the The Banff Centre.

Inspired by the need to develop better leaders, located among a wealth of artists working in a variety of disciplines, and able to take advantage of facilities and tools designed for those disciplines, the lab looks to the arts to help shape creative ideas into program innovations. The Leadership Learning Lab is surely an innovative structure to facilitate leadership development program development. The lab serves programming innovation in three principle ways.

Thought Leader Forums

First, Thought Leader Forums provide an opportunity for open dialogue on issues of importance in today's complex business world. These forums help anchor program content development, to ensure that The Banff Centre's programming is focused on the right content—what leaders need to be focusing on in their organizations. Thought Leader Forums are events that bring together business leaders, executives, Banff Centre faculty, and alumni in order to engage in discussion and dialogue of a current leadership topic or issue. The process of inquiry for the topic/ issue at hand is facilitated through various artistic mediums. For example, Thought Leader Forums have included:

- An artful awakening: the practice of artful reflection forum
- The leader as designer: a forum to explore how the future is created
- The art of developing leaders

- The voice of leadership: power, influence, and authenticity through communications
- Ethical governance—creating a climate of corporate integrity: creative inquiry through the theatre arts
- Leading for creativity and innovation: creative inquiry through the visual arts

Leadership Arts Workshops

The second way in which the Leadership Learning Lab brings new ideas into programs is through Leadership Arts Workshops. Here, artists, facilitators, and business people are invited to participate in hands-on collaborative work centered on a particular artistic medium. These workshops afford the opportunity to explore how the arts can inform our understanding of organization life and leadership development. Leadership Arts Workshops are a developmental opportunity for the community of practice of the facilitators of arts-based learning in Leadership Development. The workshops afford these facilitators an opportunity to join a network of like-minded individuals and learn new and creative facilitation techniques, as well as provide an opportunity to engage in professional development by a sharing of experience, ideas, and practices with a group of peers. For example, Leadership Arts Workshops have included:

- Powerful expression: creative writing for creative leaders
- Advancing the practice of leadership through poetry and creative writing
- Exploring the practice of leadership through opera
- Advancing the practice of leadership through movement and dance
- Advancing the practice of leadership through jazz music
- Advancing the practice of leadership through the medium of mask

The Leadership Arts Ensemble

In addition to Thought Leader Forums and Leadership Arts Workshops, The Leadership Learning Lab also has created an innovation incubator—The Leadership Arts Ensemble. This is a group of leadership development staff, faculty, creativity facilitators, and Banff Centre artists. The ensemble works collaboratively in the Leadership Learning Lab environment to explore, test, and define connections among leadership, artistic mediums, and creative process. Some of the key activities and initiatives of the Ensemble have included:

- Advancing the practice of creative leadership by working with and inventing artistic process for application within Leadership Development and other areas of programming within The Banff Centre (e.g., Mountain Culture and the Arts);
- Developing metaphor consciousness and sensibility;
- Observing and recording arts-based learning processes that contribute to new knowledge and greater understanding of Leadership Development; and
- Providing space and processes for developing Leadership Development Facilitators who are able to engage in arts-based learning.

Innovating Arts-Based Learning

The Leadership Learning Lab essentially serves as The Banff Centre's Research and Development function. The lab develops and executes a research agenda that explores the interconnections of the arts, nature, and leadership, integrating the ideas into program innovation in leadership development. The lab's research agenda is framed by three focus areas:

1. Applied Research: Using an action research approach, the Leadership Learning Lab focuses on a variety of known and emergent processes to explore how the arts and nature can inform the practice of developing leaders.

2. Program Evolution: Applied research findings inform the ongoing evolution of The Banff Centre's public and customized leadership development programs in two respects: first, through the ongoing integration of new processes and concepts into existing programs, and second, through the development of entirely new offerings to the existing suite of programs.

3. New Product Development: Applied research also identifies opportunities for developing unique new product and service offerings, as well as new opportunities for value-added work with existing and new clients.

Much applied research has been conducted at The Banff Centre, led by Colin Funk, the Director of Creative Programming, (e.g., Force & Funk, 2005; Woodward & Funk, 2004). And, outside researchers have begun conducting research at the Centre, seeking to better understand their unique approach to arts-based learning in continuing management education/leadership development (e.g., Lewis, 2006; Webber, 2007).

SUMMARY

Management education is under increasing criticism, from educators and learners, for under emphasizing the creative skills that leaders and managers require for coping with a rapidly changing and unpredictable global business and social environment. As this chapter shows, there's a growing recognition by management educators that many of these skills can be found in those creative arts that have typically existed outside the business school or field of continuing management education (Ashkanasy, 2006). This creative disillusionment with traditional management education, turned arts-inspired possibility, is being expressed in mainstream management education literature. For example, Pink (2004) provocatively suggested in the *Harvard Business Review*, "An arts degree is now perhaps the hottest credential in the world of business." And, Adler's (2006) *Academy of Management Education and Learning Journal* article heralded, "The time seems right for this cross-fertilization of the arts and leadership." She noted that the twenty-first century yearns for a leadership of possibility, and that we're beginning to see a confluence between the best skills of business and those of the artistic community in service of the largest aims of humanity.

The intersection of arts and business has given rise to the innovation of arts-based learning in management education. Simply, arts-based learning offers management education an *other* way of making sense of management challenges. While one may have dismissed the emerging practice five years ago, suggesting it was merely imaginative or a creative anomaly. Today, one can say, the educators who have fueled this movement in continuing management education, have truly transformed imagination, creative ideas, and have launched an innovation—arts-based learning.

ACKNOWLEDGEMENTS

The author would like to acknowledge the following individuals, who have acted as friends, mentors, and have encouraged my work and my living of the artful life: Dave Schwandt, Mary Jo Hatch, Peter Vaill, Justin Simmons and Amy Bennett, Steve Taylor, David Barry, Laura Brearley, Lotte Darso, Chuck Palus, Stan Gryskiewicz, John O'Brien, Bastiaan

Heemsbergen, Colin Funk, and especially—my wife, Elise, and our girls Isabel and Meredith. The editorial encouragement of Bob DeFillippi and Charles Wankel were invaluable.

APPENDIX A

Select Emerging Models Describing the Intersection of Arts and Business

Authors/Citation	Model	Description
Austin & Devin (2003)	**Artful Making**	Austin and Devin describe the arts and business intersection, suggesting that managers should look to collaborative artists rather than to more traditional management models if they want to create economic value in this new century. They call this approach artful making. "Artful," because it derives from the theory and practice of collaborative art and requires and artist-like attitude from managers and team members. "Making," because it requires that you conceive of your work as altering or combining materials into a form, for a purpose.
Darso (2004)	**Arts-in-Business**	Darso describes the arts and business intersection, documenting four ways in which businesses use the arts: (1) decoration – the artwork in lobbies/corridors, and the picture on office walls (e.g., corporate art); (2) entertainment—bringing the arts/performances into the office space (e.g., giving employee tickets to arts events); (3) instrument—when business uses the arts as an instrument for management/leadership development (e.g., teambuilding, communication skills development, etc.); and (4) strategic transformation—when the business integrates the arts in areas such as vision and values, creativity and innovation, branding, and marketing.
Davis & McIntosh (2005)	**Artistic Flow** (vs. Economic Flow)	The authors create a dichotomous understanding of arts and business, and assert an other way of looking at business and management practice, which moves beyond the traditional focus upon the economic flow of business, and suggest that business also has an artistic flow. Specifically, they identify elements of artistic flow: artistic inputs such as imagination, artistic processes such as creating, and artistic outputs such as beauty. Such a redefinition of how we conceive of business has obvious implications for the practice of management education.
Hatch, Kostera, & Kozminski (2005)	**The Three Faces of Leadership:** Manager, Artist, and Priest	The authors demonstrate how business leaders use aesthetics, specifically, storytelling, dramatizing, and myth-making, to effectively lead their organizations; and, thus, show the faces of the artist and priest alongside the technical and rational face of the manager.

APPENDIX B

Select Emerging Models Describing the Innovation of Arts-Based Learning in Management Education

Nissley (2004)	**Artful Creation**	Nissley describes five characteristics of "artful creations"— artforms made during arts-based learning.
		1. <u>Presentational knowledge/language</u>
		A means of representing knowing and expressing meaning, through expressive forms (e.g., visual images, drama, song, dance)—allowing us to see what we're thinking.
		2. <u>Mediated dialogue</u>
		The creation of an analog to mediate an inquiry into organizational life, where the analog acts as a means through which insights may be elicited.
		3. <u>Symbolic constructions that act as metaphorical representations</u>
		An approach that uses artlike representation (e.g., photos, sculpture, drawings) to elicit, reveal, and transform existing sensemaking frameworks.
		4. <u>Process of collaborative inquiry/cocreation</u>
		Using the process of artful creation for the development of shared sensemaking, where the artful creation is co-created by organization members and their inquiry is self-guided (socially constructed), not relying on expert interpretation.
		5. <u>Window to the unconscious</u>
		Engaging the artful inquiry process as a means to make hidden thoughts more discussable—where the artful creation acts as a vehicle for gaining insight by externalizing unconscious or tacit thinking.
Palus & Horth (2002)	**The Sensemaking Loop for Creative Leadership in Action**	Palus and Horth describe a sense making process which defines the essence of creative leadership. They define six creative competencies (strongly correlated with aesthetic sensibilities) that leaders use to engage in effective sense making. The competencies are:
		1. paying attention
		2. personalizing
		3. imaging
		4. serious play
		5. coinquiry
		6. crafting
Taylor & Ladkin (2007)	**Four Ideal Type Arts-Based Processes**	Taylor and Ladkin reviewed the literature on arts-based methods in development and change in organizations, and induced four different ideal type arts-based processes:
		1. skills transfer
		2. projective technique
		3. illustration of essence
		4. spiritual development

Appendix B continues on next page.

APPENDIX B CONTINUED

Kerr (2006)	Artful Learning Wave Trajectory Model	The artful learning wave trajectory model is a model of artful experiences, bridging from any one art-work event to another, like the points in a trajectory, linking an individual's perceptions of artful experiences and their appropriated benefits. The points are: capacity, artful event, increased artful capability, and finally the application and action of the capability to have product, through being artful and becoming an artful being.

APPENDIX C

Formal Postsecondary Management Education Institutions

The Banff Centre, Leadership Development Program
Banff, Canada
www.banffleadership.ca
Key Leadership: Nick Nissley and Colin Funk

Copenhagen Business School, Centre for Art and Leadership
Copenhagen, Denmark
http://uk.cbs.dk/forskning_viden/institutter_centre/institutter/ckl
Key Leadership: Ole Fogh Kirkeby

University of Essex, Essex Management Centre (Art of Management & Organization Conference)
Essex, England
http://www.essex.ac.uk/afm/emc/index.shtm
Key Leadership: Ian King and Ceri Watkins

Hartwick Institute
New York, USA
http://www.hartwickinstitute.org/
Key Leadership: John K. Clemens

Nomad University
Åbo, Finland
http://www.nurope.eu/oases.html
Key Leadership: Bengt Kristensson Uggla

Research Unit on Communication, Organizational Learning and Aesthetics (RUCOLA)
Trento, Italy
http://www.unitn.it/rucola/index.htm
Key Leadership: Antonio Strati

Stockholm University, School of Business, Fields of Flow (Arts and Business Research)
Stockholm, Sweden
http://www.fek.su.se/inst/faculty/EnProgram.asp?id=13
Key Leadership: Pierre Guillet de Monthoux

APPENDIX D

Continuing Management Education With Arts-Based Learning Programming

Arts and Business, U.K.
London, England
http://www.aandb.org.uk/render.aspx?siteID=1&navIDs=1,185,319
Key Leadership: Tim Stockil

The Banff Centre, Leadership Development Program
Banff, Canada
www.banffleadership.ca
Key Leadership: Nick Nissley and Colin Funk

Center for Creative Leadership
Greensboro, North Carolina, USA
http://www.ccl.org/leadership/index.aspx

University of Chicago
Chicago, USA
http://www.chicagoexec.net/chicago.nsf/Program.html?OpenNavigator&id=400
Key Leadership: Harry Davis

Cranfield University
Cranfield, England
http://www.som.cranfield.ac.uk/som/executive/course/overview.asp?id=203
Key Leadership: Diana Theodores and Josie Sutcliffe

Creativity Connection
New York, USA
http://ww3.artsusa.org/private_sector_affairs/arts_and_business_council/programs/
creativity_connection/default_sales.asp
Key Leadership: Harvey Seifter

Massachusetts Institute of Technology/Boston School of the Museum of Fine Arts
Boston, USA
http://www.smfa.edu/News_Exhibitions/News/
MBA_meet_MFA_SMFA_offers_MIT_Sloan_students_experimental_workshop.asp

McGill University
Montreal Canada
http://www.mcgill.ca/newsroom/news/?ItemID=13415
Key Leadership: Nancy Adler

APPENDIX E

Select Arts-Based Learning and Management Education Communities of Practice

Arts, Aesthetics, Creativity, and Organization Research Network (AACORN)
http://www.aacorn.net/

Creative Skills Training Council (CSTC)
http://www.cstc-apa.com/

REFERENCES

Adler, N. (2006). The arts and leadership: Now that we can do anything, what will we do? *Academy of Management Learning & Education, 5*(4), 486-499.

Arts, Aesthetics, Creativity and Organization Research Network. (2007). *AACORN Web page.* Retrieved January 15, 2008, from http://www.aacorn.net/

Arts and Business, U.K. (2007). *Arts and Business Web page.* Retrieved January 15, 2008, from http://www.aandb.org.uk/render.aspx?siteID =1&navIDs=1,185,319

Art of Management and Organization Conference (2007). *Art of Management and Organization Conference Web page.* Retrieved January 15, 2008, from http://www.essex.ac.uk/afm/emc/fourth_art_of_management_and_org.shtm

Ashkanasy, N. M. (2006). Special section: Art and design in management education. *Academy of Management Learning and Education, 5*(4), 484-485.

Austin, R., & Devin, L. (2003). *Artful making: What managers need to know about how artists work.* Upper Saddle River, NJ: Prentice Hall.

Barry, D. (1994). Making the invisible visible: Using analogically-based methods to surface the organizational unconscious. *Organizational Development Journal, 12*(4), 37-48.

Beckwith, A. (2003). Improving business performance: The potential of arts in training. *Industrial and Commercial Training, 35*(5), 207-209.

Boyle, M., & Ottensmeyer, E. (2005). Solving business problems through the creative power of the arts: Catalyzing change at Unilever. *Journal of Business Strategy, 26*(5), 14-21.

Burrell, L. (2007). A larger language for business: Poet David Whyte on conversational leadership. *Harvard Business Review, 85*(5), 28.

Buswick, T., Creamer, A., & Pinard, M. (2004). *(Re)educating for leadership: How the arts can improve business.* Arts and Business Report. January 15, 2008, from http://www.aandb.org.uk/Asp/uploadedFiles/File/ REI_Re_Educating_for_Leadership_Sept_04.pdf

Chalofsky, N. (1996). A new paradigm for learning in organizations. *Human Resource Development Quarterly, 7*(3), 287-293.

Champoux, J. (1999). Film as a teaching resource. *Journal of Management Inquiry, 8*(2), 206-217.

Champoux, J. (2000). *Management: Using film to visualize principles and practices.* Cincinnati, OH: South-Western College.

Clarke, T., & Mangham, I. (2004). From dramaturgy to theater as technology: The case of corporate theater. *Journal of Management Studies, 40*, 37-59.

Cohen, C. (1998). How literature may be used to assist in the education of managers. *The Learning Organization, 5*(1), 6-14.

Corsun, D., Young, C., McManus, A., & Erdem, M. (2006). Overcoming managers' perceptual shortcuts through improvisational theater games. *Journal of Management Development, 25*(4), 298-315.

Copenhagen Business School, Centre for Art and Leadership. (2007). *Centre for Art and Leadership Web Page.* January 15, 2008, from http://uk.cbs.dk/ forskning_viden/institutter_centre/institutter/ckl

Creativity Connection. (2007). *Creativity Connection Web Page.* January 15, 2008, from http://ww3.artsusa.org/private_sector_affairs/arts_and_business_council/programs/creativity_connection/default_sales.asp

Creative Skills Training Council. (2007). *Creative Skills Training Council Asia Pacific and Australia Web Page.* January 15, 2008, from http://www.cstc-apa.com/

Darso, L. (2004). *Artful creation: Learning-tales of arts-in-business.* Frederiksberg, Denmark: Samfundslitteratur.

Davis, S., & McIntosh, D. (2005). *The art of business: Make all your work a work of art.* San Francisco: Berrett-Koehler.

Denhardt, R. B., & Denhardt, J. V. (2006). *The dance of leadership: The art of leading in business, government, and society.* Armonk, NY: M. E. Sharpe.

Di Ciantis, C. (1995). *Using an art technique to facilitate leadership development.* Greensboro, NC: Center for Creative Leadership.

Ferris, W. (2002). Theater tools for team building: How an improvisational play got one software team back on track. *Harvard Business Review, 80*(12), 24-25.

Force, J., & Funk, C. (2005, December). *Navigating complexity: Understanding organizational complexity through interactive theatre.* Paper presented at APROS 11 (Asia-Pacific Researchers in Organization Studies), Melbourne, Australia.

Gibb, S. (2004). Arts-based training in management development: The use of improvisational theatre. *Journal of Management Development, 23*(8), 741-750.

Gibb. S. (2005). Imagination, creativity, and HRD: An aesthetic perspective. *Human Resource Development Review, 3*(1), 53-74.

Halpern, B., & Lubar, K. (2004). *Leadership presence: Dramatic techniques to reach out, motivate, and inspire.* New York: Gotham.

Hatch, M., Kostera, M., & Kozminski, A. (2005). *The three faces of leadership: Manager, artist, priest.* Malden, MA: Blackwell.

Heemsbergen, B. (2004). *The leader's brain: How are you using the other 95%?* Victoria, British Columbia: Trafford.

Initiative for the Development of Intercultural Relations Through the Arts (2007). *IDRIART Web Page.* January 15, 2008, from http://www.borl.org/eng/ljudje_3.html

Johansson, F. (2004). *The Medici Effect: Breakthrough insights at the intersection of ideas, concepts, and cultures.* Boston: Harvard Business School Press.

Jones, M. (2006). *Artful leadership: Awakening the commons of the imagination.* Victoria, British Columbia: Trafford.

Kerr, C. (2006). The learning wave trajectory model: exploring the nature and benefit of an artful management education learning process. In DiMilia, L. and Kennedy, J. (Eds.). *Proceedings of the 20th ANZAM Conference,* pp. 1-20. Rockhampton, Queensland, Australia.

Lawrence-Lightfoot, S., & Davis, J. (2002). *The art and science of portraiture.* San Francisco: Jossey-Bass.

Lewis, M. (2006). *Nurturing the spark: Development of creative leaders within the certificate program at the Banff Centre.* Unpublished master's thesis, Royal Roads University, Victoria, British Columbia.

Linstead, S. (2006). Exploring culture with The Radio Ballads: Using aesthetics to facilitate change. *Management Decision, 44*(4), 474-485.

Linstead, S., & Höpfl, H. (2000). *The aesthetics of organization.* London: SAGE.

Marsick, V. (1990). Altering the paradigm for theory building and research in human resource development. *Human Resource Development Quarterly, 1,* 5-24.

Mirvis, P., Ayas, K., & Roth, G. (2003). *To the desert and back: The story of one of the most dramatic business transformations on record.* San Francisco: Jossey-Bass.

Monks, K., Barker, P., & Mhanachain, N. (2001). Drama as an opportunity for learning and development. *Journal of Management Development, 20*(5), 414-423.

Morgan, G. (1986). *Images of organization.* Newbury Park, CA: SAGE.

Morgan, G. (1993). *Imaginization: The art of creative management.* Newbury Park, CA: SAGE.

Nissley, N. (2002). Art-based learning in management education. In B. DeFillippi & C. Wankel (Eds.), *Rethinking management education in the 21st century* (pp. 27-61). Greenwich, CT: Information Age Press.

Nissley, N. (2004). The "artful creation" of positive anticipatory imagery in appreciative inquiry: Understanding the "art of" appreciative inquiry as aesthetic discourse. In D. Cooperrider & M. Avital (Eds.), *Advances in appreciative inquiry: Constructive discourse and human organization* (pp. 283-307). New York: Elsevier.

Nissley, N., Taylor, S., & Houden, L. (2004). The politics of performance in organizational theatre-based training and interventions. *Organization Studies, 25*(5), 817-839.

Nomad University. (2007). *Nomad University Web Page.* January 15, 2008, from http://www.nurope.eu/oases.html

Palus, C., & Horth, D. (2002). *The leader's edge: Six creative competencies for navigating complex challenges.* San Francisco: Jossey-Bass.

Palus, C., & Horth, D. (2001). *Visual Explorer: Picturing approaches to complex challenges.* Greensboro, NC: CCL Press.

Pink, D. (2004, February). The MFA is the new MBA. The HBR list: Breakthrough Ideas for 2004. *Harvard Business Review.*

Research Unit on Communication, Organizational Learning, and Aesthetics (2007). *RUCOLA Web Page.* Retrieved January 15, 2008, from http://www.unitn.it/rucola/index.htm

Schein, E. (2001). The role of art and the artist. *Reflections* (Journal of the Society for Organizational Learning), *4*(2), 81-83.

School of the Museum for Fine Arts. (2007). MBA, meet MFA: SMFA offers MIT Sloan students experimental workshop. Retrieved January 15, 2008, from http://www.smfa.edu/News_Exhibitions/News/ MBA_meet_MFA_SMFA_offers_MIT_Sloan_students_experimental_worksho p.asp

Seifter, H., & Buswick, T. [Guest Editors] (2005). Arts-based learning for business [special edition]. *Journal of Business Strategy, 26*(5), 1-84.

Strati, A. (1992). Aesthetic understanding of organizational life. *Academy of Management Review, 17*(3), 568-581.

Strati, A. (1999). *Organization and aesthetics.* London: SAGE.

Stockholm University, School of Business, Fields of Flow (2007). *Fields of Flow Web Page.* Retrieved January 15, 2008, from http://www.fek.su.se/inst/faculty/ EnProgram.asp?id=13

Taylor, S., & Ladkin, D. (2007). *Explaining arts-based methods in development and change in organizations*. Unpublished manuscript, Taylor (Worcester Polytechnic University) and Ladkin (Exeter University).

Taylor, S., & Hanson, H. (2005). Finding form: Looking at the field of organizational aesthetics. *Journal of Management Studies, 42*(6), 1211-32.

The arts in business and society. (2001). *Reflections* [special edition]. *The Society for Organizational Learning Journal, 2*(4), 1-84.

The art of good teaching. (1997). Special issue. *Journal of Management Education, 21*(4), 443-524.

Vaill, P. (1974, May). *Management as a performing art*. Presented at the Commencement Address, School of Government and Business Administration, George Washington University, Washington, DC.

Vaill, P. (1989). *Managing as a performing art: New ideas for a world of chaotic change*. San Francisco: Jossey-Bass.

VanGundy, A., & Naiman, L. (2003). *Orchestrating collaboration at work: Using improves, storytelling, and other arts to improve teamwork*. San Francisco: Jossey-Bass.

Webber, B. (2007). *The application of curatorial practice to organizational leadership*. Unpublished master's thesis, Royal Roads University, Victoria, British Columbia.

Woodward, B., & Funk, C. (2004, July). *The aesthetics of leadership development: A pedagogical model for developing leaders*. Paper presented at the The Art of Management and Organization Conference. Paris.

CHAPTER 9

LIFELONG LEARNING FOR MANAGERS—THE BUSINESS OF EXECUTIVE EDUCATION

A Case Study of a Small University Provider

Steven Maranville and Wil Uecker

Lifelong learning for corporate managers is big business. Some estimates of the nondegree executive education market are as large as $16.5 billion. If that is correct, university providers have only a tiny fraction of the total market. The lure of such a large market, however, is irresistible to business schools in their quest for revenue to enable them to compete for the best faculty and students.

The management education literature reflects the rapid growth in executive education programs over the past decade. This literature, though, mostly reflects the perspective of large, university providers. There are only a few universities whose executive education operations achieve gross revenues in the $25 to $100 million range, the vast majority of university providers have gross revenues under $5 million.

University and Corporate Innovations in Lifelong Learning, pp. 213–236

Some of the challenges facing small university providers are the same challenges with which large university providers must grapple. Yet, small, university providers also encounter other challenges unique to their competitive situation. This study explores the challenges facing small university providers of executive education through the experiences of the Jessie H. Jones Graduate School of Management at Rice University.

INTRODUCTION

Lifelong learning for managers in the corporate world is big business. *Business Week*, which periodically ranks providers of executive education based upon surveys of companies, reported that the companies surveyed in 2003 spent approximately $210 million at business schools and nonuniversity affiliated organizations that provide executive education courses. During the same period, university and nonuniversity providers of executive education reported revenues of approximately $662 million. (Merritt, 2003, p. 88). Overall spending on corporate training and education for managers may be much higher. In 1999, *Business Week* reported that the total for U.S. corporations alone was $16.5 billion (Reingold, Schneider, & Capell, 1999). If that is correct, university providers have only a tiny fraction of the total market.

The lure of such a large market is irresistible to business schools in their quest for revenue to enable them to compete for the best faculty and students. As the top ranked university providers of executive education illustrate, there are only a few universities whose executive education operations achieve gross revenues in the $25 to $100 million range, the vast majority of university providers have gross revenues under $5 million (Merritt, 2003).

The management education literature reflects the rapid growth in executive education programs over the past decade. This literature is mainly concerned with pedagogical matters, rather than the operation of executive education programs. Moreover, this literature tends to reflect the perspective of large, university providers. Although the executive education market is intensely competitive and offers some notable advantages to large university providers with global reputations for quality education, the above market demand and trends creating that demand suggest opportunity for small university providers that carefully define their market niche and build appropriate institutional capabilities.

Some of the challenges facing small university providers are the same challenges with which large university providers must grapple. Yet, small, university providers also encounter other challenges unique to their competitive situation. What are the challenges facing small university providers of executive education? To address this question, this chapter describes the landscape of the executive education marketplace and the experiences of a small university business school, the Jessie H. Jones Graduate School of Management at Rice University, in competing in the executive education arena.

SCOPE OF EXECUTIVE EDUCATION AND ITS PROVIDERS

The pace of globalization and technological change has hastened the competitive intensity of virtually all industries. Corporations are in the hunt for sources of competitive advantage that will maintain some degree of sustainability and provide a springboard for the next generation of competitive strategy. As resources that once brought competitive advantage become more widely distributed and commonly possessed, corporations have realized that reinvention is vital. However, the ability to create new products, markets, and business models requires a new organizational perspective that comes only from new knowledge. Therefore, corporations are employing learning strategies to make sense of, and take advantage of, competitive uncertainty (Dulworth & Bordonaro, 2005).

Lifelong learning has, therefore, become a practical reality of employment, and executive education is an essential form of lifelong learning that fits within the framework developed by Holmes (2003, p. 161) and is consistent with his view that the purpose of lifelong learning is for career enhancement. Without it, career progression would be impeded in many circumstances. Executive education is more than knowledge accumulation. It is transformational in building the ability to lead and work with others.

While individuals must constantly learn new skills to remain competitive in the work place as well as to enrich their personal lives, all of which fall under the broad umbrella of lifelong learning, the focus of this chapter is on education for leadership development. We do not address the vast array of training programs designed to teach technical skills, or language skills, or to meet compliance requirements for health and safety. We do not include programs for personal enrichment such as those dealing with art, literature, or leisure activities. We also exclude all degree programs including executive MBA programs. Our focus is on nondegree programs designed to develop individuals' abilities to lead and work with others in an organizational context.

There are a number of suppliers of executive education competing for a share of the executive education market. In addition to universities, the competitors include consulting firms, corporate universities, and human resources departments, and individuals, some of whom are faculty competing with their own universities! These competitors have different business models and compete at different price points.

Corporate universities are common in large corporations. Some may be virtual organizations staffed by a small number of individuals who work with human resources to conduct needs assessments and organize training programs to meet assessed needs, while others may employ hundreds of people and have their own facilities. Their close and frequent contact with their firm's executive leadership and their intimate knowledge of their firm's operations and strategies make them formidable competitors to universities (Anderson, 2001). If they outsource to a university, it is typically to one of the universities that appears perennially on the *Business Week* ranking of top university providers of executive education. As one chief learning officer explained, "If you get a bad result with a known brand, the consequences are not as severe as getting a bad result going with a lesser known brand."

Some of the outsourcing practiced by corporate universities and human resources departments is to individuals with a particular area of expertise. Individuals typically operate as independent contractors providing short programs on the client's premises. Because they have very little overhead, they are the least expensive provider. One unfortunate aspect, at least from the perspective of the university, of this practice is that university faculties are a prime target for outsourcing to individuals. Since faculty members are allowed under their contracts to engage in a limited amount of consulting or outside teaching, they can be hired directly by companies to provide executive teaching. Universities have policies that prohibit conflict of interest behavior on the part of their faculty so that a faculty member offering a program for university executive education is not permitted to offer the same program directly to a client; however, enforcement is difficult because programs are never quite identical from client to client and faculty have no incentive to reveal their consulting clients. Universities may even compete with each other for faculty to teach executive education. Duke Corporate Education, for example, promotes as one of its competitive advantages that it can draw upon faculty from around the world to staff its executive education programs (Educators, 2006).

Consulting firms have certain advantages over universities in providing executive education. Education and training can be integrated within the context of a consulting engagement to enable the client to affect the changes being recommended. Some consulting firms such as Mercer Delta have made education and training a significant portion of their product offering (Swain, 2006). Consultants are often perceived by the client company as having more practical knowledge than faculty enabling them to offer education and training that is more applicable to the work environment of client employees. Because consultants spend a great deal of time with their clients, they are also perceived as having greater knowledge of the client's business which they can translate into more relevant material for education and training. Unlike universities, consulting firms are also prepared to follow-up with educational programs to assist the organization in deploying talent, as well as to identify under utilized talent. It is difficult, if not impossible, for universities to adopt the consulting firm model for executive education. Consulting firms make money by leveraging the work of a few highly paid senior consultants with many lesser paid junior consultants. Universities are not staffed to leverage the work of faculty and faculty members have neither the time, because of research and teaching commitments, nor the experience to manage consulting engagements.

The advantage of the university is the perceived independence that it brings to the client as well as the deep knowledge of particular disciplines that its faculty possesses. The university does not have a stake in the outcome of its educational programs in the way that consultants, whose educational programs are part of the implementation process for a course of action recommended by the consultant, do. University faculty, by virtue of their research and teaching activities also develop depth in a discipline that consultants, whose work may cause then to have greater breadth of knowledge across disciplines, do not. The university campus can also be an advantage. It is important for the effectiveness of an educational program to take participants out of their work environment where day-to-day responsibilities can interrupt the educational experience and pull them back into their work routines. While such separation can be achieved by going off-site to a hotel or conference center, participants seem to enjoy returning to the campus environment. Many of the prominent university providers of executive education have built housing facilities on campus exclusively for participants of their executive education programs.

EXECUTIVE EDUCATION AT RICE UNIVERSITY

For a small university, competing in the executive education market is particularly daunting. With a small faculty, the ability to meet the needs of large, multinational clients is limited. With few alumni in high level corporate positions, the small provider often competes unsuccessfully with large providers, even in their immediate geographic region.

This chapter presents a case study of the lessons learned by Rice University as it has attempted through experimentation to adapt to the challenges of the executive education market. Rice University is a small, prestigious, private university in a major metropolitan area, Houston, Texas. Houston is home to many of the world's largest oil and gas exploration companies and oil field service companies. It also has one of the largest medical centers in the world.

The Jessie H. Jones Graduate School of Management is one of three professional schools at Rice University and offers a full-time MBA. program, an executive MBA program, an evening professional MBA program, and executive education programs. One of the authors served as associate dean for executive education in the Jones Graduate School of Management from July 1997 to January 2005, a period of rapid growth within the school. This period spanned the dot com bubble and bust, the September 11 terrorist attacks, oil prices going from less than $20 a barrel to almost $50 a barrel, and the Enron collapse. Rice's revenues, from nondegree executive education programs during this period, more than doubled but remained well below the $5 million mark.

Although executive education launched a highly successful executive MBA program during this time period, the focus here is on the effort to expand the nondegree executive education offerings of the school. The nondegree programs offered by executive education during the period studied included traditional open enrollment programs, custom tailored programs for large corporate clients, and industry specific consortium programs in healthcare and energy. The latter are a hybrid of custom and open enrollment programs featuring industry specific content and sponsoring organizations which provide advice on curriculum, send participants, and, in some cases, contribute instructors.

The design of this case study is grounded in qualitative methods following the direction given by Stake (1998). Data has been collected through documents, interviews, and participant observation. Informants represented four categories of stakeholders: executives of corporations that sponsor participants, present and past participants, program administrators, and faculty who teach in Rice University's executive education programs. Efforts to accurately interpret this data have been facilitated by the use of multiple readers who are inside and outside the Rice Executive education program.

POSITIONING THE PROGRAM

The executive education market can be segmented in terms of program content and participant selection. Program content ranges from broad general management programs to focused content designed to build specific skills such as understanding financial statements. Program formats are either open enrollment or closed enrollment (Tirard, 2004).

Open enrollment programs are similar to degree programs in reflecting primarily the faculty's decisions of what to provide. Individuals attending open enrollment programs typically self-select and take advantage of company reimbursement programs for continuing education. The company has no input on program content and typically exercises little control on who may attend. Some open enrollment programs focus on skill development in particular areas such as negotiations. Others offer broader general management education.

Closed enrollment programs are open only to participants selected by the company to attend. They are generally referred to as custom programs, but in the chart below, a distinction is made between those that include problem-solving projects which lend greater focus to these programs than the more traditional custom program which emphasizes broader education for general management. In closed enrollment programs, the company has significant input into the curriculum design.

The challenge from the perspective of the provider of open enrollment programs is identifying what the market wants while at the same time effectively promoting what is being offered. To plan a series of open enrollment offerings requires commitments from faculty to prepare material and costly marketing activities. Faculty members know what they want to teach, but have little information on what the market wants. To retain continued faculty cooperation, however, administrators of

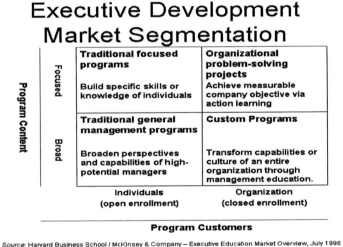

Figure 9.1.   Segmentation of the market based on customer and content.

executive education programs must not only be willing to gamble that what the faculty wants to teach will find a receptive market, but also be willing to fully compensate them for their efforts even if the number of program participants is not sufficient to cover costs.

Once faculty commitments are secured, brochures must be created, mailing lists purchased, Web sites updated, and staff must be educated to respond to inquiries from potential participants. These commitments to faculty and expenditures for marketing are made well in advance of the receipt of revenue. To cancel a program that has too few participants to cover program costs, risks alienating the faculty as well as participants who have registered. If participants, who have registered, are traveling from out of town, they may have purchased airline tickets and demand reimbursement. Consequently, our practice at Rice was to run open enrollment programs as planned in almost all cases even if all costs were not covered by registration fees.

Of course the upside of open enrollment programs is that once costs are covered, additional participant registration fees are almost pure profit. At Rice, we estimated that all costs including allocated overhead, was covered by the registration fees of approximately 15 participants and that we could cover out-of-pocket costs (faculty fees and the cost of course materials and food) with the fees of approximately 7 participants. While a few of Rice's programs consistently had enrollments in the mid-20s, most had enrollments close to the breakeven point with a number in the range from the breakeven point to the point of just covering out-of-pocket costs. While some schools are very successful with open enrollment program offerings that was not the experience at Rice during this period.

The content of open enrollment programs offered at Rice was typical of that offered at other schools. Topics ranged from general management to the development of specific skills such as negotiation skills or accounting and finance. Although content was similar, scheduling was different. To appeal to its local market, Rice had to offer shorter programs than schools that have a national and international market. Participants who have to travel a great distance to attend a program prefer to remain on site for at least a week before returning. In contrast, Rice's local participants were unwilling to take more than a few days away from their work to commute to Rice for executive education programs. Even Rice's general management program, the Rice program for managers, which was 11 days in length, was broken into 2 and 3 day segments over a 9 week period. Some of Rice's programs were scheduled in the evening to appeal to those who had difficulty getting time off from work to attend.

Attempts to schedule longer programs and attract participants from outside the Houston area failed. For example, an attempt to package the rice program for managers as a 2 week residential program drew only a handful of registrations from outside the local market and drew even less from the local market, forcing a painful cancellation of the program. Rice continues to rely on the short duration program format for open enrollment programs as is illustrated by open enrollment programs currently offered by the Jones Graduate School of Management at Rice University which can be found under the executive education tab at http://www.jonesgsm.rice.edu/jonesgsm/

The size of the local market was a major factor in Rice's struggle to achieve profitable levels of attendance in its open enrollment programs. Schools in the *Business Week* top 20 (Merritt, 2003) draw participants from around the world. However, the local market was the only viable alternative for Rice. Although Rice University is well known nationally and internationally, its reputation was based upon the quality of its undergraduate programs and outstanding research and scholarship in selected areas, principally in science and engineering, but not for business education and scholarship.

The focus on the local market for open enrollment programs had some advantages, however. Local participants did not require residential accommodations so there was no need to contract for or build such facilities—a huge expense and one that would require executive education to become involved in the hospitality industry, not a core competency. Many of the larger and better known universities offering executive education programs have such facilities. When the terrorist attacks of September 11, 2001 occurred, corporate travel was severely curtailed, and took months to recover, causing some of these larger programs with residential facilities to experience sharp drops in enrollment (Schneider & Hindo, 2001). Even less extreme events, e.g., an economic down turn, can trigger cutbacks in travel and expenditures for executive education, exposing those programs with high fixed costs to the risk of significant losses. Another advantage of appealing to the local market is that the burden of caring for participants is reduced. Since participants return to their homes after classes are over for the day, neither faculty or staff are needed for after class functions such as social events or study sessions.

To exploit its local market for open enrollment programs, Rice formed collaborative arrangements with other providers of professional education, particularly those that opened new market niches. An example of this type of arrangement for Rice was its program in healthcare management offered with the Baylor College of Medicine. Baylor offered continuing medical education for physicians to enable them to meet the requirements to maintain their medical licenses. By joining with Rice, Baylor could expand its offerings to include management education for healthcare professionals. For Rice, the association with Baylor provided the opportunity to adapt its management courses to healthcare. A critical factor in the success of healthcare management offerings was the ability to offer continuing medical education (CMEs) units for attending physicians. The Baylor College of Medicine could issue CMEs; Rice could not. Course content included negotiation and contracting in a managed care environment, leadership in healthcare, and trends in the healthcare market.

There were more challenges with the healthcare management program than expected. The first was finding qualified faculty. While Rice faculty members were good teachers of general management, none had experience in healthcare. Although many management issues are generic regardless of the organizational setting, participants invariably believe that their industry or profession is extremely unique. Physicians, perhaps more than most professionals, feel that only other physicians really understand healthcare. Consequently, it was not possible to simply ask our faculty to teach their subject matter using cases drawn from healthcare. In some cases, it was possible to pair a Rice faculty member with a physician to teach. In other cases, physicians with MBAs were recruited as instructors. Having two instructors for a class added costs. Because of their busy schedules, physicians were sometimes late in providing course materials for distribution to participants creating "rush" situations for the support staff.

Classes were scheduled in the evenings because feedback from physicians indicated that most could not attend during daytime working hours. Physician instructors also indicated that they were available only in the evenings. This schedule required that executive education staff go on a flex-time schedule so that there could be staff coverage in the evenings. Finally, the requirements for CMEs necessitated extensive and time consuming documentation by staff of program content, instructor qualifications, and participant attendance.

Although the initial enrollment in the healthcare management modules was encouraging, enrollment declined rapidly in subsequent offerings. Because the healthcare management program appealed primarily to physicians, the challenge of maintaining profitable enrollment levels was even greater than for conventional open enrollment programs. Other healthcare professionals, for example, nurses, had their own continuing education requirements that were different from CMEs and most were more price sensitive to program costs than physicians. As a consequence of declining enrollments, the program was discontinued after several offerings. Recently, healthcare offerings have been resumed and can be found along with other executive education offerings at the Web site above.

To address the challenge of sustainable levels of enrollment, a variation of open enrollment programs offered by some schools, including Rice, is the consortium open enrollment program. Such programs are sponsored by several firms that each commit to send a minimum number of participants, usually two or three. For universities, the company's commitment assures a critical mass which enables the university to sell additional seats in the class on a purely open enrollment basis with minimal risk of cancellation or loss. These programs tend to be industry focused to make it attractive for several firms within an industry to serve as sponsors. Sponsoring firms sometimes offer curriculum suggestions and may be a source of instructors to supplement university faculty who rarely have in-depth experience in a particular industry.

Given its location in Houston, Rice chose to launch a consortium program in the energy industry. With many large oil and oil field support companies in Houston, it was possible to recruit several that were willing to commit to sending two or three participants to each offering of the program for a period of time, usually a year. Companies typically renewed their commitment each year for several years. With an up-front commitment of participants that assured that the program would be offered, Rice advertised the program as an open enrollment program for additional participants. An incentive offered to sponsoring companies was registration fees that were somewhat less than participants who registered on a purely open enrollment basis paid.

Rice's energy management program faced challenges similar to those faced by the healthcare management program, but these challenges proved easier to surmount. The problem of finding suitable faculty was again a problem, but not as severe as in the healthcare management program. While regular Rice faculty had no experience in the industry, they could still be used to some extent because participants did not perceive the industry as being as unique with respect to management issues, as was the case in healthcare. To obtain faculty with in-depth experience in the industry, Rice was able to recruit recent graduates of its executive MBA program, whose careers were in the energy industry, to teach in the program. Some of the sponsoring companies also provided speakers with in-depth experience and contributed in other ways as well. One permitted field trips by participants to a highly technical oil field visualization facility. Several participated in the curriculum design.

While consortium programs mitigate the risk of having to cancel a program because of insufficient enrollment, the narrow focus of such programs creates a challenge for long term sustainability. It was difficult to retain a sponsor for more than a year during which programs would be offered two or three times. Ironically, much of the demand for industry focused programs comes not from managers in the industry, but from consultants who want to do business with managers in the industry. Care must be taken, however, not to over populate industry focused courses with participants who are not in the industry themselves because managers in the industry want to interact with other managers in the industry who share common challenges and do not want to be solicited for business. The energy program at Rice now has an underwriting sponsor. Courses currently being offered can be found at the Web site above.

Although open enrollment programs remain a growth area for some schools, Rice and many other schools experienced a shift in program mix from predominantly open enrollment to predominantly custom programs through growth in its custom programs while open enrollment programs remained stagnant. A survey of UNICON schools shows that the percentage of schools generating more than half of their revenue from custom programs increased from 46% in 2003 to 54% in 2006. Most schools continue to offer open enrollment programs but some have discontinued pure open enrollment program offerings. (UNICON, 2006) Rice continued to offer open enrollment programs because they continued to generate needed revenue and they were opportunities to sell custom programs and recruit students for the school's executive MBA program.

In custom programs, the client firm plays a significant role in the design of a curriculum for selected individuals in the firm who have been identified as high performers.

Custom programs provide the selected participants with a common language, tools, and shared experience that can transform organizational culture and facilitate organizational change. The increased demand for custom programs reflects the realization by company leadership that sending individuals to open enrollment programs does not lead to lasting change in the workplace. Instead, the pressure on the individuals to conform once back in their traditional work environment overwhelms any motivation for change induced by the learning experience in the open enrollment program. This observation is supported by research by Mercer Delta Consulting which concludes that leadership development done out of the context of the work environment is futile. The explanation for their conclusion is premised on the linkage between behavioral change and changes in the organizational environment. In essence, unless the corporate culture changes, leadership development efforts will have no effect (Swain, 2006). Custom programs, through a shared learning experience and mutual support, empower participants to change the corporate culture.

At the highest level, custom programs deal directly with organizational problems and become part of the organization's strategy for building competitive advantage. These programs have participants working on projects identified by company leadership as critical to maintaining competitiveness in the market place. While Rice held discussions with its clients about building projects into the fabric of custom programs, none were actually implemented during the period being reported upon.

A significant challenge of incorporating projects in executive education programs is that to be effective, the projects must be carefully selected by top management and must be supervised to ensure that participants have the necessary cooperation and access within the firm to carry them out. University faculty do not have the intimate knowledge of the client company or the ability to insure access and cooperation within the company; hence much of the burden falls on top management for the successful implementation of projects—a burden which top managements of Rice's clients, faced with so many other demands, were unwilling to assume.

The shift in demand toward closed enrollment or custom programs has nevertheless had a significant impact on the way program content is determined and delivered. These ways are summarized and contrasted below (Bardach, 2003).

In traditional open enrollment programs, the faculty offering the program determines the content and approach. As a result, such programs tend to be similar to degree program offerings with theory and research being prominent. The focus is on the individual learner even though lecture and case presentations are supplemented with ample break-out time where participants work in groups to assimilate the material through application exercises. The approach is a process of discovery in which participants not only assimilate the material, but more importantly, learn how their counterparts at other organizations are dealing with common issues and challenges. Because participants bring a diversity of experience to the class, questions, and discussion are often lively and insightful.

Table 9.1.   Changing Demands for Content and Delivery

Open enrollment	Custom program
Educational process	Learning outcomes
Individual work	Team work
Discovery/journey	Competencies
Power with the producer	Power with the client
Theory and research driven	Application driven by customer demand

In custom programs, the client company plays a prominent role in determining content. While faculty expertise continues to be relied upon to develop the educational material, it is common for faculty to be assigned to a counterpart within the firm, for example, a controller with accounting faculty or a marketing manager with marketing faculty to plan the content in a particular discipline. Faculty members are frequently required to incorporate company data such as the firm's financial statements in developing their materials. While this can be a learning experience for the faculty, companies typically restricted the use of these materials to their program limiting the ability of faculty to derive significant long term benefits from the learning experience.

Emphasis on specific learning outcomes based on desired competencies replaces the traditional academic focus on the educational process as a journey of discovery. Because the participants are employed in the same company, there is much greater emphasis on developing teamwork skills. Courses frequently include exercises and assignments such as computer simulations on which participants work as teams. It is not uncommon to have a faculty person designated as "team consultant" to provide instruction and counseling to enhance team performance. Rather than theory, a premium is placed on "real world" experience to insure that materials and instruction are directly applicable to participants' work environment. At Rice, we encouraged involvement by company leaders in the instructional process either by team teaching with university faculty or more commonly by holding question and answer sessions on the topics being presented by faculty to assist participants in relating the material to their work.

Not only are faculty expected to perform differently in custom programs than in open enrollment programs, but expectations of executive education staff support are dramatically higher for custom programs. At Rice, participants in open enrollment programs attended class during the day and returned home at night since most lived in the area. Activities were rarely planned for after class hours. For custom programs there was a great emphasis on total emersion so that even participants who lived in the area were expected to stay in accommodations near campus over night. Numerous social activities were planned for participants after hours which included dinners out, sporting events, casino nights, and festive activities such as Hawaiian Luaus. Such activities helped build camaraderie among participants to enable them to support one another back in the workplace to resist being overwhelmed by the existing culture of "business as usual." These activities also provided additional opportunities for leaders within the company to mingle with participants who constituted the future leadership of the company. In some cases, activities for the spouses of participants were also planned by executive education staff.

It may be surprising to the reader, but all programs provided by Rice, whether open enrollment or custom, employed a face to face, classroom learning approach. What role does distance learning play in executive education? In addressing this question, it is important to keep in mind the scope of executive education as we have defined it in this chapter. We distinguish between executive education and programs designed to teach technical skills, language skills, or to meet compliance requirements for health and safety. Our focus is on programs designed to enhance individuals' abilities to lead and work with others.

At the height of the dot com bubble, there was widespread belief that distance learning would dominate education including executive education. A number of universities invested large amounts of money building their capacity to offer distance learning and developing online nondegree executive education programs (Authers, 1999). At the time, Rice also believed that distance learning would become a major channel for executive education. A venture with a now defunct dot com was launched. The project was a course in business basics. The program was to be jointly marketed nationwide. Countless hours were spent negotiating the intellectual property rights. Just as the curriculum development was begun, the company began to experience financial difficulty and the deal fell apart, fortunately, before Rice had invested significant funds in the project. When the dot com bubble burst, most of these ventures disappeared (Moore, 2002, pp. 178-182).

Today there is little interest among clients, not only at Rice, but at other schools as well, for distance learning for executive development programs. A survey of key decision makers at Fortune 500 companies with respect to the selection of providers of executive education and preferred learning methodologies found no significant interest in Internet based learning methodologies (Spearly & Baker, 2006). The important role that building relationships and having a shared experience play in the long term effectiveness of leadership development cannot be duplicated in the on-line environment. The belief in the importance of relationships and shared experience is reflected in the comments of a client, "My simple goal with the Rice course was to create an environment that we could put people through, that was immersive ... to create a common language within our management group."

It would be naïve to assume, however, that on-line learning will not experience a resurgence. Steve Mahaley (2006) of Duke Corporate Education sees renewed interest in online learning in combination with face-to-face learning among Duke CEs clients. He attributes this renewed interest to improvements in technology and the forces of globalization.

He also notes that research comparing net generation students with current faculty finds that the two groups exhibit very different traits with respect to learning and social interaction. In the long term, executive education will have to adapt to net generation managers.

RECRUITING QUALIFIED FACULTY

The faculty is central to any educational effort. However, the demands of executive education do not afford faculty the comfort of their accustomed role. For example, the all day schedule for executive education programs requires that faculty employ multiple approaches in teaching the material because lecturing for seven or eight hours would not be tolerated by participants. Faculty must adapt by mixing lecture with case discussion, videos, business simulations, role plays, and small group break-out sessions where subgroups of participants work on a particular issue and then present their recommendations when the class regroups. Faculty must also adapt to the changing demands for content and delivery caused by the shift in demand from open enrollment to custom programs described above.

The percentage of faculty participating in the teaching of executive education programs is typically quite small, ten percent or less of regular faculty, since untenured faculty are discouraged from participating and many senior faculty are not effective in the executive classroom or choose not to devote time to executive teaching. Finding the right faculty for executive education programs is a continuing challenge. Given current trends in the educational needs of clients, the long-term role of conventional university faculty in executive education may be limited because the skills required go beyond expertise within a discipline. Faculty are increasingly expected to have broad multidisciplinary knowledge and be able to act as coach as well as teacher in order to personalize the educational experience for the participant to be relevant to his or her work environment in the company (Bendersky, 2004).

It is common for the larger providers to have dedicated faculty that are not drawn from the ranks of the regular faculty of the school. Even at small schools like Rice, some of the best instructors are from the ranks of adjunct or part-time faculty or are graduates of the executive MBA program who have in depth experience in a particular industry. Duke Corporate Education maintains a large data base of faculty with little more than half drawn from universities, the remainder being drawn from industry and the professions.

There are other factors which limit the use of regular university faculty in executive education. One is that there is simply a shortage of business

Changing Demand for Faculty Expertise

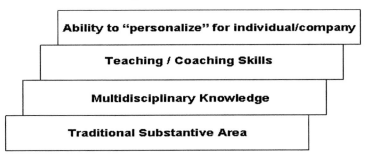

Figure 9.2.   The current shift in demand for faculty expertise.

school faculty because of declining enrollments in PhD programs in the United States and Canada during the past 2 decades and the impending retirement of many senior faculty who were hired during the rapid expansion of American business schools in the 1960s and 1970s.

Furthermore, the greatest demand for faculty is not in North America, but in the developing world, especially in rapidly growing countries such as China and India. North American faculty often lack the cultural sensitivity required to be effective in the developing world (Gandz, 2006). The *Business Week* rankings of top providers of executive education show an increasing number of providers based outside the United States—10 in the 2005 rankings; up from 5 in 2003 (Gloeckler, 2005). Adding to the problem is that the developing world cannot afford to pay North American levels of compensation for executive teaching.

Rice pursued numerous opportunities to offer programs in Asia and the Middle East. All of these initiatives failed because Rice could never make the economics work. Only when an American firm doing business in another country had to provide management training to foreign nationals as part of its contractual obligations for doing business in the country did it become economically feasible for Rice to offer the training.

Another factor limiting involvement of regular faculty in executive teaching is the view at most business schools, including Rice, that executive education is not a part of the school's mission, but rather a source of income to support the achievement of the school's mission. A business school's mission is typically focused on degree programs and academic research. And, since executive education teaching is almost always an overload for faculty, commitments to research, degree program teaching, and service, which are central to the mission of the school, often leave faculty unable to be as flexible and responsive as executive education clients desire.

At Rice, as at most schools, executive teaching is treated as over load teaching for extra compensation. Hence junior faculty who have not yet established their research credentials are discouraged from engaging in executive teaching. Unfortunately, these are the faculty who are most likely to be at the cutting edge of their fields, so their exclusion from executive education deprives managers of the latest thinking and ideas.

For senior faculty, the primary benefit of teaching in executive education is the compensation derived. At Rice, faculty members teaching in executive education do not receive any rewards beyond the compensation they earn for participating. As one senior faculty who teaches regularly in executive education observed,

> "I'm getting extra money, and it's doing something for the school. I've never had a real sense that the dean (the dean during the time period covered in this chapter) ever had any understanding of those other contributions. It (executive education) was purely a cash cow for the rest of the School."

The recruitment of qualified faculty was, and will likely continue to be, a challenge for Rice University. Rice considered trying to develop a cadre of faculty from around the country as Duke Corporate Education has done, but discovered that its local market strategy was an impediment. For many clients, it was important to have Rice faculty teaching in their programs.

Given the high research standards of the Jones School, faculty would be less likely to teach executive education courses in addition to their assigned degree courses. Allowing faculty the option of teaching executive education as part of their regular teaching load had been considered. But the availability of faculty for degree program teaching was sufficiently tight that this alternative was never considered feasible. Consequently, the faculty needed to be approached in a way that would show the relationship of executive education to the mission of the school. All faculty and staff in the school were encouraged to attend open enrollment programs on a space available basis at no charge. New hires were given salary supplements expressed in days of executive education teaching that they were not required to teach, but were asked to simply sit in on some executive education courses. These practices increased the visibility of executive education in the school and also attracted some faculty to consider teaching executive education programs.

As the School grew, a number of full time lecturers were appointed who did not have research or service obligations. These individuals were good teachers who did well in the executive classroom. In addition, Rice sought executive education staff with experience in management education. These individuals were appointed as both staff and faculty, so they could teach in the executive education programs. This not only increased the business school's faculty resources, but also allowed staff to increase their income which was important as the executive education program's staff salaries could not match those in private industry.

Part time faculty members were also a source of faculty for executive education, primarily for open enrollment programs. Graduates of the executive MBA program also became a good source for executive education faculty. Part-time faculty and executive MBA graduates could not be used as easily for custom programs; however, because their full-time employer might be a competitor of the client.

From time to time Rice outsourced open enrollment programs to consultants, forming revenue sharing agreements to mitigate risk or simply paying a day rate. Sometimes these programs were marketed as custom programs, but often the consultant was contacted directly by previous executive education participants to offer a program to their firm. Although the agreement with the consultant forbade accepting such offers, it was difficult to enforce. In instances where this behavior became egregious, Rice ended the relationship with the consultant.

FULFILLING CLIENT EXPECTATIONS

The executive education literature places great emphasis on the need for rigorous evaluation of outcomes, including the calculation of return on investment to determine the impact on the performance of corporate clients. Ironically, the demand for rigorous evaluation of executive education programs does not come from the corporate buyer or the participant. Interviews of senior executives of client firms of Rice's executive education, revealed a general attitude that measuring the benefit or return on investment from an executive program in any rigorous way was probably not possible and certainly not worth the time and expense to attempt it. When asked about evaluating return on investment from executive education, one CEO responded,

> We don't have time for that stuff. I'm not sure it's very measurable. The cost is relatively small in relationship to other stuff. You spend more time trying to measure it and proving it to yourself than you would ever benefit from the answers. I think you have to go with your judgment. If you think it's worthwhile, do it. If you don't, don't.

What this client and others want is less tangible than a return on investment measure is able to capture. For example, a CEO described his company's situation as follows.

> We looked around our organization and saw people who are running profit centers of our business who came from the field without even a college degree. They were street smart and very capable people who rose to be managers. They could make deals, knew how to make money, knew how to get jobs done, and got promoted.

This CEO saw the need to take these people who were critical to the continued competitiveness of the company and not only provide them with management and financial skills, but also the ability to work in teams. He also wanted to give them the self confidence to make decisions and defend their judgments and not be intimidated by those with advanced degrees. He saw the certificate of completion from a program at Rice as a confidence builder as well as a skills enhancer.

Another executive in a different company said that he wanted his people to "think more like a business person than a scientist." At the same time, (he observed),

> We're a very diverse company. We operate in 24 countries. So, the other part of the goal was to create a common language within our management group. So, when we talk about return on investment, we talk about the same thing across all those borders.

He also believed that there was an important benefit of bringing people together from around the world and immersing them in a shared learning experience.

Interviews of individual participants in open enrollment programs also indicated that they did not feel the need for any kind of rigorous evaluation of return on investment for programs attended. When asked whether their companies required a formal report on programs attended, they responded that at most their company wanted feedback on whether they thought the program was interesting and worthwhile so this information could be shared with others in the company who might want to attend. Regarding their motivation to take an open enrollment program, one participant replied, "You really get in a rut, if you don't do that. If you just continue on the treadmill with what you do everyday it's a problem.... [This] keeps you better informed, and you do a better job."

Despite the apparent lack of interest by client company leadership or individual participants in a rigorous evaluation of the benefits of executive education, providers of executive education and training have learned from experience that the beneficent attitude toward executive education vanishes as soon as budgetary constraints become binding. At Rice, the collapse of Enron which caused many people to loose their jobs (not only at Enron, but also at other energy companies that discontinued or severely reduced their trading activities) resulted in planned programs being cancelled, corporate universities being dismantled, and no new programs being initiated for an extended period. When the dot com bubble burst, there was a similar cut-back in executive education.

Obviously, the quantifiable affect of executive education on corporate performance cannot be ignored by either the client or the provider. But, if clients are not fundamentally concerned with holding executive education providers responsible for measurable performance improvement, what are the expectations of providers by their corporate clients?

Corporations choose their suppliers of executive education for a variety of reasons. When narrowing the focus to why corporations choose a small university as their executive education provider, there seem to be three reasons. First, it is convenient for corporations to send employees to a local site, reducing travel time and expense as well as time away from work. Second, many corporations have a desire to support their local communities in which a small university may have a prominent role. The reputation of the university's perceived level of quality, though, is critical in the decision. The selection of a university provider is not typically made as a purely altruistic desire to support a local university, but rather based on recognition that the prestige of the university reflects on the status of the corporation.

In terms of fulfilling client expectations, relationship management is the key. The relationship between the university provider and the corporate client is an ambivalent one. On the one hand, there is a stated need for a true partnership relationship—a critical friend. Ideally, the university partner learns the needs of the corporate client, participates fully in the design of the program and can challenge the client's wants in light of his understanding of the needs. There would also be long-term contracts to execute mutually agreed to plans. Unfortunately the reality is quite different. University providers of executive education are more often vendors than partners. While there is repeat business with clients, programs must typically be sold one at a time.

In the final analysis, perhaps the key to the success of a local provider like Rice is to capitalize on familiarity. As one of our corporate clients explained when asked why his company chose Rice for its custom program, "It's intangible—the atmosphere. I think the people at Rice are open. We became like family there."

CONCLUDING OBSERVATIONS

A small provider of university based executive education faces many challenges, but can still compete successfully. The faculty is obviously a key factor in the equation for success. Only a relatively small percentage of the school's faculty is typically able to deliver the kind of classroom experience that clients expect. These faculty need to be nurtured or they will become your competitors. There is also a constant need to identify and develop new faculty to provide for client growth and faculty attrition. However, it is important to note that the client experience is not solely the result of interaction with the faculty. Every staff person in executive education contributes to the total experience of the client. In custom programs, the staff is especially important as there is much activity outside of the classroom which they must support.

The relationship with the client is critical and it is important that the relationship be with executive education and not the faculty who teach in executive education. Maintaining control over the relationship is a delicate balancing act. In open enrollment programs, participants' primary contact is with the faculty. Our executive education staff, particularly the senior staff, always made an effort to have lunch with participants as well as to spend time with them on breaks. We used these times to learn about their business and seek opportunities for custom programs or to suggest other programs that the participant should consider for their own professional development. It was also a good opportunity to obtain informal feedback on the quality of their program experience. In custom programs, the faculty needs to be involved with the client in developing content and, of course, teaching the program. However, the program design and logistics should be handled by executive education senior staff with faculty input as necessary. When the program is on-going, senior staff should make a point to spend time with participants outside of class. Follow-up to discuss program outcomes and participant evaluations are essential to maintaining the relationship and identifying opportunities for additional programs.

Cross selling and cross training are beneficial. At Rice, during the period covered by this chapter, executive education and the executive MBA (EMBA) were the responsibility of one associate dean and were housed in the same group of offices. In addition to promoting other nondegree programs to nondegree program participants, we recruited many nondegree participants for the EMBA program. We also made a point of having lunch with EMBA students when they were on campus to learn about their companies and identify opportunities for corporate programs. By creating shared staffing responsibilities, we were also better able to handle peak load situations such as orientation for a new class of

EMBA students. Involvement with the EMBA program also gave executive education staff a feeling of being closely aligned with the School's focus on degree programs.

Diversification of the participant pool is an area of unrealized potential. Our participant pool was predominantly white males in their thirties and forties with college degrees and some with advanced degrees, but not MBAs. Demographic trends in this country and the dramatic increase in the number of MBA degrees awarded annually over the past decade make this a shrinking pool. Houston in particular has a very ethnically and racially diverse population with no group exceeding 50% of the population as a whole. And where were the women? Executive education's efforts to attract a more diverse participant pool during the period of the study achieved only limited success.

A stable and predictable revenue stream is impossible to deliver. Deans tend to view executive education as a revenue stream and, accustomed to the relatively stable enrollments in degree programs, expect a reliable prediction of revenues and expenses for budgetary purposes. Nondegree programs are, however, highly sensitive to economic conditions, and changing conditions within companies. Programs constituting a significant fraction of expected revenue within a budget period can be cancelled or postponed. Attendance at open enrollment programs can be dramatically impacted by shocks such as the Enron collapse or 9/11.

REFERENCES

Anderson, L. (2001). Tailor-made for life-long learning. *Financial Times,* p. 1. Retrieved January 17, 2008, from ABI Inform, Doc ID:_69995425, Document URL: http://proquest.umi.com/ pqdweb?did=69995425&sid=5&Fmt=3&clientId=480&RQT=309&VNam e=PQD

Authers, J. (1999). Wharton direct. *Financial Times.* Retrieved January 17, 2008, from ABI Inform, Document URL: http://proquest.umi.com/ pqdweb?did=37752546&sid=4&Fmt=3&clientId=480&RQT=309&VNam e=PQD

Bardach, K. (2003, April 13-15). *Summary comments.* Presentation at UNICON Spring Conference, Ashridge, England.

Bendersky, Ron, (2004, July 13). *Rethinking the design of executive education programs: Refocus on personal effectiveness of executives.* Presentation at UNICON Summer Workship, Madison, Wisconsin.

Dulworth, M., & Bordonaro, F. (2005). *Corporate learning.* San Francisco: Pfeiffer.

Educators. (2006). Duke Corporate Education Web site, Retrieved January 17, 2008, from http://www.dukece.com/employment/index.htm

Gandz, J. (2006, April 26-29). *Leadership development for a flattening world.* Presentation at UNICON Spring Conference, Toronto, Canada.

Gloeckler, G. (2005). Head of the class. *Business Week, 3956,* 76-81.

Holmes, A. (2003). *Smart things to know about lifelong learning.* United Kingdom: Capstone.

Mahaley, S. (2006, June 21). *When technology is an essential part of executive education.* Presentation at UNICON Summer Burst, Cleveland, Ohio.

Merritt, J. (2003). The executive education edge. *Business Week, 3854,* 86-92.

Moore, T. (2002). Emerging competitors in executive education. In C. Wankel & R. DeFillippi (Ed.), *Rethinking management education for the 21st Century* (pp. 157-182) Greenwich, CT: Information Age.

Reingold, J., Schneider, M., & Capell, K. (1999). Learning to lead: Tech is driving the demand for executive education—and creating lots of new options for companies. *Business Week, 3651,* 76-80. Retrieved January 17, 2008, from ABI Inform, Document URL: http://proquest.umi.com/ pqdweb?did=45666900&sid=1&Fmt=3&clientId=480&RQT=309&VName=PQD

Schneider, M., & Hindo, B. (2001). *Business Week, 3753,* 110-114. Retrieved January 17, 2008,, from ABI Inform Document URL: http:// proquest.umi.com/ pqdweb?did=84169515&sid=5&Fmt=3&clientId=480&RQT=309&VName=PQD

Spearly, J. L., & Baker, V. L. (2006, April 26-28). *An investigation into the major factors that influence the selection of a custom executive education provider.* Presentation at the UNICON Spring Conference. UNICON: http:// www.uniconexed.org/

Stake, R. E. (1998). Case studies. In N. K. Denzin & Y. S. Lincoln (Eds.), *Strategies of qualitative inquiry* (pp 86-109). Thousand Oaks: SAGE.

Swain, J. (2006, April 26-28). *Executive leadership development: Mercer Delta perspectives & approach.* Presentation at the UNICON Spring Conference. UNICON: http://www.uniconexed.org/

Tirard, A. (2004, April 18). *ROI: The client's perspective.* Presentation at UNICON Spring Conference, Atlanta, Georgia.

UNICON. (2006, November 21-23). *Benchmarking Survey #12.* Presentation by Mike Malefakis, UNICON Fall Conference, Northwestern University, Kellogg Graduate School of Management. UNICON: http://www.uniconexed.org/

CHAPTER 10

LIFELONG LEARNING AS THE HIGHWAY TO GLOBAL COMPETITIVENESS FOR LITHUANIA

A Bumpy Road

Arunas Augustinaitis, Egle Malinauskiene, and Charles Wankel

Lifelong learning (LLL) is of great importance in transitional nations such as Lithuania as a vehicle in the restructuring of the nation's knowledge to bridge the gap between formal education and the real needs of work, while the fuller reform of its educational system is still underway. This study provides a holistic approach to LLL and its role as a catalyst for structural changes in society, the climate for innovation, work organizations, and management. Particular attention is paid to the role of Lithuanian universities in the development of LLL activities and the associated transformation of their functional abilities to develop efficient knowledge processes for society.

The most prominent theme is the role of universities in the deepening crisis of the educational system, specifically their inability to establish sustainable and efficient knowledge partnerships with other sectors. How

University and Corporate Innovations in Lifelong Learning, pp. 237–266
Copyright © 2008 by Information Age Publishing

soon and how effectively Lithuania completes its postcommunist economic transition depends on how the nation's human capital can develop the requisite knowledge structure.

INTRODUCTION

Lithuania aims to become a global competitor by becoming a knowledge society. To attain this end, learning must be restructured and education modernized. A key element is LLL. LLL has become a key element of the public discourse about the optimal organization of education and training for the twenty-first century (Hake, 1999). This chapter considers the role of LLL over the last 17 years since Lithuania's independence, particularly its usefulness as a vehicle to help catch up with globally oriented Western nations. LLL is seen as an important catalyst, spurring changes in society, the environment for innovation, work organizations, and management.

The backdrop for the role of universities in providing LLL is the deepening crisis of the Lithuanian educational system. This crisis is abetted by the underdeveloped state of LLL and the relatively low level of partnering of Lithuanian universities with other societal sectors. However, in this period of late modernity LLL has become a condition for the survival of economies (Hake, 1999). For one thing, it supports intergenerational learning. A holistic approach to LLL for older workers is a typical focus (Tikkanen, 2005), as is providing the education requisite for competent participation in a democracy's political processes. Ideally, a nation's LLL partnerships might include ones among educational institutions, the media, businesses, and local government (Bîrzéa, 2000).

Emery, who coined the idea of an "educated community" has said that killing the desire in adults to learn, while attempting to foster in children a love of learning, is misguided in the focus of its financing of formal education (Emery & Baburoglu, 2000). Institutions of higher education in Lithuania that are taking on robust LLL programs are probably among the best situated to foster the needed integration of the education and business knowledge environments (Davies, 2000). To undertake LLL properly, Lithuanian universities must modernize their curricula to cogently bring together knowledge from all societal arenas and actors, creating and sustaining interdisciplinary knowledge. Only interdisciplinary knowledge has a ready capacity to be used across the diversity of social contexts and arenas in Lithuania's society and economy, including the public sector and business. It is incumbent on twenty-fist century universities to abandon Humboldtism and academic Taylorism by moving to curricula based more on learner needs through action-research approaches (Greenwood & Levin, 2000).

The topics that are intended to be examined in this chapter are as follows:

- The current state of the transformation of the Lithuanian system of higher education as a baseline of LLL activities;
- Specific characteristics of the Lithuanian knowledge environment and the forms of knowledge circulation conditioned by the extent of social and political ruptures and continuities with the post-Soviet period;
- Statistics and facts of LLL in Lithuania, with illustrative case studies of university-based LLL.

The chapter will clarify problematic contextual elements including managerial attitudes and the status of technological innovation development and management, through the prisms of Europeanization and globalization.

LLL AND THE KEY FORCES OF LITHUANIAN GROWTH

Heightened interest in LLL is fostered by its being perceived as the best way to integrate social capital with the needs of business given the changing social structure, including increasing community power, and given the limitations of the current state of the economy's restructuring. With its membership in the European Union (EU), Lithuania has been thrust into the European context and the global economy. However, it is still searching for a viable combination of self-sustainability and global competitiveness.

At first blush, Lithuania's development over the past 2 decades looks like a success story. Average gross domestic product growth in 2002-2006 was 8%. The unemployment rate in 2006 was somewhat under 6% (Department of Statistics of Lithuania) but the number of the officially registered unemployed was only about 4% of the working age population in April 2007 (Labor Exchange of Lithuania). Also impressive are data on the real earnings of employees, exports and imports, foreign direct investment, and so forth. Similarly notable is the progress in political democracy since the time of national independence in the early 90s to its 2004 accession to the EU. Lithuania is very active in the Lisbon processes seeking global competitiveness for the EU through knowledge-based jobs and innovation. Since joining the EU, wages have risen about 30%. Still, despite accelerating Europeanization and aspirations to surpass the average of EU economic prosperity and quality of life, Lithuanian societal development has its own logic. Criteria developed for measuring the original members of the EU today do not capture completely the breakneck sprint of postcommunist societies rushing into the also rapidly changing global and technological realities. The extremely low rate of unemployment is unfortunately not the result of ongoing economic growth but rather a high emigration level (more than 400,000 have emigrated) and a higher proportion of older persons in the population. Since 1992 (independence) the population of Lithuania dropped from 3.7 to 3.3 million (2007). The proportion of older workers (55-64 years of age) rose from 39 to 49% from 2001 to 2005, compared with the EU average of 42% in 2005 (Lithuanian Department of Statistics).

Despite a relatively high proportion of well-educated professionals, innovation is at a low level in Lithuania. Lithuania has 15 state and 6 private universities (Lithuanian Department of Statistics). The proportion of students in the society ranks in the top 10 in the world, with more than 70% of secondary school graduates immediately undertaking higher education. In 2004, 25% of those aged 25-34 were in higher education in the EU25 contrasted with 35% in Lithuania (Statistical Office of the European Communities, 2006).

Paradoxically, indicators of business innovation activity in Lithuania are extremely low. That is, there is a huge discrepancy between robust measures of higher education and its conversion into economic, social, and technical innovations. Lithuania has one of the highest rates of education in Europe but lags in research and development, innovation, and patenting activities. Only 1% of Lithuanian enterprises develop strategically significant innovation.

DOMINANT LAYERS OF KNOWLEDGE FORMATION IN LITHUANIA

Lithuanian society is no longer insulated from uncontrolled flows of global knowledge. The coming of the information age has initiated in a postmodern revolution of Europeanization and globalization. As knowledge flows into Lithuanian businesses and government, it is incorporated into day-to-day decision-making without reflection on the decision-making apparatuses or how they might be adapted to better process and act on such information. However, given the nation's transition from communism to capitalism, the contexts of learning are appearing in haphazard forms and places. For example, Aidis and Praag (2007) ask whether the experience of former black market entrepreneurs has developed the entrepreneurial know-how requisite for high motivation and performance as legitimate entrepreneurs in the above-board business context.

The absence of the unbroken and long evolutionary experience of business that many Western nations have had seemingly could have been countered by Lithuanian businesses leapfrogging from the decrepit state Socialist quagmire of the communist era directly into the rapid streams of world-class twenty-first century business. However, such a possibility is premised on the development by Lithuanian businesspeople to obtain the requisite know-how to leverage new forms of knowledge and human capital. Investigating the extent of the emergence and growth of a small and medium-sized enterprise sector and its ability to foster innovation, experimentation, and adaptation in the new business environment, the dynamic growth of the new private sector has in fact been one of the key driving forces behind the economic recovery in the former Communist economies of Central and Eastern Europe. It might seem that the transition period in Lithuania has been unduly extended, though new technologies of knowledge such as Web applications are helping to connect transitional societies such as Lithuania to the speeding train of globalization and its ongoing associated changes (Figure 10.1).

The structure of knowledge in the still transitional Lithuanian society has the following peculiarities:

- Knowledge of science, values, and practice exhibits many discontinuities and contradictions from knowledge grounded in the old system existing along with knowledge grounded in the new system;

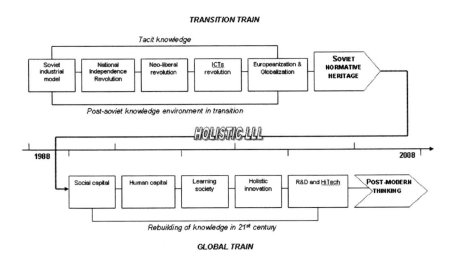

Figure 10.1.   The knowledge that graduates identified as insufficient for their future careers.

- Lithuania is a "black hole" for knowledge, pulling it in indiscriminately in immense quantities, absorbing information, value systems, cultural influences, and practices without the filtering and selectivity normal in more mature societies;
- The rapid rate of knowledge accumulation from global sources is breaking down and transforming existing value systems;
- Lithuanian organizations, to a large extent, are attempting to connect their knowledge to the new global and domestic realities they are encountering, while still blindly encumbered by stereotypes and now inappropriate decision criteria of the Soviet industrial system;
- Though there is an increasing amount of information policymaking, it is largely ideological display rather than practically fitting the knowledge environment to the real contemporary demands for information.

Learning processes in Lithuania can be characterized as wedged between the pressures of rapid modernization and nascent political and managerial development. In terms of learning, the situation in Lithuania is complex and postmodern, despite the dearth of knowledge management abilities and competences to handle this complexity, including the interface of the multiplicity of business arenas, actors, and stakeholders. This societal stage has been characterized as "postmodern postcommunist" (Saulauskas, 1996).

This chapter shows how to bring mixed, flexible, and dynamic learning environments into instruments of the integration of the managerial knowledge disseminated by a LLL system to accelerate societal change in a transitional nation such as Lithuania. Of course, what this change will ultimately look like is unpredictable. It is challenging to convert Lithuania's dormant knowledge potential into socioeconomically important processes that neatly might be subsumed under the system of formal Euro-indicators.

Criteria of knowledge assessment should be able to evaluate the different learning forums informal education and the knowledge environment's extent of facilitation of informal learning. Also, knowledge assessment of the impact of LLL design and deployment on intergenerational and senior citizen learning is important.

THE ROLE OF LLL IN THE LITHUANIAN EDUCATION SYSTEM

The challenges for the Lithuanian education system were delineated in the study *The Lithuanian Nation: Analysis of its Situation and Development*

Prospects (Kraujelyte & Spurga, 2007). The challenges brought by Europeanization, globalization and ever more advanced information technologies assign new tasks for Lithuania's education policymakers such as to ensure the technological literacy of its citizens, restructure the current education system, and guarantee access to high quality education, create favorable conditions for LLL not only by establishing the necessary infrastructure but also by promoting the need for knowledge and learning within the community.

Key contemporary problems of the Lithuanian education system include a decline in the quality of education, an overly vague and underdeveloped state of partnership between universities and businesses, and slow investment into nondegree continuing education by employers who largely consider it as personal whimsy not meriting financial encouragement by firms.

Another problem is that there is a widespread lack of motivation on the part of individuals to undertake nondegree and e-learning coursework. One reason for this is the absence of the kind of official certification system of continuing education that many nations have. Also current online course offerings are paltry and inferior, as well as out of alignment with the needs of the market and beyond the means of most people.

The Lithuanian academic community is made out to be the villain for not developing the potential of LLL. However, a root cause is the legacy of the communist era when training employees devoid of initiative, critical thinking, decision-making ability, and so forth, was seeming the objective. The educational reform process in Lithuania has been underway since 1992, though its administrative structure still seems quite Soviet.

The Lithuanian education system is also confronting the challenges of a graying society, occasioned by a high emigration rate and a low birth rate. For example, currently the Lithuanian labor system is ill-equipped to assist older workers who might like to work part-time or on a flexitime schedule. The survey "The Working Needs of Adults in Villages and Little Towns" (Tamosiunas, Sutiniene, Filipaviciene, & Guseva, 2004) found a negative correlation between increasing age and interest in learning. In general, there is a dearth of information on the status of senior citizens, possible models for their retirement, further employment, and LLL.

Universities and other institutions of higher education should be playing a key role in providing students with a foundation for LLL. Universities should be helping to nurture values supporting ongoing learning as part their professional responsibilities and ethics. However, the report "The State of Informal Adult Education and the Attitudes of Citizens and Employers to it" has shown that more than half of all young specialists coming from universities and colleges must be provided additional education before starting their work in the new workplace.

According to another report "The Competitiveness of Higher Education Graduates in the Context of Supply and Demand of the Labor Market" (2004) the majority of graduates also were dissatisfied with their preparedness for their future careers: 51% saw their educational background positively while 49% gave a negative opinion (Darbo ir socialiniu tyrimu institutas, 2004).

The qualifications and competencies that were identified by graduates as deficient are shown in Figure 10.2. As it can be seen the majority of respondents lack practical readiness, according to 80% of graduates and 75% of employers.

Among those who mentioned business competencies, 64% said they lacked adequate information technology (IT) skills, 51% reported insufficient knowledge of business administration, and 60% reported inadequate financial knowledge. Among other practical skills graduates were deficient in initiative, critical analysis, creativity, time management, computer literacy, and foreign languages (83%). Sixty-five percent of graduates reported inadequate preparation in teamwork skills, management know-how, and communication skills.

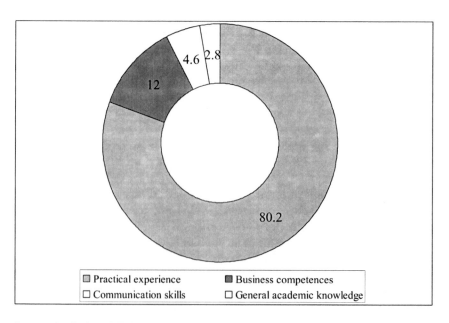

Source: Darbo ir socialiniu tyrimu institutas (2004).

Figure 10.2.   The knowledge that graduates identified as insufficient for their future careers.

The results of the employers' assessment of what knowledge is requisite for their personnel and what knowledge young specialists really brought from the universities dovetailed with the survey of the graduates (see Figure 10.3). Employers have emphasized that their new hires coming from the higher education system have inadequate preparation in law, business administration, and psychology, and have a lack of initiative for both individual and team work. They also report that these entry level employees lack critical and analytical acumen. They do not practice time management. And, they have rather poor foreign language skills. To a greater extent than new graduates, employers considered young people entering the work force to be relatively computer illiterate.

When talking about the employment possibilities, respondent opinions were unevenly distributed. A majority of recent graduates stressed that internships during their studies need to be better organized (Figure 10.4). The proposal to rev up the intensity of study in higher education was unpopular (Figure 10.5).

Forty-seven percent of Lithuanian employers have some form of partnership with the universities. However, most of these partnerships involve passive benevolence rather than active collaborative involvement. According to the survey, 91% of employers reported that they notify

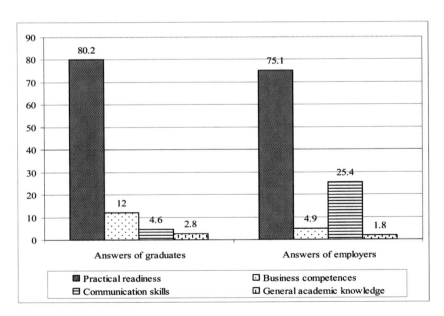

Source: Tamosiunas, Sutiniene, Filipaviciene, and Guseva (2005).

Figure 10.3.   The comparison of graduates' and employers' surveys.

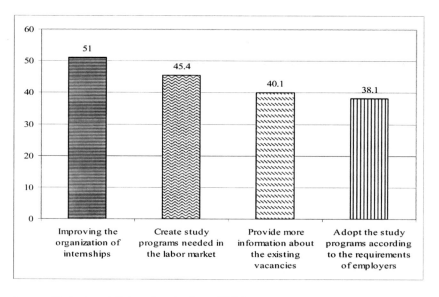

Source: Darbo ir socialiniu tyrimu institutas (2004).

Figure 10.4.   The main means to increase the employability of the graduates.

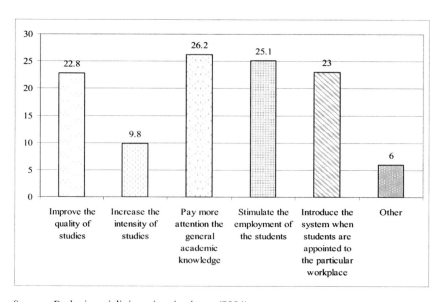

Source: Darbo ir socialiniu tyrimu institutas (2004).

Figure 10.5.   Other means to increase the employability of the graduates.

universities of position openings. 80% reported interest in the academic programs of universities. But, 76% stated that they are not interested in getting directly involved in the education programs of students. However, the prospect remains that business and academe might come to develop collaborations in projects and research of mutual interest.

LLL in Lithuania is offered in a fragmented way, hit or miss by this or that department, rather than as a planned, integrated, and complete continuing studies program through a unit of the university or other higher education institution dedicated to that purpose. Similarly, continuing education courses and programs are not coordinated interinstitutionally or nationally. Also, continuing education and development offered in industry is not clearly defined in relation to continuing education offered by higher education institutions or self-directed individual studies.

What the best model should be for Lithuanian universities to follow to overcome the current crisis in higher education is a point of controversy. Some hold the premise that universities should be the key driver of new knowledge development in Lithuania. If universities are indeed the main actors in knowledge development, should they also be the engine driving LLL activities bridging education, business, and government and not-for-profit organizations and their needs? (Figure 10.6).

Conceptual Development of LLL in Lithuania

According to Rubenson (1998) three "generations" of LLL conceptual development can be identified: (1) LLL as a master concept and guiding principle for restructuring education with a major role for civil society; (2) LLL as a lever for increasing productivity in organizations, and (3) LLL focused on active citizens increasing their employability.

Lithuania, as well as the majority of countries in transition, seems to have ideologically adopted the general vision of latter concept of LLL. On the strategic level as defined in Lithuanian education policies, the goals of LLL are consistent with the main statements of the EU documents on LLL. For instance, in the EU's strategy for lifelong learning, LLL is defined as "all learning activities undertaken throughout life, with the aim of improving knowledge, skills, and competence, within a personal, civic, social, and/or employment-related perspective" (Commission of European Communities, 2001). The objective would be to optimize the deployment of all requisite resources of government, business, communities, nongovernmental organizations, and individuals to develop a unified and trustworthy LLL system including both formal and informal education. The main problems identified by the EU were a

MULTILEVEL LEARNING ENVIRONMENTS

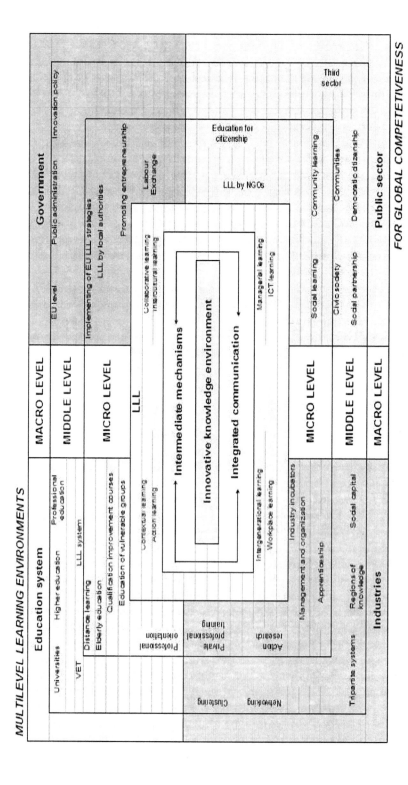

Figure 10.6.   Holistic model of LLL to achieve in Lithuania.

dearth of certification and other requirements for vocational and ongoing professional training, accessibility to learning resources, infrastructure, management of education and coordination of vocational policies, financing, qualification of educators, regional differences, and quality assurance.

Formal LLL programs must be a key part of Lithuania's anticipated successful meeting of the challenges currently facing it such as globalization, coping with the need to develop and deploy information via new technologies in ever-increasing amounts, and the positive and strong contributions of the intensifying democratic and economic forces of the country. Lithuania's National Education Strategy for 2003-2012 sees learning as a boost for proper individual and societal responses to the challenges. Lithuania needs to become more serious in its focus on doing what is needed to provide the nation with the education required for participation in the EU and the world as a world-class actor rather than a laggard. This would include making education available to all who need it to fit with the changing needs of jobs and organizations, developing an LLL infrastructure, and assuring that the quality of such education meets existing European standards, as well as the needs of today's Lithuanian society. This corresponds very closely to Hake's (1999) statement on the character of the EU's LLL policies regarding nations in transition: "Not only is lifelong learning firmly established on the policy agenda of many inter-governmental organizations and multi-national enterprises, it is now also one of the core policy principles of the EU and many of the member states. Former Communist countries, such as Estonia and Slovenia, have recently declared themselves as lifelong learning societies" (pp. 77-89).

LLL is included in Lithuania's National Common Strategy as a priority for productive human resources to support a knowledge society. The main objectives of LLL are seen as retaining and attracting people to the national labor market and to support the ramping up of the quality of specialists in the labor force. However, with reference to Rubenson's (1998) typology, Lithuanian government still focuses mainly on the organizational, institutional and technological issues of LLL more characteristic of its first phase, focused on restructuring education. The question is what are the best criteria and principles to assess Lithuania's existing policies of LLL? LLL policies are only partly based on improving employability, human resource qualifications, and global competitiveness. They are also aimed at increasing active citizenship and the quality of life. So LLL, rather than just a way to develop human resources to increase organizational productivity, is more properly seen as holistically affecting all facets of society as an integrated knowledge environment (Griffin, 1999, 2007).

There are many formal policies in Lithuania regarding adult education, vocational training, and different forms of informal learning including the Law of Non-Formal Adult Education, the Law of Vocational Education, and the Strategy for the Implementation of Information and Communication Technologies in the Education of Lithuania. The Law of Non-Formal Adult Education provides a legal basis for participants, coordinators, and social partners active in nonformal adult education. The main trends of nonformal education in Lithuania are the development of individual abilities and professional skills. The law proposes various adult education courses and faculty to be deployed using various types of media for both on-campus and distance learning and for full-time and part-time study.

The Law of Vocation Education similarly emphasizes the need of LLL for all. The main objectives are the insurance of high quality vocational studies with a focus on their fit with the requirements of the specific occupation. This should be designed to assist citizens to earn the qualifications and competences they need for successful careers in the current technological, economical, and cultural environments.

The strategy for the implementation of information and communication technologies in the education of Lithuania is an integral part of the overall education strategy of Lithuania. According to this strategy the educational system and society are to be networked, including through distance learning technologies. Also the wider deployment of information and communication technologies (ICT) is hoped to improve the quality of student life and enable cutting-edge educational content and pedagogy.

One of the indicators of the Lithuanian government's changing understanding of LLL is the strategy of professional orientation. This aims to better align educational programs with the careers they are supposed to be preparing for. Additionally, readily available and robust career advisement services need to be deployed in higher education institutions to dispense information on what the specific requirements are of various occupations and professions and how and to what extent various courses of study and degrees prepare students for those occupations. Individuals should be made responsible for their own career development but encouraged and shown how to be entrepreneurial and seek out the educational preparation needed to support their career visions.

Unfortunately, despite the Lithuanian government's promulgation of highly promising LLL policies, actual practice in Lithuanian education still has limited collaborations and partnerships with business and other organizations. A salient flaw of Lithuanian higher education is the chasm between the official declared strategic priorities including the development of the country as a knowledge society and its seeming inability to make meaningful progress in that regard. This situation corresponds with the postmodernist framing of LLL by Griffin (1999, 2007). In Lithuania's case, the entrenchment of formal educational programs constrains the development of the requisite level of innovation required for a world class business competitiveness. The dated Lithuanian education system currently does not have the capacity to meet such needs.

LLL in Lithuania is treated as an insignificant subsidiary of the larger educational enterprise. It is still close to the format of the Soviet-initiated "qualification improvement system." In contrast to world class approaches, Lithuanian LLL is still far removed from social learning and work-based learning. The most remarkable particular of this is that LLL is not focally connected to the needs of the labor market. It is not a bridge mediating formal, nonformal, and informal education, nor does it foster a networked knowledge environment.

Lithuanian Implementation of LLL

According to the Lithuanian Department of Statistics (2007), the percentage of Lithuanians involved in any form of education nearly doubled from 28% in 2003 to 55% in 2006. Seventy-two percent of those responding aged 25-64 were studying on their own. About one third of them were involved in some form of nonformal education such as courses, seminars, and so forth. Six percent of citizens were studying in institutions offering formal programs of higher education while 3% of citizens aged 25-34 were participating in education (formal, nonformal, and informal). The overall distribution of adults aged 25-64 in some form of education is shown in Figure 10-7.

Sixty-two percent of the respondents, who participated in nonformal education, attended qualification improvement courses; 46% attended seminars and conferences; while 27% studied in their workplace. Half of the adults attended some sort of training annually, 35% did so two or three times per year, while 15% did so four or more times. Fifty-four of those in this additional learning had a degree from a higher educational institution.

The most popular training courses were in business, law, and sciences (Figure 10.8).

The majority of the employees participating in nonformal education came from management, logistics, and service (Figure 10.9).

A positive LLL trend in Lithuania involves informal education. In 2003, only 25% of individuals studied as nonmatriculates. By 2006, this had increased to 45%. Such study was particularly popular with those with

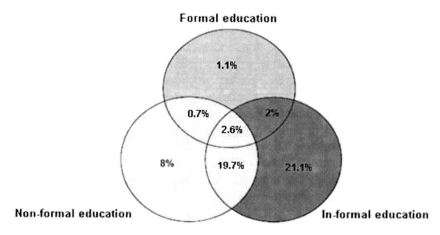

Source: Lithuanian Department of Statistics (2007).

Figure 10.7.   Participation of adults aged 25-64 in all forms of education.

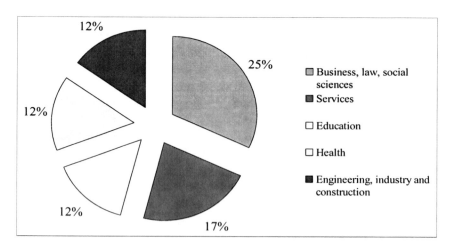

Source: Lithuanian Department of Statistics (2007).

Figure 10.8.   The most popular training courses.

a higher education degree. Also younger people were more eager to participate than older citizens (Table 10.1 and Table 10.2).

Only 16% of those adults who had not undertaken studies during the research period stated that they wanted to increase their level of qualification and deepen their knowledge of some areas. The remaining

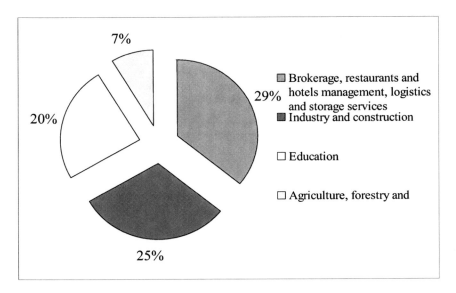

Source: Lithuanian Department of Statistics (2007).

Figure 10.9.   Occupations of the adults involved in LLL activities.

Table 10.1.   Percentage of Informal Students According to Their Educational Background

		Educational Background			
	Total	University or Higher Education	Secondary	Basic Education	Primary or Unfinished Primary
The percent in comparison with all students	100.0	44.5	48.9	6.2	0.4
The percent in comparison with all 25-64 years people having particular education	45.3	69.4	38.9	22.7	11.0

Source: Ministry of Education and Science of the Republic of Lithuania (2006).

84% expressed disinterest in additional study. This shows that in Lithuania too many people remain indifferent to education or embrace the stereotypical cliché that learning is for the young. Willingness to undertake additional study and having an understanding of the advantages that accrue from knowledge varies with the age of a person, their educational background, and whether they live in a rural or urban

Table 10.2.   Percentage of Informal Students According to Their Age

		Age Groups		
	Total	25-34	35-49	50-64
The percent in comparison with all students	100.0	31.0	44.7	24.3
The percent in comparison with the people in the particular age group	45.3	53.4	47.4	35.5

Source: Ministry of Education and Science of the Republic of Lithuania (2006).

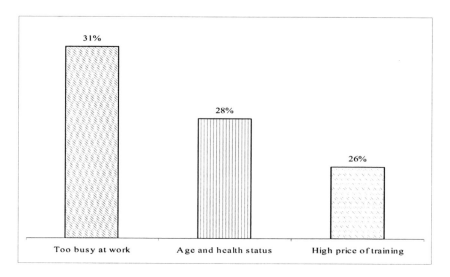

Source: Lithuanian Department of Statistics (2007).

Figure 10.10.   The distribution of adults not involved in any forms of education according to the reasons.

community. Figure 10.10 shows some of the obstacles that hinder the continuing education.

Beyond the official statistics on LLL in Lithuania, there seems to be more of a focus on giving degrees and certificates per se than as proof of having attained certain levels of knowledge, experience, or innovative capacity. According to the Lithuanian Department of Statistics, the two main motivations for the continuing education and qualification improvement identified by Lithuanian citizens were: employment (89%) and personal (11%) needs. Reasons put forth for embarking on nonformal study included work performance improvement, obtaining qualification certificates, fear of losing a job, and an employer's insistence.

**Table 10.3.   The Benefits That Employers see in
the Nonformal Adult Education to their Organization**

Nonformal Staff Education	Very Important	Important	Difficult to Tell	Not Very Important	Not Important
Improved qualifications	67	30	2	1	–
Increased productivity and quality	48	40	8	2	1
Decreased shift of personnel	20	34	37	4	5
Improved work organization	38	48	12	1	–
Better communication skills	32	46	19	4	–
New career possibilities and rooting in the organization	40	41	14	3	1

Source: Ministry of Education and Science of the Republic of Lithuania (2005).

It can be seen from the statistics that most people are interested in LLL largely for employment-related reasons and that employers play a key role in promoting LLL. A study "State of non-formal adult education and the attitudes of citizens and employers to the non-formal adult education" conducted in 2004 showed that the majority of employers recognized the benefits of nonformal adult education to their organizations (Table 10.3 above) and invested in personnel training (Figure 10.11). However, the scale and intensity largely depended on enterprise size (Figure 10.12). Large and middle-sized organizations tended to recommend employee training more than small ones did. Also, public sector organizations tended to have more continuing education.

Despite a positive attitude by employers about adult education, many problematic issues persist including a dearth of financial resources since many available courses are pricey, many are offered by far-flung educational institutions, there is a concern that employees might leave after obtaining a prestigious certificate with the organization not getting the benefit of the investment in the education (see Table 10.4).

Lithuanian employers as well as employees mostly focus on the superficial bestowal of certificates rather than more objective measures of knowledge enhancement. Many support education when it is completed outside of regular working hours and financed by individuals themselves. According to the Lithuanian Department of Statistics, 51% of respondents were studying during their normal working hours. Sixty-one percent had their training courses fully paid for by their employers, 13% partially, and 15% paid from their own resources.

The majority of respondents studied in higher educational institutions (Figure 10.12). Over the course of a year, 7% of all working people had

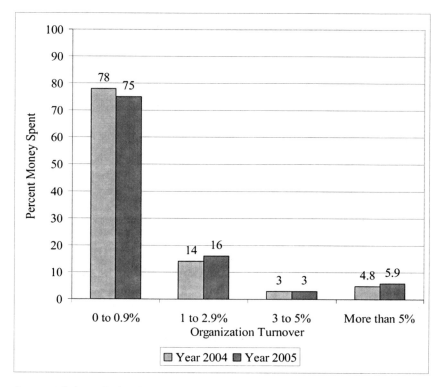

Source: Ministry of Education and Science of the Republic of Lithuania.

Figure 10.11.   The percentage of the money spent from the turnover of organizations in 2004 and 2005.

participated in study abroad. A positive trend is that 98% of all respondents thought the knowledge they gained in various training courses was useful and would be successfully applied in their professional tasks. Only 2% of people did not use their new knowledge in practice.

Another problem of Lithuanian LLL is its fragmented administration by several agencies (the Ministry of Education and Science, the Ministry of Social Security and Labor, and the Ministry of Economy) over several levels of administration for several target groups. University-based continuing education, the training regimes of labor exchange institutions and vocational training centers function as separate entities with separate objectives and frameworks (Figure 10.13 above). Also the apprenticeship system is not well established.

The resignation of universities to a subservient role vis-à-vis government and paltry moves toward partnering with business and other

Table 10.4.   The Main Problems Faced by Employers in Organizing the Nonformal Education of the Staff

Problems	Distribution (%)
The institutions of education are far away from the organization itself	24
Not modern educational infrastructure	13
High price of the courses	43
The majority of the certified staff changed their job to the better paid one or have found a job abroad	21
A lack of the needed training courses	35
Low quality of the nonformal education	15
Trained staff require higher salaries	15
Employees have no motivation for the continuing education	16
Learning takes too much of *expensive* working time	27
Other problems	6

Source: Ministry of Education and Science of the Republic of Lithuania.

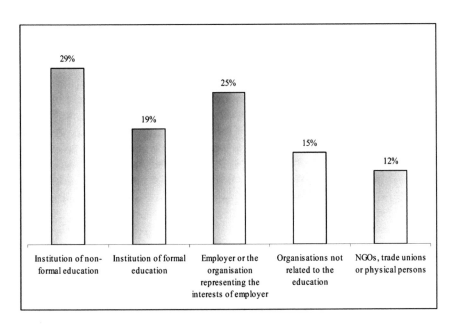

Source: Lithuanian Department of Statistics.

Figure 10.12.   The Percentage of people involved in the trainings at the various types of organizations

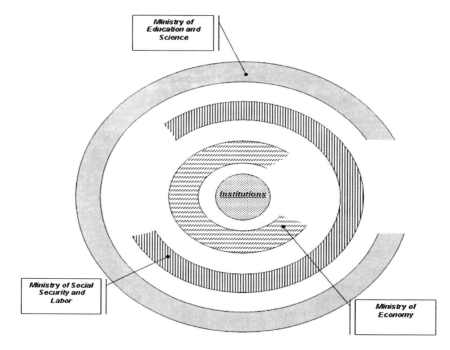

Figure 10.13.   Fragmentation and gaps of the Lithuanian LLL system.

organizations is inherently a basic cause of the current crisis of the Lithuanian education system since universities are the largest and most important part of the nation's educational system. A stark fact is that the diminution of the role of universities within the larger educational system has made them less able to put resources and energy into developing collaborative LLL. The flipside of this is that the inability of universities to establish and sustain organic networking and partnering with other public and private sectors is itself one of the roots of the crisis of the national educational system.

As is shown in the Figure 10.13, in these circumstances the state education system under the governance of the Ministry of Education and Science is losing the initiative and the leading role in the development of LLL. The formerly monolithic control over LLL by the central government has eroded as new LLL niches and methods are appearing. The Lithuanian Labor Exchange (LLE) has become of the largest institutional players in this field. Though the LLE purports to provide knowledge according to the demands of the labor market, its focus is constrained to professional training and retraining. The Ministry of Economy of Lithuania is developing the other significant LLL system.

The Lithuanian LLL system does not have a clear policy for LLL but rather reacts to EU funding opportunities regardless of the extent that they align with the nation's needs. In contrast, the Finnish LLL program TYKES (Finnish Workplace Development Program) functions holistically in providing LLL by integrating it with learning networks joining university-based research and workplace forums. The TYKES network brings together people from different geographical areas, industries, positions in the value chain and beyond the experts (Alasoini, 2005, pp. 158-161).

The Role of the Lithuanian Universities in Fostering LLL

The majority of university graduates continue their education as matriculates in university graduate degree programs, rather than taking continuing education courses such as those offered through the LLE or private training institution (Figure 10.14).

In Lithuania, LLL is seen as derivative from formal degree programs and is largely limited to distance learning programs, which recently have

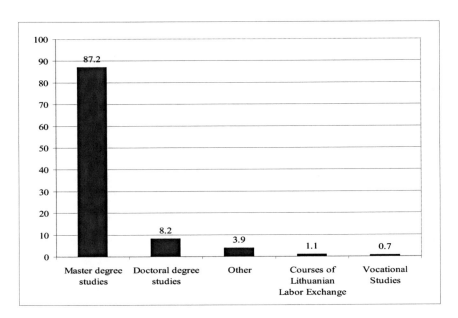

Source: Institute of Labor and Social Research.

Figure 10.14. The percent distribution of graduates according to various forms of continuous education.

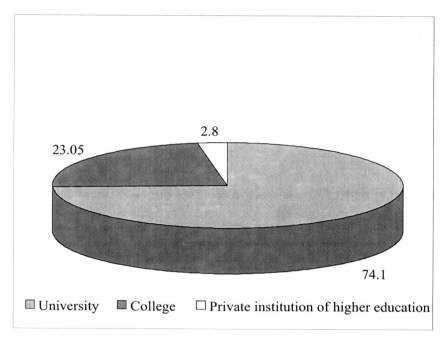

23.05

2.8

74.1

▨ University   ▧ College   ☐ Private institution of higher education

Source: Nuotoliniu studiju (2005).

Figure 10.15.   The percentage of distance modules in Lithuanian institutions of higher education.

been burgeoning. A study of distance education in Lithuanian higher education (*Viesosios politicos ir vadybos institutas,* 2004) found 53% of the state universities and 60% of the state colleges were preparing distance learning programs or courses. Twenty-one of the 40 higher education institutions that participated in the survey were providing 642 modules of distance learning: 74% of them offered by state universities, 23% by the state colleges, and only 2.8% by the private higher educational institutions (see Figure 10.15 above).

The subject areas of these distance education modules were social sciences (38%), engineering (27%) and physical sciences (17%) (Figure 10.16). The average percentages of courses provided online were: 48 in state universities, 18 in state colleges, and 12 in private institutions of higher education.

The number of students who finished distance courses in some manner is shown in Figure 10.17.

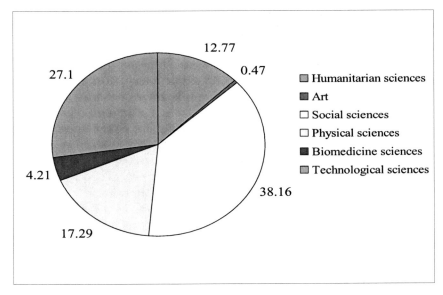

Source: Nuotoliniu studiju (2005).

Figure 10.16.   The percentage of distance modules in various sciences.

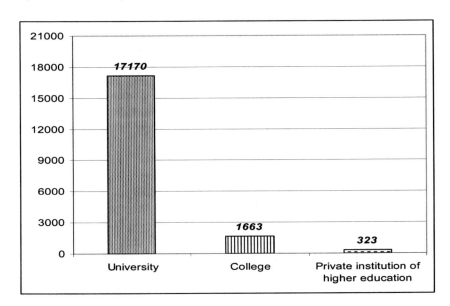

Source: Nuotoliniu studiju (2005).

Figure 10.17.   The number of students who have finished at least one distance module.

In 2004-2005 distance education programs were offered only by the state universities. There were 10 programs: 6 in the social sciences and 4 in engineering sciences with 697 students involved.

Lithuanian universities are strongly focusing on improving continuing education to develop an academically credentialed workforce and to enable members of the workforce to improve their qualifications and to meet the need for new knowledge and skills. Continuing education is oriented to the improvement of general skills like communication, IT, foreign languages, and career management, through special vocational training. Second, arrangements are made for instruction to be provided for the personnel of groups of businesses. Finally, they propose programs for vocational training to develop particular competencies.

At the moment Lithuanian universities have centers for continuing studies, career development, and personal development with an array of offerings, including business management, law, education, psychology, and engineering. These offerings are usually graduate level courses or vocational studies programs. Some universities including Mykolas Romeris University offer requalification courses and special courses designed for senior citizens ("University of Third Age").

Lithuanian universities continue to develop their curriculum on their own or through negotiation with a professional association (Davies, 2000). This influences course quality, course delivery, reception by students, and further development towards the LLL paradigm under which curricula development is a collaborative endeavor with involvement of employers to better meet business needs while simultaneously maintaining conformance to accreditation requirements (Figure 10.18 and Figure 10.19). However, new approaches for extending university-grounded endeavors into business enterprises are emerging in Lithuania.

CONCLUSIONS

This study shows how a country completing its transition from the Soviet higher educational system to one suited to thrive in a capitalist economy and also foster the thriving of that economy. This involves the development of LLL with a holistic approach enabling the creation of a panoply of knowledge environments on different levels and for different purposes. Such a holistic orientation not only reflects the ongoing transformation of Lithuania into a knowledge society but also validates accomplished social changes and orients them to the development of global competitiveness.

How might university-offered LLL facilitate the redevelopment of Lithuania's economic, cultural, and social situations help with the

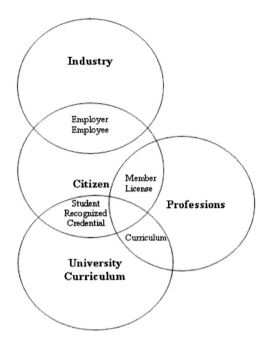

Source: Adapted from Davies (2000).

Figure 10.18.   Traditional paradigm of universities.

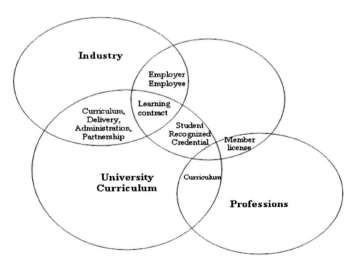

Source: Davies (2000).

Figure 10.19.   Organizational and LLL paradigm.

reconstruction of its knowledge environment? First, one must gauge the extent to which the increasingly diverse range of university LLL stakeholders possess the prerequisites for network-based forms of knowledge hybridization and synergy. However, the underdevelopment of Lithuanian civil society constrains the social innovation and related forms of social capital that might otherwise enable the flowering of ambient knowledge through LLL.

Second, Lithuania's formal system of education does not adequately meet the real needs of business and the labor market. LLL as deployed by the bureaucratic educational apparatus is not designed to enable people in organizations to be adept at cutting-edge workplace innovation, and even hampers usage of accumulated practical know-how. Although the entire Lithuanian educational edifice is undergoing reform, the way this is being undertaken actual strengthens its formal premises, hierarchy, and control mechanisms. Specifically the approach to reform focuses on the management of human resources and knowledge development. Furthermore, the formalization of the educational system including LLL side-steps the potential inclusion of tacit knowledge and curtails educational innovation by imposing inflexible bureaucracy over the system.

Third, LLL in Lithuania still reflects the legacy of Soviet structures under which various sectors of society were like silos where meaningful dialogue and partnering among different parts of society, including education and work, was discouraged. Thus the current Lithuanian system of LLL is not what it would be like if it was developed from scratch with a mind to fostering a knowledge milieu aimed at maximizing innovation and productivity. Although by EU standards Lithuania has a relatively high proportion of its population qualified with higher education, the workforce's type and quality of competencies are not aligned as well as they should be with the needs of business and society, causing a shortfall of dynamic and agile entrepreneurial types that knowledge economies need.

Fourth, Lithuanian LLL does not address the needs of an aging population adequately. For example, the provision of intergenerational learning, say through ICTs, has not been championed (Augustinaitis, Ennals, Malinauskiene, & Petrauskas, 2007).

Fifth, LLL has not realized its potential as a catalyst for nurturing post-Soviet democracy and citizenship (Bîrzéa, 2000) nor for other social and technological innovations.

Our final conclusion is that the well-developed network of Lithuanian universities should move to develop a robust LLL system in partnership with business and government.

REFERENCES

Aidis, R., & van Praag, M. (2007). Illegal entrepreneurship experience: Does it make a difference for business performance and motivation? *Journal of Business Venturing, 22*(2), 283–310.

Alasoini, T. (2005). Learning networks as creators and disseminators of generative ideas. In T. Alasoini, E. Ramstad, & N. Rouhiainen.(Eds.), *The Finnish workplace development program as an expanding activity* (pp. 136-168). Helsinki: Ministry of Labor. Retrieved January 15, 2008, from http://www.ist-africa.org/Conference2006/default.asp?page=paper-repository&fltyear=all&flttheme=all&flttype=all&flttitle=&fltauthor=ennals&pagesize=100&submit=Search

Augustinaitis, A., Ennals, R., Malinauskiene, E., & Petrauskas, R. (2007). eRedesigning of society: Towards experiential connectivity of generations in Lithuania. P. Cunningham & M. Cunningham (Eds.), *IST-Africa 2007 Conference Proceedings*. Dublin, Ireland: IIMC International Information Management Corporation.

Bîrzéa, C. (2000). Education for democratic citizenship: A lifelong learning perspective. *Project on "Education for Democratic Citizenship."* Strasbourg: CDCC. Retrieved January 17, 2008, from http://www.okm.gov.hu/letolt/nemzet/eu/Education%20for%20Democratic%20Citizenship.pdf

European Commission. (2001). *Communication from the commission: Making a European area of lifelong learning a reality* (COM (2001) 678 final). Brussels, Belgium: Author.

Darbo ir socialiniu tyrimu institutas. (2004). *Aukstuju mokyklu absolventu konkurencingumas darbo rinkoje darbo jegos pasiulos ir paklausos kontekste* [Research on the competitiveness of graduates from higher education institutions in the labor market in the context of labor force supply and demand]. Vilnius: Darbo ir socialiniu tyrimu institutas.

Davies, A. (2000). Enterprise-university partnerships and the emergence of a new paradigm of organizational and lifelong learning. In O. N. Baburoglu, M. Emery, & Associates (Eds.), *Educational futures: Shifting paradigm of universities and education*. The Netherlands: Springer.

Department of Statistics of Lithuania. (2007). Retrieved May 1, 2007, from http://www.stat.gov.lt/en/?PHPSESSID=b6fa6425b16704ff424f18672be05fd8

Emery, M., & Baburoglu, O. N. (2000). Education systems and universities as seen by Fred Emery. In O. N. Baburoglu, M. Emery, & Associates (Eds.), *Educational futures: Shifting paradigm of universities and education* (pp. 3-16). The Netherlands: Springer.

Greenwood, D. J., & Levin, M. (2000). Recreating university-society relationships: Action research versus academic Taylorism. O. N. Baburoglu, M. Emery, & Associates (Eds.), *Educational futures: Shifting paradigm of universities and education* (pp. 19–30). Istanbul, Turkey: Sabanci University.

Griffin, C. (1999). Lifelong learning and social democracy. *International Journal of Lifelong Education, 18*(5), 329-342.

Griffin, C. (2007). Lifelong learning: Policy, strategy and culture. In *Working papers of the global colloquium on supporting lifelong learning*. Retrieved January 15,

2008, from http://www.open.ac.uk/lifelong-learning/papers/393B8319-0006-659F-0000015700000157_CGriffin-Paper-LifelongLearning.doc

Hake, B. J. (1999). Lifelong learning in late modernity: The challenges to society, organizations and individuals, *Adult Education Quarterly, 49*(4), 77-89.

Kraujelyte, A., & Spurga, S. (2007). Kurianciosios žiniu visuomenes pletra [Development of a creative knowledge society]. In M. Adomnas, A. Augustinaitis, T. Janeliunas, D. Kuolys, & E. Motieka (Eds.), Lietuvos tauta: bukle ir raidos perspektyvos [Lithuanian nation: Analysis of the situation and development prospects] (pp. 165-208). Vilnius, Lithuania: Versus Aureus.

Labor Exchange of Lithuania. (2007). Retrieved May 1, 2007, from http://www.ldb.lt/LDB_Site/index.htm

Rubenson, K. (1998). *Adult education and training: The poor cousin—An analysis of reviews of national policies for education.* OECD, University of British Columbia and Linkoping University.

Saulauskas, M. P. (1996). *Customizing iron cage: Postmodern postcommunism? Lithuania and the Baltics* (Working Paper). Norway: University of Bergen.

Statistical Office of the European Communities. (2006). *EU integration seen through statistics.* Luxembourg: Office for Official Publications of the European Communities.

Tamosiunas, T., Sutiniene, I., Filipaviciene, D., & Guseva, O. (Eds.). (2004). *Kaimuose ir miesteliuose (gyventoju skaicius iki 30 000) gyvenanciu suaugusiuju mokymosi poreikiai. Socialinio tyrimo ataskaita* [The learning needs of the adults from the rural areas (population less than 30,000)]. Vilnius, Lithuania.

Tamosiunas, T., Sutiniene, I., Filipaviciene, D., & Guseva O. (Eds.). (2005). *Neformaliojo suaugusiuju svietimo bukle ir gyventoju bei darbdaviu poziuris i neformaluji suaugusiuju svietima* [The state of informal adult education and the attitudes of citizens and employers to it]. Vilnius, Lithuania.

Tikkanen, T. (2005). Reconciling learning, human resource development and well-being in the workplace. *The British Journal of Occupational Learning, 3*(1), 33–53.

Viesosios politicos ir vadybos institutas. (2004). *Nuotoliniu studiju kokybes vertinimo Lietuvos ir uzsienio aukstosiose mokyklose analize* [Quality assessment of the distance learning in Lithuanian and foreign institutions of higher education]. Vilnius, Lithuania: Author.

ABOUT THE AUTHORS

Elena Antonacopoulou is professor of organizational behavior at the University of Liverpool Management School. She is director of GNOSIS, a dynamic management research initiative that focuses on the cocreation of knowledge for action. Her principle research interests are organizational learning and change and the dynamic complexity of social practices. She has led and participated in international interdisciplinary research programmes on these topics and has published in international journal on all these areas. She has been elected and appointed in numerous prestigious positions including: Senior Fellow, Advanced Institute of Management Research, Academy of Management Board of Governors, European Group for Organization Studies Board where in all cases she had the opportunity to deliver impactful results through the initiatives she has led always motivated to make a positive difference.

Steve Armstrong is professor of organizational behavior and director of research at Hull University Business School in the United Kingdom. He is also a council member of the British Academy of Management, chief editor of the *International Journal of Management Reviews*, and 2006/07 president of the Management Education and Development Division of the Academy of Management. He holds a a PhD in organizational behavior from the University of Leeds. Recent journal articles have appeared in *Academy of Management Learning and Education, Journal of Management Studies, Journal of Occupational and Organizational Psychology, Small Group Research, British Journal of Educational Psychology, Personnel Review,* and *Educational Psychology*.

Arunas Augustinaitis, PhD, is a professor at the Mykolas Romeris University (MRU) (Vilnius, Lithuania). The research areas are knowledge society, economy, and management; communication and information; public policy and e-governance. In 1986 he defended the doctoral thesis in communication and information; in 2004 habilitated the thesis in management and administration. In 1991 he established faculty of communication at Vilnius University, he also headed the Department of Communication and Information Theory. In 2002-2005 he worked as director of Knowledge Society Management Institute at MRU. He has implemented eight bachelor and master study programs. He is the author of more than 50 scientific articles.

Maria Avdjieva teaches business management courses for the Bachelor Of Business And Information Management ((BBIM)) degree at the University of Auckland Business School. This highly structured degree was introduced in 2001 in response to growing demand for graduates able to effectively bridge the worlds of business and information technology. Drawing on her research program on quality of teaching and learning in higher education, in 2005 Maria's teaching team won the University of Auckland Teaching Excellence Award for Innovation in Teaching. Her learner-centered curriculum designs creatively facilitate the development of students' capacity for lifelong learning in the knowledge era.

Schon Beechler is academic director, Duke Corporate Education, and faculty director of POS Leadership Programs at the Stephen M. Ross School of Business, University of Michigan where she works with executive education clients and faculty to design and deliver executive education programs globally. She was previously on the faculty of Columbia University and served as the faculty director of the Columbia Senior Executive Program for 14 years. She has published widely in the fields of global management, HRM, and global leadership and her work has appeared in leading academic journals, including the *Academy of Management Learning and Education Journal*, the *Academy of Management Review*, the *Journal of International Business Studies*, and H*uman Resource Management*. Her current research is on global leadership in Western and Asian countries.

Jared Bleak, EdD, Harvard, is an executive director at Duke Corporate Education, a unit of Duke University that focuses on creating customized educational solutions for corporate clients. In this capacity, he works to use education as a tool in solving clients' strategic challenges and has taught across the United States and in Europe, Africa, and Asia. His research focuses generally on issues of organizational culture, leadership, and learning. Currently, he is leading research aimed at improving the learning environment in corporations by translating the methods and culture of top-rated teaching hospitals to the corporate environment. He is the author of the book, *When For-Profit Meets Nonprofit: Educating Through the Market* and coauthor of *The Leadership Advantage: How the Best Companies are Developing Their Talent to Pave the Way for Future Success*.

Rachel Ciporen is currently completing her doctorate in adult learning and leadership at Teachers College, Columbia University. Her dissertation examines the supports and barriers leaders experience as they attempt to transfer learning from executive education programs back to their organizations and personal lives. Rachel is as an executive coach in a variety of leadership development programs. She is a practicum supervisor and board member with the Gestalt Center for Organization and Systems Development in Cleveland Ohio.

Robert DeFillippi is professor of management, director of the Center for Innovation and Change Leadership, and academic director for the Innovation and Design Management Executive MBA concentration at Suffolk University's Sawyer Business School in Boston. He is the author of over 35 journal publications and 7 books. His research, teaching, and consulting practice focuses on creative collaborations and knowledge-based perspectives on innovation. Professor DeFillippi's empirical research typically compares United States and European practices and he lectures regularly in Europe, with presentations at the following European business schools: Bocconi University, Cambridge University, Erasmus University Rotterdam School of Management, Free University of Berlin, Linkoping University, London Business School, Manchester Business School, University of Hull, and University of Sussex. Moreover, he is a four time visiting professor at City University (now Cass) Business School (London), an Advanced Institute of Management International Visiting Fellow at Tanaka Business School of Imperial College of London, a research fellow at the Freeman Innovation Center, Universities of Sussex and Brighton, and four time visiting lecturer at Institut d'Administration des Enterprises- Aix-en-Provence, Universite de Marseille. Dr. DeFillippi is also associate editor for the *International Journal of Management* and he has served as guest editor for special issues of *Management Learning* (2001), *Organization Studies* (2004) and *Journal of Organizational Behavior* (2007). E-mail: redefilli@suffolk.edu.

Robert M. Fulmer is currently academic director for Duke Corporate Education and distinguished visiting professor of strategy at Pepperdine

University. He was previously a visiting scholar at the Center for Organizational Learning at MIT and taught organization and management at Columbia University's Graduate Business School. For 6 years, Bob was director of executive education at Emory University. He held endowed chairs at William & Mary and Trinity University and was responsible for worldwide corporate management development for Allied Signal, Inc. He has also served as president of two management consulting firms specializing in human resource issues and authored or coauthored 12 business books including *Growing Your Company's Leaders (2004)* and *The Leadership Advantage (2007)*.

Paolo Landri is researcher at the Institute of Research on Population and Social Policies of National Research Council of Italy (CNR-IRPPS). His main research interests concern educational organizations and policies. He has published in a range of journals and edited books, including *Il Ministero Virtuale. La pubblica istruzione online* (with Roberto Serpieri, Liguori, 2004) and *New Society Models for a New Millennium. The Learning Society in Europe and Beyond* (ed. Kuhn, M., Peter Lang, 2007). Address: Institute of Research on Population and Social Policies, National Research Council, Via Vittorio Emanuele, 9/11, 84080 Penta di Fisciano (SA), Italy. E-mail: p.landri@irpps.cnr.it

Egle Malinauskiene is a PhD student at Mykolas Romeris University (MRU) (Vilnius, Lithuania) doing the research in the field of e-government. She also teaches the subjects of e-health, public e-services, and information technologies in e-government in the same university. She is also a bachelor of computer science and master of software engineering. For several years she was involved in IT projects at the same time teaching software engineering for IT students.

Steven J. Maranville, associate professor, University of Houston, earned a BA and MBA at Brigham Young University and received a PhD in business administration from the University of Utah. Professor Maranville is UH-Downtown's active-learning faculty specialist, providing consultation on teaching improvement to other faculty. Accordingly, his teaching philosophy embraces an active-learning methodology. Professor Maranville is the editor of the *Journal of Applied Case Research*, sponsored by the Southwest Case Research Association. Professor Maranville is a member of Beta Gamma Sigma, the academic honor society for Business Schools accredited by AACSB-International. Most recently, he was honored by the Federation of Business Disciplines with the Outstanding Educator Award.

Charles McClintock is dean, School of Human and Organization Development at Fielding Graduate University in Santa Barbara, California, and professor emeritus of policy analysis and management at Cornell University where he taught and served in various administrative positions for 27 years before joining Fielding in 2001. His academic interests include management, program evaluation, social policy, and a current research study of transformational learning in distributed education.

Nick Nissley currently serves as executive director of The Banff Centre's leadership development programs, located in Canada's Banff National Park. Nick earned his EdD from the George Washington University (Washington, DC, United States) in human resource development. He has served as a university professor (University of St. Thomas, Minneapolis, United States), and in executive roles in the mining, health care, and education sectors. Most recently, before coming to Banff, Nick served as vice president, organization effectiveness at his alma mater, the Milton Hershey School, in Hershey (United States). Nick has chronicled the emergence of the field of arts-based learning, and serves as a proud spokesperson for the field.

Giuseppe Ponzini is a senior researcher at the Institute of Research on Population and Social Policies of National Research Council of Italy (CNR-IRPPS). He has extensively published on Italian journals on welfare systems and European citizenship. He is coeditor (with E. Pugliese) of the Rapporto sullo Stato sociale in Italia 2007 (Donzelli Editore, Roma). He is responsible of the Research Unit on Welfare Systems and Social Policies, and team leader of the Research Group on Welfare Systems in New Member States of European Union at CNR-IRPPS. Address: Institute of Research on Population and Social Policies, National Research Council,Via Vittorio Emanuele, 9/11, 84080 Penta di Fisciano (SA), Italy. E-mail: g.ponzini@irpps.cnr.it

Lindsay Ryan is director strategic partnerships with the University of South Australia, the university's corporate education unit. Lindsay has been undertaking global research on corporate education and lifelong learning as part of his PhD on the strategic management of university-corporate education partnerships. Prior to joining the university in 2001, Lindsay was a management consultant specializing in marketing management and strategy.

Judith Stevens-Long is associate dean for curriculum and lifelong learning at Fielding Graduate University in Santa Barbara, California, and also served as full professor at California State University, Los Angeles, and University of Washington. In 1996 she designed Fielding's organizational management and development program, one of the first entirely online master's degree programs in the United States. Her scholarship focuses on human development and learning, including the graduate textbook, *Adult Life: Developmental Processes* (4th ed.), and contributions to the *Handbook of Online Learning*. Her current research is a survey of transformational learning in distributed education.

Denise Thursfield is a lecturer in organizational behavior at Hull University Business School. Her research interests are in the areas of management and organizational learning and critical HRD. She is a member of the university forum for human resource development. Previous work has been in the area of applied research. This includes evaluation research of U.K. policy initiatives such as individual learning accounts, employee development and workforce development. She has published a range of book chapters and articles in peer reviewed journals such as *Human Resource Development International, Journal of Vocational Education and Training, Employee Relations and Management Learning*.

Wil Uecker is the Harmon Whittington professor of management in the Jessie H. Jones Graduate School of Management at Rice University. He has taught in the MBA and MBA for executives programs, served as a member of a faculty team in the school's innovative action learning project curriculum in the full-time MBA program, and has taught corporate programs for companies in the energy, health care, and information technology industries. He has been recognized for the frequency that his published works are cited in leading research journals in managerial accounting and auditing. Dr. Uecker received his BA in economics, MBA, and PhD from the University of Texas at Austin.

Charles Wankel is associate professor of management at St. John's University, New York. He received his doctorate from New York University. Dr. Wankel has authored and edited many books including the best-selling *Management* (3rd ed.) (Prentice-Hall, 1986), *Rethinking Management Education for the 21st Century* (IAP, 2002), *Educating Managers with Tomorrow's Technologies* (IAP, 2003), *The Cutting-Edge of International Management Education* (IAP, 2004), *Educating Managers Through Real World Projects* (IAP, 2005), *New Visions of Graduate Management Education* (IAP, 2006), the *Handbook of 21st Century Management* (SAGE, 2008), and *Being and Becoming a Management Education Scholar* (IAP, 2008). He is the leading founder and director of scholarly virtual communities for management professors, currently directing eight with thousands of participants in more than 70 nations. He has taught in Lithuania at the Kaunas University of Technology (Fulbright Fellowship) and the University of Vilnius, (United Nations Development Program and Soros Foundation funding). Invited lectures include 2005 distinguished speaker at the E-ducation Without Border Conference, Abu Dhabi and 2004 Keynote speaker at the Nippon Academy of Management, Tokyo. Corporate management development program development clients include McDonald's Corporation's Hamburger University and IBM Learning Services. Pro bono consulting assignments include reengineering and total quality management programs for the Lithuanian National Postal Service. E-mail: wankelc@stjohns.edu.

Lyle Yorks is an associate professor in the Department of Organization and Leadership, Teachers College, Columbia University where he teaches courses in strategy development, human resource development, and research. His current research centers on action learning/research, collaborative inquiry, complexity, and management development.

9 781593 118105